A GREAT VISION

A Militant Family's Journey
Through the Twentieth Century

Richard March

HARDBALL

PRESS

Published by Hard Ball Press.
ISBN: 978-0-9979797-3-2
Exterior and interior book design by D. Bass.
Information available at: www.hardballpress.com

Library of Congress Cataloging-in-Publication Data
March, Richard
A Great Vision - A Militant Family's Journey through the
Twentieth Century
1.Labor Union—Nonfiction. 2. American oral history. 3.
Communist Party USA oral history. 4. Croatia oral history. 5.
Brooklyn oral history. 6. Chicago oral history.

Dedication

But we have a glowing dream
Of how fair the world will seem
When each man can live his life secure and free,
When the Earth is owned by labor
And there's joy and peace for all
In the Commonwealth of Toil that is to be.

From "The Commonwealth of Toil" (1918) by Ralph Chaplin
(composer of "Solidarity Forever")

A GREAT VISION

A Militant Family's Journey
Through the Twentieth Century

Richard March

GRBAC-MARCH FAMILY TREE

Ivan Grbac(1866-1930) married Maria ("Nona")
Sokolic(1872-1961)

Kristina Grbac (1892-1989) - married Tony Karlich
Lena Grbac (1893-1991) -married Dominic Sokolich
John Grbac(1896-1934) – Katarina Hrončić
Maritza Grbac (1897-1988) - married Celestin Cavedoni
    Virgilio Cavedoni
Kreso Grbac (1899-1971) - married Eva
Richard Grbac (1901-1939*) – married Aleksandra
Groshenko
Tony Grbac (1903-1943) – married Ana Dominic Grbac
(1905-1941*)
Joseph Grbac(1908-1998) – married Kate McGowan
Agnes Grbac (1910-2005) – married Nicholas Daniels
Jane Grbac (1912-2004) – married Herbert March
    Robert March (1934-2015)
    William March (1939-) – married Carolyn Reddick,
        daughter, Sara Elaine
    Richard March (1946-)

Benjamin Fink (1889-1973) – married Rose Haber
(1891-1930)
    Herbert Fink (1912-2002) (adopted the surname
        March)
    Morton Fink (1915-2008)
    Irving Fink (1922-1967) (adopted the surname March)

Contents

Introduction

Members of my family have long embraced a passionate—some might say misguided—idealism. We have never accepted the state of society, there are too many injustices and inequalities. We feel it isn't honorable to live our lives in the world as it is, we have a duty to improve the human condition.

As a boy I remember feeling duty-bound to challenge every schoolmate's racist comment or teacher's jingoistic statement. In time I learned you didn't have to fight all the time, you could pick your shots. But to our family, turning a blind eye to injustice was unacceptable, you needed to speak up.

We had a vision of a beautiful society in which everyone was equal and free from want, and everyone behaved ethically and contributed to the general welfare. The solution to humanity's problems was socialism, which would eventually evolve into an ideal communist society. This ideal world would not be modeled after authoritarian regimes that betrayed the socialist principles to which they paid lip service. A slogan that encapsulated our beliefs was, "From each according to his abilities, to each according to his needs." It was our Golden Rule. I recited it once to Miss Ford, my third-grade teacher when she was trying to elicit "Do unto others..." from someone in the class. She was taken aback. When the teacher got another student to offer the recitation she was looking for, I thought, well, that rule was all right, but ours was better.

While raised to be proud of our idealistic viewpoints, growing up in the 1950s and early 1960s I learned that ours was a persecuted group. I grew up keenly aware that the FBI was regularly monitoring us. Our views had to be presented with care and only in circumstances that would not endanger us and might be favorable to advancing our goals. Above all, we could only invoke the word "communism" in the circle of comrades who comprised my parents' close friends. Even now, as I type the word, I experience a twinge of trepidation that I am being reckless. By the 1950s, the typical American notion of "communism" was vicious totalitarianism, and "communists" were seen as dangerous Soviet spies menacing the country.

The actual communists I knew were not ominous people. They were my family's many friends. It was a big network that spanned the country. The lively, colorful people in it played crucial roles in shaping and enriching our lives. As a persecuted group, we sought security, solace and mutual support from like-thinking people. The title of a solemn song we sang, "Beloved Comrade," expresses the warmth and significance of our friendship ties. Mom said that the network of family and comrades was essential for her to endure the years when their lives were in danger.

Our community of communists tended to be idealistic, generous, open-hearted people with a willingness to devote themselves to advancing world peace, social justice and equality. If they had a fault, it was a naïve, overly optimistic view of the perfectibility of the human spirit. If only everyone were just like them, perhaps a utopian communist society could be possible.

When they converted to the cause, our comrades were inspired by the Russian Revolution. The Bolsheviks had actually overthrown the ruling class and taken possession of the farms and the factories in the name of the workers. Later on our friends admired the enormous sacrifices and courage of the Soviets as they defeated the fascists in World War II. They had not yet heard of the anti-democratic, authoritarian practices of the Soviet system. Later on, they remained unconvinced much too long, thinking anti-Soviet reports were just capitalist propaganda. In contrast, they had personally witnessed, as well as felt on their own skins, the viciousness of the American capitalist system. Since their imagined Soviet Union was supposed to be capitalism's antithesis, they were in denial about accepting the Soviet Union's failures.

Within communist ranks there was a contradiction, nearly incomprehensible to me as a boy—not all communists were our allies! Some actually opposed our efforts. I heard my parents criticize these rigid, doctrinaire, sectarian types. They interfered with our revolutionary efforts, offered ignorant criticism and threatened disciplinary action, even expulsion from the fold and ostracism. These dogmatic people generally lacked genuine contact with working people. They quoted Lenin and Marx to justify the current Party line, and through astute internal maneuvers achieved paid positions and personal power in the Party. They drove people like us out of the organization and ultimately made a hash of the cause.

My parents, never doctrinaire Marxists, didn't believe in violent revolution. Complex ideological polemics bored them. They had a red-bound set of the works of Lenin, but the books never looked worn from wear. Non-sectarian, they worked as progressives with whomever they shared a particular goal. In their formative years they were appalled by the extremes of wealth and poverty they saw about them and became determined to do something about it. Pa devoted his life to union organizing and Mom was a community activist. Pa readily acknowledged that there were energetic members of his union who subscribed to various schools of radical thought, Socialists, anarcho-syndicalists, Trotskyists and Communists. He noted, moreover, that there were devout Catholics, black preachers and politically conservative workers who were staunch unionists as well. They could argue about their differences, but facing their class enemies, the bosses, they all needed to stick together.

Experiences in their formative years led my parents to become radicals. Pa was raised in a Brooklyn neighborhood that was a leftist hotbed. Rent strikes, protests and soapbox speakers drew him into a life of struggle. As a community organizer in Chicago's Depression-ravaged Packingtown district, Mom followed in her grandfather's and parents' footsteps. In their Croatian homeland they had been community leaders who organized fellow villagers in mutual assistance efforts before immigrating to the US. With a vision of a just, egalitarian society, they organized a Croatian school, a co-op, a credit union and a cultural society in the face of Italian hegemony.

In Chicago my parents held onto the fervent belief that by organizing militant, democratic labor unions and strong, inclusive community organizations, they could end racial discrimination, achieve world peace, and build an egalitarian society.

#

The impetus to write this book came from my marriage partner, historian Nikki Mandell. In 2004, when I was getting acquainted with Nikki, I showed her the half-hour documentary about my cousin Sasha produced that year by Croatian television. The documentary chronicled part of my family history. Croatian nationalists, we were forced to leave Nerezine, our home village on an island in the northern Adriatic Sea, after the region was awarded to Italy in 1920.

The family settled in Chicago and prospered until we were battered by financial catastrophe in the Great Depression. Disillusioned with American capitalism, in 1931 Sasha's father Gavde and two of his brothers (my uncles) journeyed to the Soviet Union to join "Seattle Commune," a utopian community founded in southern Russia in 1923 by a group of Americans. But the Soviet Union proved to be no utopia. Sasha's father perished in a prison camp, his uncles died in World War II. Sasha and his Ukrainian mother survived the ensuing turmoil of Soviet history. Now, seventy years later, Sasha was in touch with his American relatives and spending most of his time in his father's native village on the Adriatic recording a documentary about our family.

My cousin Gemma gave copies of the documentary to family members. I translated the Croatian sound-track and made DVDs with English overdubbing.

After viewing the documentary, Nikki exclaimed, "Oh my God, Rick, you've got to write about this! Your family has been involved in many important developments of the twentieth century." To me it was just our family story—one that many people might find disreputable. She already heard about my father's union organizing and my mother's community efforts. She knew of my participation in the civil rights and anti-war struggles of the 1960s and 1970s. Nikki thought my contribution could reveal a loving family with generations of passionate activists.

There are many histories of American radical and labor movements by professional historians. These works present well documented information and good analysis. There also are sundry memoirs penned by radicals who recalled the stirring events of their lives. What the histories and even the memoirs seldom convey, however, are the personalities and habits of the people and the tenor of family life in those movements. As a family of radicals, we had our daily routines, just like other people. We established our homes, cooked meals, went to movies, sang songs and enjoyed other simple pleasures. We raised our kids, sent them to school, read them stories, sang "Happy Birthday" and blew out the candles. And in the process we passed through generations our values and the great vision that inspired us.

The family stories that comprise this book, some gripping, some commonplace, described and gave meaning to our lives. They convey the normality of real people, living day-to-day immersed in a movement for social justice.

While the great vision was shared by most of our family, the life path of each member was unique. Only a few devoted themselves to sustained struggle. My mother's parents were accepted leaders of the nationalist movement in their village community, a lifelong role inherent in all their actions until they were exiled. My father's father voted Socialist but, worried about repercussions on his job, kept it secret. My parents were ardent grassroots organizers in the broader working class community where they lived, while Mom's sister and brother, less assimilated immigrants, participated in progressive efforts mainly within their Croatian ethnic community. Circumstances led my mother's three brothers to emigrate to the USSR to the commune where they imagined their efforts would advance the workers' state. Mom's pharmacist brother expressed our values in a less conspicuous ways, the highly ethical manner in which he practiced his healing profession.

There are internal and external factors that determine how deep an individual plunges into activism. A person needs to have the character and temperament to put oneself at risk. There are powerful forces of the existing order arrayed against those who would dare challenge it. It is a rare activist who has not paid a price for his or her engagement. Timing and location are crucial outside factors. My parents came of age in the 1930s, during the depths of the Great Depression, a time when desperate people became ready to fight for change. Industrial Chicago was a key location for the struggle.

I became a teenager in 1960, just as the Civil Rights and Peace Movements were emerging, with exciting roles for young foot soldiers. By the end of my teen years, the New Left and counter-culture movements were shaking staid American political and social mores, especially where I lived in California. In the late 1970s, a few veterans of the Old Left and the New Left launched public folklore, a movement for cultural democracy in which I was able to have a rewarding three-decade career.

This story concentrates on my grandparents, my parents and myself, as well as the uncles, aunts and other relatives, revealing differing life paths that incorporated to a lesser or greater degree the pursuit of our great vision.

Our great vision has yet to be attained. There have been victories we can cherish and defeats that we mourn. My grandparents were leaders in what we learned to call a bourgeois anti-colonialist movement. Their hopes for self-determination and sustaining the Croatian culture of the common people in their village have been largely realized. My parents, socialist revolutionaries, worked towards similar goals, made advances and suffered setbacks.

The lasting fruits of my father's struggles were two decades during which the union made working in a Chicago packinghouse a family-supporting job. Those immigrant and African-American workers attained a financial base that enabled their children to take advantage of educational opportunities that propelled them into the middle class. The community organization that Mom co-founded, the Back-of-the-Yards Neighborhood Council, still exists and still advocates for the interests of its immigrant inhabitants, now, mostly Latinos.

As to the struggles of my generation, the Civil Rights Movement succeeded in eliminating the worst manifestations of institutionalized racism. The New Left played a significant role turning public opinion against the Vietnam War, the '60s counter-culture made Americans more tolerant and enabled the Women's Movement to make important strides against sexism.

But our increasingly unequal, still racist and highly militarist nation has defied efforts at fundamental change. As a man of 70 years, I believe that we dreamers can pass our vision to forthcoming generations, that one day our descendants may finally achieve the great vision of a just society.

# # #

This book is a story, a saga, a tale. While it is subjective, hopefully it is fair. It is not an historical survey. I offer some background information drawn from historians' works to put my family's experiences into context, emphasizing happenings which greatly affected my forebears that likely would be unfamiliar to American readers, like D'Annunzio's seizure of Rijeka and the Trieste crisis.

Trained in the field of folklore, I value the humble narratives of ordinary people. Most of what I know about my family is through such narratives, the kind everyone has, more or less embellished, that sum up a life. I draw on the stories of my parents Herb and Jane March, Grandmother Maria Grbac, from aunts, uncles, my two older brothers and my numerous cousins.

I had a boyhood fascination with family stories. As a child, my grandmother was often the sole person available when I came home from school. She was in her 80s and inclined to reminisce about younger days in her home village. I was all ears.

I also have a head full of stories from my father. We talked often during my childhood and adult life. In addition, oral historians took an interest in dad's life of organizing in Chicago. On their transcripts and tapes, lo and behold, a dozen of Pop's polished stories sum up his life from 1930 to 1955—his defining quarter century. Dad started as a teenage radical, an organizer of the unemployed on the dusty Great Plains. He became an organizer in Chicago and a principal founder of the United Packinghouse Workers of America (UPWA-CIO). Ultimately he was persecuted and pushed out of the union by anti-communist witch hunts of the 1950s, as well as the Communist Party's own nonsensical policies.

I emphasize Pa's union career. He was a significant figure in American labor history, and although he is mentioned in studies of the meatpacking industry, there is no work that fully focuses on his life and career.

His stories dealt with confrontations, violence and intimidation he encountered as a union organizer, about arrests and beatings, and strikers killed on the picket line. But also workers out-smarting the bosses, pushing back when united militant action carried the day.

Pa was an able narrator. The quotes from his interviews are a direct window to his own voice, his irony and understatement. Pa portrayed himself as an honest man, navigating in a menacing world of threatening bosses, venal police, and opportunistic politicians. His stoic tone matched his real-life actions. Aware of the threats to his life, he was completely undeterred.

I am fortunate also to have such a window to my mother's own words. Regrettably, the historians did not interview Mom, despite the historical importance of her community organizing efforts. I try to remedy that oversight in this work.

Mom expressed herself mostly through the visual arts, painting and print-making. In 1991 at age 78, she enrolled in a community-education writing class. Recently I discovered file folders and spiral notebooks with her compelling but unfinished writing. I know the most about my family's past through hours of hearing Mom's stories, so I am delighted that she also left these manuscripts, scrawled on lined paper, words crossed out, arrows to change the order of clauses, with afterthoughts in tiny script squeezed between the lines. Unlike Pa's understatement, Mom had a darker, dramatic tone about those same times, emphasizing travails and her fear, but also her determination to overcome.

In the manuscripts Mom accentuated her earliest memories of surviving starvation in the home village. She reflected on older childhood and teenage experiences as a new immigrant in Chicago and her process of becoming a dedicated radical activist. Sadly, Mom never finished these writings nor shared them beyond the writing class. But I have remedied that. With gentle editing, excerpts are included in this book, allowing my father and mother both to address readers in their own words. It is a family story, told by those who lived it.

I was able also to pierce the veil of mystery that surrounded my three uncles' lives in Russia. Their letters to the family in Chicago were brief. Fortunately another writer offered more detail. E.M. Delafield, an English travel writer, visited and expansively described Seattle Commune near the time when my uncles lived there. I rely heavily on her account.

When this story reaches the era I can remember well, the 1950s, I present a narrative of my own formative experiences and my involvement in the causes that have been important to me. The saga spans more than a century, including material on five generations of the family, from my great-grandfather to my niece.

Pink Violets and Starvation

As a child I knew my mother was Croatian. Every day I heard her and my maternal grandmother Maria Grbac, whom I called Nona, conversing in the clipped cadences and drawling diphthongs of their island dialect. Nona and Mom were from a place that seemed mythical to me, Nerezine, a village on the island Lošinj in the Adriatic Sea. Our world atlas didn't have a detailed map of that little known corner of the world, so Mom had to point to Lošinj on a map of southern Europe, a truly miniscule speck in the sea not far from the famous city of Venice, Italy. "That's where I'm from," she'd say.

Nona was born there in 1872, my mother in 1912. Mom's native island is in Kvarner Bay, near the peninsula of Istria which separates the major port cities of Trieste and Rijeka, the northernmost part of the Adriatic Sea. In this strategic location, the nearest part of the Mediterranean coast to Central Europe, the Slavs to the east and Italians to the west fought for control. Even at the local level Mom's home village was fiercely divided between supporters of Italian and of Croatian language and culture.

My great grandfather Gavde Sokolić and his son-in-law, my grandfather Ivan Grbac were local Croatian leaders. They established a Croatian school, a credit union and an agricultural cooperative.

While serving in the Austro-Hungarian Navy as a valet to an admiral in Budapest, my grandfather Ivan learned fluent Hungarian and German, as well as shoe and boot making skills, fashioning fancy boots for the admiral. Returning home after seven years, he ran a shoemaking business as well as an *ošterija,* an inn for travelers, in his spacious house located on the island's main road in the village's hilly Podgora district. My grandparents' home was the beehive of local Croatian political and cultural activity. The Croatian school held classes there and offered a Croatian reading room, a small library of books and periodicals for adults.

Because of his language skills, Ivan served as the sales representative for the local cooperative, marketing medicinal herbs to pharmacies in Vienna and Budapest. In 1912, his political enemies accused him of embezzlement. He was briefly jailed, then released without charges. Ivan decided it was the prudent moment to emigrate to America, leaving behind my grandmother Maria, pregnant with my mother, who months later became the youngest sibling of the 13 children in the family.

In her late 70s, Mom described her early life. Here are my mother's memories of that mysterious island in the hard year of 1919 after the region had been ravaged by war.

The little green meadow had high spring growth. In the areas around the bright yellow Spanish broom were great patches of blue wood violets. My sister and I were sent to gather the violets to be dried for an aromatic tea. It was fun to pluck the sweet-smelling blooms. Some, especially those that had nectar oozing on their pretty faces, we put in our mouths to savor.

Quietly wandering some distance from my older sister, who was supposed to watch me, I spotted some pink violets, which are very rare. We always competed to see who would find the most. In this spot there were lots of them. I would surely have the most!

I was six years old and just recovering from almost three years of starvation caused by the war. It was good to go up into the hills after years of being kept indoors and pick the most pink violets. I carefully placed them in my apron pocket separate from the blue ones. I wandered further and further into thickets of sweet-smelling bushes and herbs, intent on finding more pink violets. Finally, feeling triumphant, sure I had more than my sister, I called, "Agata, Agata, come see the pink violets I've found."

There was no response. The bees and flying insects were buzzing around me. An occasional bird sang. Everything was very still. I called and called.

The little grassy area where we had started picking was nowhere in sight. The bushes around me were thick. I thrashed about trying to find a high place from which I might see the blue sea below. I knew if I walked towards the sea I would find the path down the mountain to our house. I began to cry. Scratches from the bushes were smarting. My basket caught on a branch and spilled my blue violets. As I gathered them up, I cried. I wandered, trying to find the path. Exhausted, I sat on a rock, sitting for a long time.

Still sniffling, I dried my face with the apron and stood up. Some of the precious pink violets fell out of the apron pocket. I began to count them. I was elated. I had found more than anyone. I knew I had!

Before long, I heard my mother's voice echoing my name from the mountain: "Jacinta! Jacinta!" It came from where the sun was going down. I picked up my basket, tucked the pink violets into the big apron pocket and walked toward the sun. Soon I saw my mother. After a hug, she scolded me for straying away from Agata. But her tone was quiet and subdued, not harsh. Even though I had strayed, really she was glad I was again able at last to go to the beautiful flower and herb covered areas above our town.

It was spring of 1919. It hadn't been long since the November 11, 1918 Armistice. Once again ships were able to come to our little port. The men had come home from the war. The mines around our harbors had been deactivated and removed. Food was coming in, not much, but at least some polenta, flour, rice and beans. I loved the rice as I had never had any before.

But everything was horribly expensive. The Austrian money paid to my mother for cooking and washing for the soldiers forcibly billeted in our house was worth nothing. I remember one day when mother came home empty-handed from shopping at the piazza. She went to a kitchen storage area. Pulling out a big basket, she reached in, grabbing hands full of Austrian Kroner banknotes. She ripped them up and threw them into the fire on the hearth to boil the bit of corn flour we still had. She turned to me, angrier than I had ever seen her, and shouted, "Don't ever work for this!" Not understanding her outburst, I started to cry. She caught me in her arms and cried with me, singing, "Jacinta *roba fina*, don't you cry."

Years later I understood mother's frustration. All that money, but it could buy nothing. The Austrian state backing those bank notes was gone. In the chaos after the war, people bartered their household goods, the pots and pans they had hidden from the army that was confiscating all metal items. They even took the digging tools needed for working the land. The greatest tragedy, they took the bells at the

Franciscan monastery, the church on the piazza, and the small road-side church by our house. The town and surrounding small villages had paced their lives by the ringing of those bells.

After bartering linens, dishes, or hand-knitted clothing during the war for a cup of beans, flour or a few dried figs, my mother had little of value left. When Austria-Hungary started to lose the war against the Allies, they abandoned our islands. We had been valuable to them as suppliers of herbs, medicinal plants and flowers. Wool, olive oil, dried figs, grapes and wine were extracted from us, their Croatian coastal colonies.

Early in the war, they took away males from 16 to 60 and boys from 8 to 15. The men were drafted for the army. The older boys, 13 to 15, were given to ship's captains to replace older crews drafted to fight. The youngest boys, 8 to 12, were sent to work on farms. On our island there remained only old men, women and young children. To Austria-Hungary we were totally expendable.

Two of my brothers, Dick and Tony, were taken by ship's captains. Two others, Dan and Joe, went to farms. My eldest brother John had gone to Chicago the year before the war, in 1913, where my father Ivan had immigrated in 1912. The same year, 1912, my two eldest sisters, Kristina and Lena were sent for. Years earlier, when they were still little girls, their husbands-to-be, Tony Karlić and Dominic Sokolić, who were leaving for America's Pacific Northwest, arranged with our father to pay their passage to America and marry them as soon as they were old enough. When her boys were taken away in 1915, Mother was 43 years old, on a rocky limestone island with three daughters, Maritza, 17, Agata, 5 and me, not yet 3 years old.

On an early morning during the war, the air was cool, the sun rising from the east shed a golden light on the window. I awakened and walked downstairs and out the back door. No one was in the cobble-stone courtyard. The outdoor stone bread oven was warming the air. I had come to relieve myself.

I stepped out on the weedy yard, pulled up my long nightgown and bent down. Three scrawny chickens squawking loudly ran toward me. They had seen long spaghetti-like tape worms coming out. One chicken pulled away on a worm that hadn't come out completely. I was terrified. I ran and fell beside the outdoor oven. I had no strength to get up. I just lay there, crying softly. My sister Maritza came outside and took me into our kitchen.

She dipped water out of a big tub. It was sea water. We used it for washing. There was a drought and we had very little drinking water. She tenderly washed and dressed me, and helped me lie down on a bench near a window. The sun warmed me.

She put warm water into a cup from a small pot that stood on our hearth. She stirred in some ground acorn "flour" for a soft mush. In all this time not a word was spoken. She too was weak from starvation. Words required energy. She lifted the spoon to my mouth. I gagged. She put down the cup and spoon, held a smaller cup for me to drink a little warm water. She tucked me under a coverlet. She sat and ate some of the foul acorn mush, washing it down with water. There was nothing else to eat in the house.

Our mother had gone two days before to a cove ten hours walking time from our house. Usually she came back in a day and a half. Sister wasn't concerned yet. She knew many things could have delayed our mother. The smuggling and gun-running boat on which our brother Gavde was a crew member could have come later than anticipated. Or maybe it didn't make it to the hidden cove, so mother might have gone to a nearby village to see if anyone had a few crusts of bread or dried beans they'd trade for something she had brought from the house.

That evening, Maritza, Agata and I were looking down the road from a window, hoping to see our mother returning. Instead we caught sight of a man, a stranger. He stopped at the path leading to our house. We were alone, a teenager and two toddlers, three frightened girls. The man was coming to our door. There was no one to protect us. The house across from us was vacant, its windows shuttered and nailed. The house above us also was closed; the children had died of starvation, their mother had gone mad and had been taken to an asylum.

There was a loud knock; my sister put her finger to her mouth, her large eyes pleading for silence. After more knocking with no response from us, the man walked around to a window and shouted in, "I've come with a message from your mother." Maritza bade us to stay in the kitchen while she walked through the large terrazzo-tiled room which led to the front door. Opening it just a crack, she asked, "What do you know about our mother?"

He assured her he would explain, "But please, let me come in. I have walked for ten hours and have had no water since morning. Maritza opened the door to admit a lean old man. His eyes were pale blue-gray, sunken into boney sockets. He in turn saw me and Agata, two pot-bellied, hairless little girls with running sores on our heads and faces. He collapsed into a big chair. The setting sun through the window showed a man with much pain and yet compassion on his old wrinkled face.

He must have seen many such starveling girls, abandoned in shuttered houses. My sister ladled warm water into a small cup. "We have very little water for drinking. The drought dried up the springs that feed the big well in our piazza. Now they only let us get water once a day and allow just a liter or so for all of us.

He drank slowly. He sat silent for a long time. We stared at him, not daring to ask about our mother. Finally, in a deep, soothing voice, he said, "Your dear mother will be delayed, but I am sure she will be all right." That wasn't much information, but as sick and hungry as we were, this message from a kind, scrawny man made us feel great relief. Being very young I had little comprehension of what he said, but I sensed from my sisters' faces that it was something good.

We sat in silence for a long time. He looked quietly out our window, over the rooftops, down to the sea. Such beauty. Such tragedy. Finally he roused himself and opened his knapsack. He took out a small cheesecloth-covered bundle. Addressing Maritza, he asked, "Do you have some plates? Small ones will do. I have polenta and a little cheese we can grate on it."

My sister flew to the cupboard, brought plates, set a pretty embroidered white cloth on a small table. This called for a celebration. We had not had anything to eat from a plate for a long, long time. He cautioned, "Only eat a few spoon-fuls, especially this little one with the big brown eyes. An empty stomach used to nothing in it can't take a big surprise." Maritza agreed I couldn't stomach much. She would mash my share into some warm water.

After eating, darkness came to the kitchen. Maritza lit a candle, one we almost never lighted to save it. But now our honored guest was going to be led to his room and we sisters were going to bed.

Mom was a couple months less than two when World War 1 broke out. She was a couple weeks less than six when her wartime ordeal ended. It is phenomenal how many details she remembered from that traumatic time. Surviving starvation affected her for the rest of her life. As a boy, I remember her telling me, "Wasting food is a sin!" strongly emphasizing the last word. It was the only thing my mother, a declared atheist, ever told me was a sin.

Mom often remembered her starvation time. She told me how they managed to capture sparrows by propping up a flat rock with a twig and scattering some seeds or meal underneath. Once, looking at the fruit developing on the small pomegranate tree in our backyard, Mom commented that they had a pomegranate tree in Nerezine too. During the hunger time, she and Agata would stare at the green fruits, licking their lips, impatient for the day Nona might say they were ripe enough.

Paging through an issue of Life Magazine in the early 1960s, we saw pictures of starving children with distended bellies, victims of the Nigerian Biafra war. "That was me and Aunt Aggie," Mom stated. "We had big bellies like that." From her starvation stories I had the impression that Nerezine was a place of unrelenting privation. Until later I didn't realize Nerezine wasn't always like that.

In a file from her creative writing class I found a short incomplete item in which Mom described a recurring nightmare. In the dream she was uncontrollably vomiting purple ooze. When she spoke of it to her mother, Nona told her the dream was true. One day when Nona returned from seeking food, she found little Jacinta was ill because she had gobbled up too many of the black mulberries that had fallen from the tree in front of their house.

This story reminded me that when I first visited Nerezine as a teenager. It was in early summer and the many mulberry trees along the village streets were loaded with fruit. Since the age of eight I had lived in Los Angeles, where you rarely saw a mulberry; it was quite a novelty. I borrowed a pot from my cousin Antonija, and went around town climbing trees, picking mulberries. The Nerezinci thought it quite funny. The American kid was picking *murve*. They hadn't bothered to pick *murve* for years. They let them rot on the ground. I offered berries to the people whose houses were near the trees. I only got one taker. Obviously, in the 1960s, with money from tourism starting to come in, Nerezinci weren't starving any more.

While Nona struggled during the war to save her girls from starvation, her sons, who were taken away, also faced challenges. Mom's brother Gavde, a strong swimmer like all the Grbac boys, was the sole surviving sailor from a ship sunk in the northern Adriatic. Joe had just turned 7 in 1915 when he was taken to Virje in the Podravina region of northern Croatia. They were already suffering from food scarcity on Lošinj. Nona lied about his age so he could go where there was enough to eat. It was his first train trip, in a rattling passenger car with dozens of other boys from the Kvarner region. The others were at least eight years old, so Joe was the smallest. Once they arrived in Virje, they gathered in a hall where the local villagers came to pick boys to work for them. The people seemed different and strange. Joe noticed the women's costumes were very different from island women's garb. At first he could hardly understand their speech. They spoke *kajkavski,* a very different Croatian dialect from his čakavski idiom.

The villagers were looking for strong workers so the biggest boys were snatched up first. A householder's name would be called and he would step forward and put his hand on a boy's shoulder. They departed together. Joe was the last boy left. An elderly couple came forward and said, "I guess we'll take this little fellow. He looks pretty sad."

"They were so kind to me," Joe declared. Over time he learned their dialect and willingly did whatever work he could around their farm. They never overworked or mistreated him. His daily task was to take a cow to pasture, and Joe always had enough milk and cheese.

The elderly couple discovered that Joe could read. Their eyesight was failing so Joe read the Bible to them every evening. He became knowledgeable about the scriptures through three years of Bible study, which according to his daughter Kathy, "made it difficult for the Jehovah's Witnesses who came by on their rounds (in later years in California) and were brought into our living room to be 'converted' to agnosticism by Dad." Joe always loved a good recreational argument.

If Joe received good treatment, the opposite was true for his brother Dominic. He was sent to a different village where he was assigned to a sadistic pig farmer who abused him. At the end of the war, elder brother Krešo came from Zagreb where he was a university student to reclaim his little brothers from the farmers. While he was out herding the cow, Joe was ecstatic to see Krešo jumping over fences to find him. That was a happy reunion. On the other hand, when Krešo came for Dominic, he found his brother in bleak circumstances, bruised and beaten and forced to stay, like an animal, in the loft of a foul-smelling farrowing shed. Krešo berated his abuser and took his brother home. Because Dominic later suffered from mental illness, Nona and his siblings speculated that the mistreatment he endured as a boy, especially beatings to the head, was the cause. He also lost his hearing, which they attributed, improbably, to his exposure to loud squealing pigs all day.

At the end of World War 1, Nerezine and its entire region remained in turmoil. During the war, in a secret agreement, Italy had been persuaded to join the Allies with the promise of vast territorial rewards in the eastern Adriatic—essentially the entire Croatian coast. The conferees at Versailles didn't honor the unjust secret agreement and assigned most of the coast to the new kingdom of Serbs, Croats and Slovenes (later Yugoslavia), infuriating Italian expansionists. In open defiance of the pending international agreement, the Arditi, a militia of Italian chauvinists led by the adventurer/poet Gabriele D'Annunzio, invaded Rijeka in September, 1919, occupying the city and asserting control over Istria and the islands. The Powers condemned D'Annunzio, but otherwise they dithered. They refused to intervene, foreshadowing the weakness of diplomatic solutions in the face of aggressive nationalists that plagued Europe in coming decades.

The Treaty of Rapallo was signed by Italy and Yugoslavia in November, 1920, awarding Istria and the islands, including Nerezine, to Italy. Rijeka was supposed to become a neutral free port, but the idea proved unworkable. In 1924 Italy was awarded most of the city and harbor with Yugoslavia obtaining only the eastern suburbs.

D'Annunzio and his thugs initiated repressive practices soon to be employed by Mussolini's Fascists: black-shirted terrorist gangs, burning homes and businesses of adversaries and forcing arrested opponents to drink large quantities of mineral or castor oil, to humiliate, torture and sometimes kill them.

From D'Annunzio's invasion through the long period of Mussolini's rule, there were intensive efforts to Italianize the population of Nerezine and the entire region. It was forbidden to use Croatian anywhere. Croatians were required to speak Italian, be educated in Italian, conduct all business in Italian, and even Italianize their surnames or else they were driven out. It was "ethnic cleansing."

In the uncertain times before her town was awarded to Italy, and for a year thereafter, Nona remained in Nerezine with her children. Her older sons, Gavde, Anton and Dominic, departed in 1919 to work as merchant seamen, eventually jumping ship to join their father in Chicago.

The eldest son John crossed the ocean in the opposite direction. He had been in America since 1913. He enlisted in the US Army during World War 1, but he didn't arrive in Europe until after the November, 1918 Armistice. After serving in the occupation forces in Germany, he was discharged in 1919. He chose not to go back to the US immediately, making his way home to Nerezine for a long sojourn. He arranged to marry Katarina Hrončić, a young woman from a remote sheep camp settlement, Punta Križa. They married in 1921 and soon after departed for Chicago.

Krešo, who went on from a Franciscan school to study medicine at Zagreb University, spent the war years in Zagreb. He now found himself in a new country, Yugoslavia, with an international boundary drawn between him and his family.

Like his brothers, Krešo was an avid swimmer. A family anecdote has it that after the Italians had taken control of Lošinj, he wrapped his things in an oilskin bundle, then swam for miles across the two channels that separated the island from the mainland, avoiding border controls. He made it home for a visit to Nerezine, returning to Zagreb the same watery way.

Maria Grbac, a Strong, Honorable Woman

After the war ended, Mom and her siblings remained in Nerezine with Nona from November, 1918, to November, 1921. Mom wrote of an incident that happened in the winter of 1918-19.

After the war Jewish peddlers came to our island to sell pots, pans, needles and notions. According to custom, they were forbidden to spend the night.

One late afternoon a fierce wind blew, the northeast wind we called the Bura. Rain was falling as if spilled from a pail of water. We heard a loud knock on the back door, near our cavernous kitchen. My mother, mumbling who on Earth would be out in this torrent, walked to the door. She came back into the kitchen with a small man so drenched that water was dripping down his face. She led him to the bench by our raised hearth. She brought a homespun wool blanket, told him to wrap up and take off his wet clothes. While he changed, my two sisters and I were sent to another room. Mother brought some dry men's clothes from a trunk to our rain-soaked guest.

The man had a big canvas bag. He was a peddler. Mother served him hot minestrone from the footed iron pot that was bubbling on the coals. Now that the war was over, we had some food to cook. When he had eaten, he showed my mother his wares. All she wanted or had money for was needles. She told him she spun wool from our two sheep and flax that grew wild on the hills. All the while, his wet clothes were drying on a rack near the fire.

With a fine voice and sympathetic lively eyes, the peddler had much to tell about the awful conditions people in the towns and cities were still suffering in the wreckage of war. The small towns like ours where one could raise food were recovering more rapidly.

The rain continued. The wind had died down. Eventually, our pleasant guest got up and said it was time to leave. Mother asked him where he would go. The peddler said he supposed he could find a shelter along the road, probably in a stone sheep or goat shed. My mother, usually so quiet and soft-spoken, and with her face and body still thin from the starvation years, burst out, "What! Are you a *beštija* (a beast)?" The *beštija* word came out so bitterly, my sisters and I were shocked that our mother could speak so harshly.

He said, "I am *Jevrej* (Jewish). I may not stay overnight in any inn or home around here."

My mother asserted, still speaking in an angry tone, "You can here! I do not care what rules they have! You are a man, aren't you?"

Still, the peddler continued picking up his sack and putting on his coat. "You'll have trouble with your neighbors. I don't want to do that to you."

Mother firmly took his sack and leaned it against the wall. She hung his coat over a chair. "My neighbors already know that I am a free-thinker. I'm called Embroidered Mara because my father insisted that my sisters and I go to school like the boys. We were the first in this town. Don't concern yourself about me."

I was just six years old. I was very impressed, not so much by what mother said as by the sudden change in her. Her blue eyes seemed to take on a fierce bright glow. Her body was tense. She used her hands, gesturing to emphasize everything she told the peddler.

The beaten-down, forlorn, hungry, stern-faced mother I had known during the war years wasn't there anymore. She seemed beautiful. I saw she had a lovely glow on her high-cheeked face. I never forgot it.

I learned one could choose to be different, to defy convention, to be unconcerned about those around you who might scorn or condemn you. You could act according to your sense of humanity and be transformed by doing so. It made you beautiful.

Nona's courage was a catalyst transforming timid little Jacinta Grbac into the mother I knew, Jane March, an assertive seeker of justice. At times Mom continued to be startled by Nona's assertiveness. She was shocked when Nona chastised her grown-up son John after he returned to Nerezine in 1919. He complained about the breakfast of polenta with olive oil. "In America we have eggs for breakfast."

"Here, you'll eat what we have. If you don't like it, you can eat your own eggs," she snarled, implying the slang meaning of eggs, testicles.

Mom remembered striking incidents like the peddler's visit but also mundane, charming childhood memories. When she was seven, Nona assigned Mom the duty to chaperone her elder sister Maritza during visits from her fiancé. Nerezine was recovering from war and drought. Jacinta's health had rebounded. Conditions had improved and now it was possible even to enjoy a few little luxuries.

Rules of courtship were strict in her hometown. My mother wrote about the trials those restrictions put on her...

Courting

My sister Maritza was courted by a young man, Celestin Cavedoni, shortly after he came home from the war. I had recuperated from the years of starvation. To me the most pleasant time of day was just before sunset, when I could go into the hills with my mother when she went to milk the sheep.

But now, suddenly I wasn't allowed to go. I had to stay home whenever Celestin came to our house. In the late afternoon, when he finished his work in the carpentry shop, he'd come to court Maritza. When he did, my mother ordered me to stay home to be their chaperone. The customs of Nerezine, our island town, were very strict. There had to be another person with an unmarried girl when she was being courted.

It was boring for me to sit quietly while the two love birds whispered to one another. It was as if I were not there. Sometimes I would wander to the door, hoping to see someone, anyone, walking by. But our house was set far enough back from the road that seldom could I see anybody, and if I did, I couldn't get their attention. Then, while peering out the front door, abruptly I'd remember that I was supposed to remain in the kitchen, near Maritza and Celestin.

After three or four visits a week, I became upset. Every time, before Celestin arrived, I'd ask my mother to let me go with her to the hills, please. But she would answer, "No, no," firmly. I was reminded that I had a duty to stay in the kitchen where the two of them always sat, near our big fireplace.

A Great Vision

Our fireplace was a big stone structure. It had a covered hearth at least six feet long and was very deep. On each side, there was a bench, a good place to keep warm in the winter, or now, in warm weather, to sit or lie down. I liked to curl up to daydream on the cool hearthstones.

In my daydreams, I could imagine skipping along a rocky path behind my mother. Beside the path, in my mind's eye I could see the aromatic plants and pretty flowers among the big rocks. I loved to climb the slopes of our mountain, Osorščica. And while my mother was milking the sheep, sometimes I had a chance to hug a little lamb.

Emerging from reverie, I would realize, disappointed, that I wasn't on the mountain with mother. I reluctantly reminded myself that mother insisted it was my duty to stay in the kitchen. It was a contribution to our family that mother worked hard to keep fed and clothed. Nonetheless, it was a hard task I had been allotted. Those two hours seemed like torture, especially if I heard my friend Ana, a neighbor girl, playing outside.

I'd walk a few steps to look out the kitchen window, and this inattention to them would elicit quick kisses and hugs between Celestin and Maritza. My power was amazing. I nearly laughed how they would

Grbac family, Nerezine, 1906

24

separate quickly whenever I returned to my bench.

One day, in front of Celestin, I begged my mother to let me go with her. "You have to let me go with you! I don't want to stay here! I will help in the garden, clean, wash, anything!"

"I am not able to change the situation," she stated calmly, as she led me to the hall outside the kitchen. "You are the only one who can be here now. You have to be patient. I wish you could go to school and could be busy with books. But never mind, it won't be long before we go to America where you'll have nothing to do except go to school."

The following day, down the road I spotted Celestin's tall thin frame and his thatch of black curly hair. He was hurrying, almost running to our door with some things under his arm. When he came inside, his smile was wide and mischievous. His dark eyes were sparkling in his boney face.

"Well, well, are you going to cry again, my little sister, because the big bad man is keeping you cooped up in the kitchen?" As he said this, Celestin took my hand, led me into the kitchen. Maritza had put a beautiful embroidered cloth on the kitchen table. She had put on her pretty blue dress with a white lace collar. The fine skin of her round, smooth face was flushed.

Celestin gallantly bowed and presented a wrapped bundle to her. Turning to me, he placed a small package in my hands and said, "See here, little sister. This is a box of bon bons. Go outside and enjoy a few with your friend."

I was so charmed by Celestin, I skipped out the front door, then thought better of it and ran back in the house and up the stairs to my bedroom. I opened the box, extracted two of the candy-coated Jordan almonds, a pink and a yellow one, and put them in my apron pocket. I opened a drawer and hid the precious box within. It must still contain a fortune of twenty bon bons! Only once before did I have a bon bon. I was able to pick one up as they were thrown at the bride at a wedding. That prized item I had kept hidden in the drawer for nearly a month. Furtively I'd feel the silky smooth surface and smell the tantalizing aroma of almond oil. Now I had a treasure trove of them!

I went downstairs and outside to find Ana. I swore her to secrecy about my leaving the house. She elected the pink bon bon. We played for perhaps an hour, enjoying the sweet nutty taste in our mouths.

Presently, I heard Celestin calling me. As I entered, Maritza was taking some cups to the sink. Celestin sat me on his lap. Very gently feeling my hair, he started to tell me how he had come home once during the war. He came to visit us just as my brother and cousin were preparing to lance a boil on my head.

"There you were, with no hair, your brother and cousin had you stretched out on a long table in the big *sala* getting ready to operate. That's the room I used to come to for Croatian language classes. Did you know that this was a school once?" I nodded.

"Well, you probably don't remember that day."

"Yes I do. I still can see the shiny knife cousin Stane held to a match while brother Gavde held me down. Gavde had a glass in his hand to catch the puss. It scared me so much, I couldn't even scream."

"Oh you do, you do remember! You couldn't have been more than four years old. But look at you now. Your hair is below your ears, there are no lice, and the sun has tuned your hair the color of silky strands of flax."

Maritza had come to listen, watching intently. She knew Celestin was putting on this performance for her benefit. In our town, a man's character was judged by his ability to be charming and gentle with children.

"It was nice that you went to play with little Ana. She was all alone because her mother had also gone to milk sheep."

Celestin paused then slyly whispered, "But let me ask you not to tell your mother that we said you could go to Ana's house. It'll be our secret, OK?" I nodded again.

The sun was setting. My mother came back from milking the sheep carrying a bucket balanced expertly on the top of her head. A large bundle of firewood for cooking the evening meal was strapped to her back. Her hands were kept free to knit. As she walked to and from her chores, mother always knitted socks or underwear from the wool or flax she carded and spun.

Celestin met her in the yard and helped her, carefully taking the milk bucket off the small donut-shaped pillow on top of her head, asking, "Do the sheep have plenty of milk?"

Mother was a sturdily-built woman nearly fifty years old. Her face already bore marks of worry and suffering from the war years. Sitting down, she quietly answered, "Yes, there is good pasture after the rains last winter. The hardy plants that survived the drought are getting new shoots. We should have plenty of branches to cut for the goat."

As he departed, Celestin smiled, "Well, goodbye Mother, goodbye Maritza," and with a tone in his voice denoting that we had a little secret, he added, "And goodbye to you too, little Jacinta."

Celestin and Maritza married around the time Nona and her three youngest children departed for America. They remained in the roomy Grbac house until the 1950s, doing their best to fill it again with the births of their three sons and a daughter.

Mom's First Communion

In 1921, after years of delay the letter came that made it definite our family was to join our father in Chicago. I was not quite nine years old. I had never seen my father except in an old photo. I was his thirteenth child and was born several months after my father immigrated to the United States.

In a small town, everybody knows your business. The letter created a lot of excitement. Our house stood near a little church where the older women came to Vespers and the word spread. Soon everybody in town was talking. It was almost pandemonium. My brothers and sisters talked about nothing except the marvels that awaited us in a new life in America.

As I was helping my mother prepare our evening meal, I saw no sign in her of the elated reaction others were having to the momentous letter. With face set, lips pursed, she kept stirring the polenta, sometimes beating it so hard I was startled.

She had paid no attention to all the talk whirling around her. She referred questions from neighbors and relatives to my oldest brother, who had come back from America a year or so ago, shortly after serving in Europe as an American soldier. Could it be that the happy news she had awaited so long was not welcome?

I had always clung to my mother. As her youngest and frailest child she kept me close. She had me accompany her on trips to milk sheep each day up on the sweet-smelling meadows in the hills. I knew her every expression and mood. Now there was nothing on the intense face with the bright blue eyes. As I was helping her set the table, without warning she took my hand, pulling me out the door, saying nothing, just holding my hand and rushing downhill along Mandalenska street towards the town square. We halted in front of the priest's door.

Mother knocked. As we waited she whispered, "You have to have your communion." The door opened. I, a frightened, skinny little girl still bearing the ravages of wartime starvation, stood before the priest.

In a firm tone, mother told him, "You must give her communion before we leave for America. We cannot wait until the spring ceremony takes place."

It was customary for all of the town's nine-year-olds to take first communion on the same Sunday in spring. I was clinging to my mother's skirts. Listening to her demanding words to the priest, I almost fainted.

"We have passage for America on the S.S. Wilson from Trieste in November."

The priest protested, "It cannot be done. She has to have training, her Catechism."

"Then train her. You must!" Her voice was so strident; I couldn't believe it was my mother, speaking like this to a priest. No one talked that way to a priest. I was in shock.

Many times during the war, my mother had scolded poor hungry women for taking their last scrawny chicken to the priest and his housekeeper. "Better to keep your chicken for an egg or so. The priest will manage."

And the priest was aware of her views. She wasn't among his daily visitors to Mass. If she made it, even on a Sunday, after all her work, it was a miracle. She sent us though, her children. We walked barefoot down the rocky Nerezine streets, shoes in hand. We put on the precious footwear only when we reached the church door.

Now, here she was, shouting at the priest, "You will! You must! I can't take her on a dangerous ocean voyage without her communion! She will be nine years old very soon. She can come to you every day for Catechism. She doesn't go to school." Indeed, I didn't. For the last two years the only schooling allowed was in Italian. My oldest brother strictly forbade that his little brother and sisters should go to the Italian school. He said, if Franz Joseph let us go to Croatian school, why can't that black-shirted D'Annunzio let us have our own school? He went on and on about it.

And mother went on, "You will! You must!" I cringed, standing in the priest's doorway, wondering when we would be struck dead. Mother was so agitated, the priest finally said, "All right, all right. She can come to me after morning Mass, all this week. On Sunday she can take communion."

Mom wrote that she could remember neither her sessions with the priest nor the first communion and her manuscript trailed off. I don't think she turned it in to her teacher. It seems, out of embarrassment, she couldn't write the rest of the story. But we kids had heard it from her. On the fateful Sunday she went to church with her mother and sisters. Carrying their precious dress shoes, the girls walked barefoot down the rocky road to the church door, putting them on before entering. The Mass was celebrated and little Jacinta, for the first time, approached the priest who placed a communion wafer on her tongue.

Mom had learned her Catechism well. She knew she was not to allow the wafer to touch her teeth. To chew it would be a great sin. She was totally dry-mouthed, a bundle of nerves, afraid that she accidentally might commit a horrible sacrilege. On the entire walk home, the wafer did not dissolve. When she reached Podgora, jumpy nerves and a full bladder sent her in the direction of the privy before entering the house. Their pig pen adjoined the privy. Without warning, she let out an uncontrollable cough. The communion wafer flew out of her mouth directly at the pig, which gobbled it up in an instant. Jacinta was mortified. This must be a sin too horrifying to contemplate. It was her fault. All because she could not control her cough, the body of Christ had been consumed by a swine! Mom said she carried the guilt for years. She never managed to confess it to an intimidating priest.

Nona, however, was not in awe of priests. She commented wryly, "I wonder why the priests always hire as housekeepers young girls from the most remote settlements around here. And the housekeepers never stay more than a few months. Could it be that they send the girls home before their pregnant bellies start to show?"

The letter from Chicago with ship tickets enclosed was pulling them to America. Also, untoward events were pushing them out. The Croatian school was banned, and Nona and her eldest son John wouldn't hear of sending the young family members to the Italian school. Their freedom was restricted. John had been arrested for violating curfew because he and a few friends had observed the old custom of shivaree, blowing horns and banging on pans outside the house of a newly married couple on their wedding night.

The use of Croatian was banned. Mom told of whispering *"pane, pane,"* the Italian word for bread, to a country woman, trying to buy bread in the store. Nervous and flustered, she had forgotten the word, though she knew it was forbidden to ask for bread in Croatian.

D'Annunzio's black shirts had their recruits also on the islands and the Grbac house was a potent local symbol of Croatian resistance to Italian domination. Although the reading groups were no longer allowed, the words *Hrvatska Čitaonica* (Croatian Reading Room) were still chiseled into the lintel over the front door. Nona had been pestered by local *Taljanaši* (Italian supporters) to remove the sign, or face consequences. Of course, she ignored them.

I heard two versions of the story of Nona's confrontation with the Black Shirts at her front door. I'll relate Mom's version first:

Because she wouldn't take off the Croatian sign, one night a gang of Black Shirts came pounding on our front door. Mother opened the door. They were carrying torches. Some of their black shirts had a white skull and cross bones emblem. I was hanging onto Mama's skirts, as usual, and Aggie and Joe were right behind. One of the Black Shirts said, 'All right, we've warned you to get rid of that sign. Now we're telling you, take it off now or we're going to burn down the house.' Mother just looked him in the eye and said, 'All right then, burn it down. We'll be inside!' And she slammed the door. Well, they didn't burn it down. They left, and they never came to our door again.

I always thought this was an amazing story. I could scarcely believe it. I had the idea that the Black Shirts were alien malevolent invaders, like Nazis. Would they have hesitated to burn my family to death? One afternoon in Nerezine, I was trudging down the Podgora road, passing the old Grbac house. I noticed Ivan

Satalić, the nearest neighbor, alongside his house. We started to chat. I thought of the Black Shirt story and I asked him if he remembered something like that happening. I reckoned he would have been a teenager at that time.

"Oh yes! Your Nona really got mad at those guys. She was shouting at them. All of us could hear her. She called each one in turn by their names, 'You, during the war, you were so hungry, and you came around here and I gave you food to eat! And now, you're doing this to me? If that's the way you're going to be, all right, burn it down. We'll be inside.' She made them ashamed. They went home."

Mom told me the story in English. I heard much the same story in Nerezine dialect from Satalić, who added an important aspect Mom had left out. In her version, the Black Shirts were an anonymous threatening force. In Satalić's recollection, the ethnic quarrel in Nerezine was between well-acquainted fellow villagers. Some of the young men swept up in the Black Shirt fever weren't rabid Italian chauvinists. They had been friendly, some even benefitting from Nona's generosity during the difficult war times. They might have been willing to intimidate Nona to curry favor with the new rulers, but they were not prepared to murder her and her family.

Leaving Nerezine

Despite facing intimidation in Nerezine, Nona had reasons for a lack of enthusiasm about their upcoming departure for America other than Mom's first communion issue. It was only a few months until Nona's 50th birthday. She had lived in Nerezine her entire life. She knew everyone there. She spoke only Croatian. She had mastered the many skills needed to make a living on the rocky island. She was respected for her needlework skills and her free-thinking ways. She had never lived in a city, much less a gigantic foreign city like Chicago. Could she learn English and big city ways?

Moreover, she had been apart from her husband almost a decade. For nine years she had been the head of the family in the old house in Podgora. How would it be to live with the headstrong

Ivan again? Had he changed during the nine years in America? She knew she had been changed by the ordeal of the last several years.

But there was no alternative. She might be able to fend off those disgusting Italians and *Taljanaši* so that they'd leave her in peace. But Ivan couldn't come back here, he was too much of a threat to them. Plus, John, home for more than a year, had married Kata Hrončić and was going to take her with him back to Chicago.

Most important of all, Nona had to think of the three younger children. They needed schooling. She couldn't bear to send them to an Italian school. No, it was better to go to Chicago. Ivan and three of her sons already there were counting on their arrival. The young kids would get schooling in English. They were bright, they'd learn quickly, and English was a neutral language—not connected to their national struggle. Besides, in America they could speak Croatian freely among their family and other Croats there, not like here where it was prohibited. She could read books and newspapers in Croatian in America. Here they were banned.

And maybe it wouldn't be forever. These Black Shirts would be driven out one day. A return could be possible. Maria and Celestin are marrying and they will stay in our house. The big house in Podgora would be here for us to come back to in better times. Now it was time to get ready to go.

On a blustery morning late in November, 1921, a truck came to the Grbac house to pick up Nona, the three children and their baggage for the short trip to the harbor in Mali Lošinj. A swarm of friends, neighbors and relatives crowded around to see them off. There were kisses and hugs and heartfelt farewells. Many of the women and girls were crying, wailing and keening in the way women were expected to do at funerals. "They're leaving, they're leaving! We'll never see them again. Never. What will we do without Teta Mara? She's the best woman in town. We could always go to her. Our best people are leaving!"

Some of the children ran after the truck until they were panting and out of breath. Engine roaring, the vehicle disappeared in a cloud of dust.

In a few minutes they had traversed the curvy road to Mali

Lošinj and unloaded their baggage on the quay beside a passenger boat bound for Trieste. Standing beside the gangplank were two Italian gendarmes in ostentatious uniforms checking the identification papers of passengers as they entered.

For the trip, the Grbac children were wearing new clothes that their brothers had sent from Chicago. Jacinta's outfit was an American sailor's suit with red, white and blue piping on the cuffs, lapels and along the edges of the big square collar that hung in back. As Jacinta approached the gangplank, one of the gendarmes hollered, "Halt!" and blocked her way. Nona stepped up to the dandified official to see what the problem was.

"She can't board this ship wearing those Croatian colors," the gendarme insisted.

Nona and the relatives who had brought her started to argue, "The suit is from America. Those are American colors, red, white and blue, it's from the American flag!"

"I don't care. The Croatian flag is red, white and blue. Those are Croatian colors as far as I am concerned, and that girl will not set foot upon this boat with them on her!"

Nona sized up the situation, and pointing to their shipping case, asked her cousin, "Help me open this trunk." She dug her hands in the chest until she felt her sewing box and pulled it out. She opened the cloth-covered box and extracted a small pair of sharp scissors. "Come here Jacinta, I'm sorry, we have to do something."

"No, no, Mama, this is my present from brother Gavde!" Mom sobbed.

Nona hugged her. "Hold still, my darling. I have to take off this trim. I can put it back in America." Mom, crying all the while, did her best to hold still as Nona carefully cut the thread that had fastened the red, white and blue track to the navy blue suit.

There followed several hours of travel on a rough sea. The boat made a stop in Pula on the tip of Istria. Other passengers marveled at Pula's Roman arena, clearly visible from the docked ship. "I couldn't see it," Mom said. "It was just a gray blur to me." Mom was beginning to realize how near-sighted she was.

Nona had instructions to stay in Trieste at a hotel where Ivan himself stayed years earlier. The four of them shared a room. They learned that the departure of the S.S. Wilson would be delayed due to bad weather, so they had to stay at the hotel a couple extra nights. The weather was rainy, blustery and cold, so they didn't go out much. Nona wanted to guard the baggage and they were timid about roaming the unfamiliar big city streets.

On the night before they sailed, Nona learned there was a movie theater close by. Admission wasn't expensive, especially for the kids, so they made it a special treat, their first time to see a motion picture. It was a Charlie Chaplin comedy. Mom found it disconcerting. Because of her poor vision, all she could make out was flashing lights. It startled and disturbed her how the men in the audience were howling with laughter. What was so funny? The seats were ordinary long wooden benches. A group of men near her were laughing so hard that the bench flipped over backwards.

Grandpa Ivan had waited to send for them until he had enough money for his wife and children to travel in a small stateroom and not in steerage. Nona and the girls stayed in the room most of the time, feeling queasy during the whole voyage. But thirteen-year-old Joe had the audacity to roam around exploring the ship.

Mom got another indication of her bad vision when they sailed into New York harbor. As the other passengers marveled at the New York City skyline and Lady Liberty, all she could see was a blur. She remembered that in Nerezine, other people would comment on things in the distance that she couldn't see. But in Nerezine, on the well-known paths of her familiar village it didn't seem to matter so much.

In New York, because of Ivan's advance arrangements, Nona and the children did not have to go through Ellis Island. They were met by Nona's brother Luka who had been living in New York for several years. He took them to his home on the West Side, the Hell's Kitchen district. Not a prosperous neighborhood, but it was not the horrible slum its name seemed to indicate.

After resting a day with the New York relatives, they continued by train to Chicago, arriving on December 1. Mom's initial impression of the city was not favorable. It was cold, the crusty snow coated with black soot. She thought everything looked filthy.

The family's reunion with Ivan proved to be upsetting. He seemed to have forgotten the gracious comportment he had learned as a young man in Budapest. His years of struggle to make a living in a Southside Chicago immigrant ghetto, living in an all-male household with his sons, none of them good housekeepers, apparently brought out a coarser aspect of his character. He was unshaven, unclean and had gained a lot of weight.

Nona chastised him, "I have gone through Hell for the last nine years keeping body and soul together for these children. And this is the way you greet us? When we had no food, no money, nothing, at least we were clean. Even when we didn't have water we used sea water to wash."

Their house on Ashland Avenue was Ivan's shoe store. The residential quarters above were crude, dreary and black with coal soot. A coal stove in the kitchen served for cooking and heat. There were bare gas jets on the walls for lighting. The bed sheets were gray and stained with blood from squashed bedbugs. Within days, Nona dragged the mattresses to the back yard and burned them. "We are not going to live like *beštije*," she asserted.

Cousin Virgilio

It took a second world war and another international crisis in their area to drive the remaining family members from Nerez-ine—Celestin, Maritza and their children. Virgilio Cavedoni, their second son, with wife Lina and two daughters immigrated to California from Italy in the early 1960s. We gave them household items, furniture and a car to get set up. Virgilio, a skilled cabinet-maker in the Cavedoni family tradition, initially worked at Todd shipyards in San Pedro, but later for a builder of recreational craft where his cabinetry skills were more appropriate.

Virgilio told us about the conditions in Nerezine during and after World War II that eventually led to their departure. He was conscripted into the Italian navy and until September, 1943, when Italy capitulated, was in a small unit stationed above Nerezine on the summit of Osoršćica operating a maritime communications center.

Between the fall of Italy in 1943 and the eventual end of the war in 1945, units of nearly every military force involved in the multi-sided Balkan conflict set foot on the islands: Četniks, Partisans, British commandoes, Germans and Ustaši, the Croatian Nazis.

The Nerezinci suffered a harsh occupation, enduring searches, looting, liquidations and revenge killings for German casualties. In August, 1944, the Germans forcibly mobilized young men, including Virgilio. Because of his nautical skills, Virgilio was ordered to pilot troop transport ships. Moved by our family's inclination to resistance, while transporting a unit of Ustaši troops led by a German officer, Virgilio decided to sabotage their mission. Intimately familiar with the waters around the islands, he knew the location of a submerged rocky ridge. He crashed the ship directly into it. Swearing at him, an Ustaši pulled his pistol, pointed it at Virgilio, but before he could fire, the German officer had a pistol trained on the Ustaši and ordered him not to shoot. "It was an accident," the German insisted. "And besides, we need this man to get us off these rocks. None of you knows a damned thing about ships!"

Virgilio managed to free the damaged ship from the rocks and they limped back to port. On the way, the German whispered to him, "When we get back, you'd better get the hell out of here." Virgilio took his advice. Under cover of night, with Kirin Ljerković, a friend from his Podgora neighborhood, Virgilio appropriated a small boat. They made their way to the Partisan-held island of Rab and joined up. Years later, Kirin's wife Lidija once merrily declared, "Oh, they had a great time on Rab, singing, partying and romancing the Partisan girls!" I never heard either of them deny it.

In April, 1945, the Partisans retook the islands, and the war soon ended, but Celestin, Maritza and all the Nerezinci found themselves again in contested territory, a situation akin to the conflict over Rijeka after World War 1. Because of its mixed population, from 1945 to 1954, Italy and Yugoslavia had contesting claims to Trieste and its region. It was an early flashpoint of the Cold War. Tito's Partisans and British troops reached Trieste almost simultaneously.

The long, uneasy face-off between Tito's forces and the British became a major international issue. In March, 1946, in his famous speech in Fulton, Missouri, Winston Churchill intoned, "From

Stettin on the Baltic to Trieste on the Adriatic, an Iron Curtain has come down over Europe." The compromise to establish a neutral, multi-ethnic Free Territory of Trieste proved unworkable. In 1954, an agreement was reached allowing Italy to take over the city and Yugoslavia got the surroundings, including Nerezine.

Although they had a Slavic background, many Nerezinci who had been Italianized during Mussolini's rule felt more secure moving to Italy than waiting to see how life might be in Communist Yugoslavia. Though ardent Croatians, Celestin and Maritza eventually decided to opt for Italy. The local economy was stagnant and the cities of impoverished post-war Yugoslavia had little to offer them. By the time they went in the 1950s, Maritza and Celestin had a large community of Nerezinci awaiting them in Genoa. The last Grbac child had departed from the old home in Podgora.

Not long after their arrival in 1955, Celestin was stricken by an incurable disease. He didn't survive long. Two years later Mom urged Maritza to come to America right away. Their mother was ailing and Maritza's help caring for Nona was needed.

Maritza joined our household in Hollywood. We put a second bed in Nona's room for her. With Mom and Nona, Maritza, knowing no English, became the third native speaker of Nerezine dialect in the house. It was good for me, I learned more of the language.

Maritza was an animated Mediterranean personality. We got a kick out of her reactions to America. We chuckled at a supper soon after she came. She asked what was the big occasion—we were using paper napkins with the meal. In Europe then, reusable cloth napkins were for everyday use, disposable paper napkins were an extravagance. Maritza cooked most of our meals, and polenta made a big comeback in our diet. She also took over the laundry chores. Thanks to her I may have been the only student at Le Conte Junior High who had blue jeans ironed with a crease up the leg like dress slacks. Maritza lived with us until Nona died in Spring, 1961.

Herb March: A Son of Brooklyn

As much as my mother's family spoke endlessly about their ethnic heritage and the fates of our far flung family, my father Herb March was the polar opposite about such matters. When I was growing up, unless prompted he seldom talked about his background. Even during family visits with his brother Irving, I never heard them reminisce about old times. More of the information I know about Pa's family actually came from Mom: He had a big extended family, most of them in New York or Florida. He left home at age 17, shortly after his mother died, on bad terms with his father. My parents married as teenagers; it seemed my father adopted my mother's cohesive Grbac clan of his own volition.

Whenever I asked about his background, Pa asserted, "I'm from Brooklyn," with a goofy feigned Brooklynese lilt. Pressed for more details, he added that he was born at home in 1912 in his parents' apartment in a tenement building. They lived on Howard Avenue in the Brownsville section of Brooklyn. He reckoned the nearby corner of Pitkin and Amboy as the center of his neighborhood. As I learned more about his neighborhood and the kind of community it once was, for his Brownsville no longer exists, I realized that Brownsville had shaped Pa just as completely as Nerezine had shaped my mother. Nerezine was my mother's village, and Brownsville, my father's. Pa's character was wrought by the character of his community.

Historian Annelise Orleck described early 20th Century Brownsville as "a community bonded by militancy, an activist hotbed." Unlike the Nerezinci, whose historical consciousness about their home town extends back to Greek and Roman days, the Brownsvillers, mostly Russian Jewish immigrants and their American-born children, reckoned Brownsville's history, as far as it concerned them, only started in the 1880s, when they rapidly transformed the rural farming area into a densely populated urban

Jewish neighborhood. From the start, there were two seemingly contradictory faces of the Brownsville Jewish community. There was devotion to Jewish religious and secular traditions, along with strong proletarian class consciousness that made the community a breeding ground for radical politics.

Rabbi Alter Landesman, the long-time director of the neighborhood's Hebrew Educational Society, has been called "the Brownsville historian." Although he concentrated on more recent times, Landesman wrote briefly about the early days. Like everywhere in North America, Native American people were the original inhabitants. The Canarsie Indians lived there prior to European settlement. Nowadays an adjoining Brooklyn neighborhood is named Canarsie. In the 17th century, the Dutch farmers who arrived grew crops and raised livestock 200 years.

The idea to develop the urban settlement that became Brownsville originated with a Connecticut Yankee, John R. Pitkin. In 1835 he bought land from Dutch farmers intending to divide it into house lots. Pitkin's idea was thwarted by the financial crisis that hit the country in 1836. When he lost the land, the Dutch continued to farm there for another quarter century.

In 1859, another entrepreneur, New Yorker Charles S. Brown, purchased 150 acres of level, well-drained land which he divided into city lots plotted on thirty-foot-wide streets. He sold lots for $50 and in 1863 built and sold rows of wooden houses. Brown's effort to found a town succeeded, unlike Pitkin's, so the locality is Brownsville, not Pitkinville. Nonetheless, Brown honored Pitkin's vision by naming the main business street Pitkin Avenue. The rural village of Brownsville grew incrementally for another quarter century.

By the 1880s, Jewish people began to disembark from Europe, including my great-grandparents. Driven out of Europe by lack of opportunity, crowded conditions, poverty and pogroms —organized murderous attacks on Jewish communities, especially in the so-called Pale of Settlement (the section of the Russian Empire where Jews were allowed to live)—Jews arrived in the US in burgeoning numbers. My father's paternal grandparents came from the vicinity of Minsk in 1889; his mother's parents came in 1888 from Kraków in the Austro-Hungarian province of Galicia.

Jews from the Russian Empire arrived in an unprecedented wave of immigration. In Russia they had endured restrictions that made it difficult to eke out more than a bare existence. During the 19th Century, their hopes were successively raised and dashed as their rulers eased then tightened restrictions.

There had been repression and pogroms before, there had been poverty and inequality always. Now there was a place to go. Needing laborers, the rapidly-industrializing United States allowed essentially unrestricted immigration.

My great-grandparents understood that America's streets were not paved with gold. Nonetheless, they were poor and oppressed in Minsk and Kraków, and as young married couples soon to have their first children, the USA beckoned as a place to make a better living in a more open society. Crossing the Atlantic, still horrid and unpleasant in the steerage of ocean liners, had become a reliable trip. And when they arrived there were growing communities of Russian and Austrian Jews to join.

New York City, especially its Lower East Side, was the most prominent destination. Families crowded into ill lighted, ill heated, ill ventilated tenements, most lacking running water. Barrels of garbage lined the sidewalks and the air was polluted with smoke from coal stoves and coal-powered locomotives of the elevated trains running through the neighborhood.

By the mid-1880s a few Jews managed to abandon the teeming Lower East Side. Some headed for the pastoral setting of Brownsville. Isaac Krupitsky, a tailor, was one of the first. Jacob Cohen, a manufacturer of boys' knee pants, started a small factory there with six sewing machines.

While most immigrant Jews arrived owning next to nothing, that wasn't true of Elias Kaplan. Kaplan came to New York in 1882 with the means to establish a garment factory on the Lower East Side. Elias soon found that the tailors he employed who had immigrated earlier resented working for a newly arrived "greenhorn." They proved to be an unruly workforce, which prompted Kaplan, like other garment manufacturers, to shift away from employing skilled tailors. He divided the garment making process into simplified steps that could be executed by less-skilled sewing machine operators.

In 1887, a real estate developer persuaded Kaplan to relocate his factory to Brownsville, providing a potential workplace to new immigrants like my great-grandfather Max Haber, a tailor. Other garment makers soon set up operations there. According to the 1890 census, Brownsville's population had mushroomed from less than 6,000 a decade earlier to 30,000. Seventy-two per cent of the residents were foreign-born or their American-born children. Initially they were transplants from the Lower East Side, but increasingly immigrants straight from Europe. The rapid growth continued. By 1930 the population was 130,000. Seventy percent of employed persons were garment workers, while construction workers made up another 11 percent of the jobs. During the 1890s, cheap wooden houses were erected along dirt streets, built at a breakneck pace, providing them employment. A New York *Landsmanschaft*, the Minsker Society, a club for former residents of the Minsk region, purchased land from a Dutch farmer and began to erect houses for its members.

While the hastily constructed wooden shacks on dusty or muddy streets represented an improvement for Jews escaping Lower East Side tenements, social reformers of that era commented with dismay that Brownsville was beginning to resemble an East European *shtetl* (a poor Jewish village). Jacob Riis, the noted photographer and author of the pioneering book *How the Other Half Lives*, caustically characterized Brownsville in the later 1890s as "a nasty little slum."

Nonetheless, Brownsville was a desirable escape from the overcrowded Lower East Side. The Williamsburg Bridge, which opened in 1902, contributed greatly to Brownsville's expansion. Even before the bridge was completed, 10,000 people were displaced when their tenements on Delancey Street were pulled down to clear the approach to the bridge, and many relocated to Brownsville. Piecework needle workers could continue their trade there. Express wagons brought them work for 10 cents a bundle.

After the bridge opened, the journey from Manhattan to Brownsville was shortened from hours to just minutes. The neighborhood rapidly urbanized, ironically to resemble the Lower East Side. As the Brownsville building boom continued, the original wooden shacks were replaced by multi-story brick tenements of the sort in which my grandfather Benjamin and my grandmother Rose were raised.

There were some Italians, Greeks and even a few Scots and Germans who had settled there prior to the Jewish influx, but the overwhelming majority in vastly-expanded Brownsville were Jews. European Jews tended to gather in compact communities in America. They were accustomed to living segregated in Europe. Nor were they welcome everywhere in the United States. They sought the security of predominantly Jewish neighborhoods where they could live close to relatives, speak Yiddish, find jobs, and practice their religion. Most of the Jews were from the Russian Empire, especially the Minsk region. They called themselves Litvaks (Lithuanians) because the Minsk area had been part of the historical Grand Duchy of Lithuania. Next most numerous, about 15 percent, were the Galitzianers (Galicians), like Max and Yetta Haber, my paternal grandmother's parents.

Though I know little about my paternal relatives, my mother's notes for an intended piece about her father-in-law indicate that Benjamin "had been born in 1889, a big healthy baby, just as his

Ben Fink, Brooklyn, 1930s

mother got off the boat from Minsk. His mother was a big, strong, blonde Polish-looking woman who could work harder than a man. She even loaded coal when necessary." Mom wrote that her health declined from bearing seven children in quick succession. Four boys and a girl survived. Benjamin was the eldest.

Ben's father, a coppersmith, died when Ben was not quite twelve years old. As the eldest boy, he went to work to support his now sickly mother, three younger brothers and a little sister. One of his early jobs was to haul fresh printer's type from a type foundry to print shops, pulling it along sidewalks on a small wagon.

While most Brownsville Jews were employed as workers, some became business owners. Merchants ranged from owners of substantial stores to pushcart peddlers on market streets. Like the rows of tenements, the crowded street markets of Brownsville came to resemble the Hester Street and Mulberry Street markets on the Lower East Side. At these markets, my great-grandparents haggled to get the best deal for their pennies and nickels.

Census information shows that my Grandmother Rose's father tried his hand as a storekeeper, so in 1908 he may have been among the store operators who complained bitterly about unfair competition from pushcart peddlers who paid no rent for a store. Brownsville storekeepers complained at the local precinct house that the peddlers were a public nuisance. On one market street, Belmont Avenue, there were about 350 rickety stands in only four blocks. Some peddlers were using baby carriages to hawk their wares. The local Police Captain Isaac Frank, the first Jew in that position, disappointed the grumbling store owners. He contended that this avenue had been a market street for over ten years and always had disputes between peddlers and storekeepers. Frank saw no reason for change, although he did order more frequent washing of the streets.

Holding political aspirations, Captain Frank figured there were more votes from peddlers and bargain-hunting customers than from storekeepers. A dozen years later, Frank was elected city alderman with the support of the Brownsville Peddlers Association, thanks to "the just and humane manner in which he had treated the pushcart men during the years he was in charge of the precinct...."

Religion, Anarchism and Strikes

Like other Brownsville Jews, my immigrant forebears and their American-born children strived to forge American identities, navigating between the religious and secular and the radical and moderate influences contending in the community.

Religious practice was established early. The first Jewish services in Brownsville were held in the garment factories. Religious practice remained largely at a grassroots level. A 1928 community survey prepared by Rabbi Landesman reported there were more than 70 "synagogues" in Brownsville, 50 of which had no building. They met in homes and basements. Of the 20 that had buildings, only 6 had "impressive" structures specifically built for that purpose.

Reckoning that a majority of Brownsville Jews attended synagogue only on High Holidays, in September, 1927, Rabbi Landesman enlisted a Boy Scout troop to make the rounds of 40 larger services to count attendees. Results showed only about 8 percent of Jewish men and boys attended non-holiday services, and the number for women was considerably lower.

It seems my grandparents Ben and Rose, like many other Brownsville Jews, were nominally faithful but scarcely observant. In 1926, my father turning 13, his parents figured he ought to have a Bar Mitzvah. But they had never sent him to Hebrew school. Ben managed to locate a rabbi who consented to teach Pa by rote the ritual Hebrew phrases he would need to utter in the ceremony. Pa got through the rite, only needing prompts from the rabbi a couple times. On the whole, Pa was unimpressed with the experience. He felt muttering incomprehensible syllables was "a bunch of foolishness," and the Bar Mitzvah only enhanced his developing atheism.

For decades there had been ferment in American Jewish communities about the place of religion and whether one should even practice Judaism. The old European Jewish notion that a man's highest aspiration should be to study the Talmud, with his wife and family providing material support, flew in the face of the powerful American notion that it is a man's duty to support his family. Indeed, census forms indicate my forebears and their Jewish neighbors as early as 1900 listed the husband as the employed head of household, while the occupation of wives was typically reported as "none."

There were developments that made the community distrustful of rabbis. The Isaacs brothers, who operated a Brownsville wholesale butcher's shop, brought Rabbi Judah Wistenetzky from Europe and paid his salary as long as the Rabbi agreed to certify as kosher only the meat from *their* business. This forced retail butchers to purchase all their wares from Isaacs at unfavorable prices. Ultimately the butchers rebelled. Aided by friends and family, they surrounded and overturned the carriage of Rabbi Wistenetzky and gave him a sound beating. The rabbi returned to Lithuania.

In an explicitly anti-religious action, New York's Jewish anarchists scheduled a "Yom Zom Kippur Ball" in September, 1890 in downtown Brooklyn. Instead of the fasting and prayers of atonement that would happen in Jewish services all over the Borough, the anarchists advertised their event would feature music and dancing and a lunch buffet including bologna and ham! New York's Jewish leaders persuaded a judge the "Ball" would lead to a riot, gaining a court order to prevent the event.

Confrontational anti-religious action did not typify Jewish anarchist behavior in Brownsville. Well-respected community leader Dr. Michael Cohen was the leading anarchist spokesman there. He was born in Poland in 1867 and escaped to America in 1888 to avoid conscription into the Tsar's army. Settling initially in Baltimore, he came into conflict with local Jewish leaders because of his anarchist views. Dr. Cohen married a grocer's daughter, Anne Netter, who was as passionate as he in her radical views. The renowned anarchist Emma Goldman characterized their family's home in the rear of their Baltimore grocery as "an oasis for the radical element, an intellectual center," and affectionately referred to Anne as "dear little Netter."

Michael and Anne moved to Brownsville, where Dr. Cohen established a popular, lucrative medical practice. He invested in real estate and is reported to have owned the first automobile in Brownsville.

Emma Goldman remained a close friend, frequently attending

anarchist gatherings at their home. She did not, however, match Dr. Cohen's business success. Charmed by Brownsville, Emma and her friend Ed Claus opened an ice cream parlor in the neighborhood, which went out of business in only three months. They returned to the Lower East Side.

Dr. Cohen served on the board of the Hebrew Educational Society, gave to local philanthropies and was a sustainer of the local radical newspaper, *Freie Arbeiter Stimme* (Voice of the Free Worker). In the 1920s he became absorbed in a movement that made a big impression on my father, the effort to prevent the executions of Sacco and Vanzetti. Though Dr. Cohen normally wrote anarchist theses in Yiddish, he published a pamphlet on the Sacco and Vanzetti case in English and traveled to Boston to protest.

Leftist politics in Brownsville were not limited to the intellectual discussions and writings of Dr. Cohen's cohort. Agitation for socialism, practical socialist reforms, as well as militant labor struggles and rent strikes were an ingrained part of Brownsville life. An early struggle that indicated prevailing views in the Brownsville community on labor issues was the long and violent cloakmakers strike of 1894. Great-grandfather Max Haber, a garment worker, would have been one of the strikers. The garment factories in Brownsville were shut down so tight, no scabs dared enter. To prevent striking Brownsville garment makers from scabbing in Manhattan, the strike committee required a pass to leave town, with pickets guarding the El station day and night. Here is an account of the strike from the memoirs of Abraham Rosenberg, a garment maker:

> A few Brownsville residents who did work as scabs in New York were packed into sacks during the night and taken away in a butcher's express [wagon]. A few scabs dared to come to Brownsville during the strike to visit their families [on a weekend]. They were escorted by a "funeral procession" never to be forgotten. They were brought in a patrol wagon, guarded by a half dozen policemen on horseback, riding in front and behind. All the men, women and children of Brownsville

followed them with black candles, crying, "*Tze-dakah Tazil Me-Movit*" (Righteousness saves from death). And when the scabs reached their homes alive, they did not dare step out during the entire weekend. Policemen guarded their homes day and night. When the time came to return to New York on Monday morning, the same funeral procession followed.

My grandmother, a striker's daughter, was no doubt among the children in the anti-scab "funeral processions." Rosenberg noted that some scabs wanted to move away to New York, but there was no expressman in Brownsville who would consent to transport their belongings.

In this instance, labor activism and religious convention converged. *Tzedakah*, meaning righteousness, an important principle of Judaism, served to justify the strikers' solidarity, condemning strike breaking as immoral.

That labor struggles, Jewish principles and Socialist politics went hand in hand is evident in the careers of Brownsville Socialist politicians like Abraham Shiplacoff. Born in the Ukraine in 1877, at age 12 Abe came with his parents to Woodbine, New Jersey, to settle in a planned Jewish agricultural and industrial colony. His parents remained in the Woodbine colony only a short time, relocating to Brownsville the next year.

At age 16, Abe entered the world of work and politics, joining a local socialist organization. Although Abe labored as a garment worker for seven years, he nonetheless managed to complete his education and become a teacher at P.S. 84, right in Brownsville. He taught school long enough to obtain his life-long nickname *Der Bronzviller Melamed* (the Brownsville teacher). But devotion to the labor movement drew him to work for unions. In 1915 Abe became secretary of United Hebrew Trades, a union of construction workers excluded from mainstream craft unions because they were Jewish. Later he was an organizer for the Amalgamated Clothing Workers and president of the International Leather Goods Workers Union.

Abe attained his greatest prominence through his political

career in the Socialist Party. In 1915 he became the first Socialist elected to the New York State Legislature. Abe represented his Brownsville district in Albany for two terms, 1915–19. He was one of the Socialist leaders indicted for sedition under the Espionage Act, but the indictment eventually was dismissed. Charles Solomon was the Socialist colleague who succeeded Abe in the legislature. In March, 1920, during a period of "anti-Red" hysteria, Solomon and all five of the elected Socialist representatives were expelled from the New York legislature. New elections were held six months later and all five Socialists were elected again. Ignoring democratic principles, the Legislature expelled three of them. The remaining two Socialists resigned in protest.

Solomon, one of the twice-expelled representatives, made the sort of impassioned statement to the New York Evening Telegraph that inspired Pa's revolutionary convictions. Solomon stated, "The new era is coming. It is too late to stop it. We refuse to go to the battlefield until we have fought it out at the ballot box, but if we ever do go to the bayonet, the blame will be on your head."

No longer in the state legislature, Abe Shiplacoff represented Brownsville as a New York City alderman from 1920 through 1923. He and other Socialists aldermen advocated nutrition for school children, public ownership of utilities, and for the City to sell at cost necessities such as fuel, ice, bread and milk. They opposed public transit fare increases and rent profiteering, and demanded the publication of full transcripts of aldermanic board proceedings.

In January, 1917, while still serving in Albany, Abe was the first New York legislator to introduce a bill to legalize distribution of birth control information. The issue had great relevance in his district. At the urging of working-class women from the neighborhood, birth control crusader Margaret Sanger opened her first clinic in Brownsville in 1916. After one hundred fifty women waited in line for the clinic's opening, Sanger wrote, "I was scarcely prepared for the popular support, the sympathy and friendly help given us in that neighborhood."

At the moment Shiplacoff's unsuccessful bill was introduced, Sanger and her sister Ethel Byrne were in the New York City jail known as the Tombs, having been arrested for distributing birth control information. Ethel was on a hunger strike. The clinic managed to remain open for only nine days. Nonetheless, women of the Brownsville Birth Control League enthusiastically greeted Sanger and Byrne's release in March, 1917.

Birth control was far from the only woman's issue in Brownsville. In 1913, shortly after my father's birth, Clara Lemlich Shavelson and her husband Joe moved to Brownsville. Clara had been a union activist in the 1909-10 New York shirtwaist maker's strike and was blacklisted by the manufacturers. In Brownsville, the Shavelsons found a sympathetic community to settle in and raise their children. Clara became a housewife and a fervent leader of a housewives' movement to value homemakers' labor and for issues that mattered to them, like education, health and especially consumer concerns.

Brownsville housewives organized several consumer boycotts. A powerful soapbox speaker and a committed organizer, for the next three decades in Brooklyn Clara instigated boycotts, sit-ins, demonstrations and political lobbying. She was among the leaders in an early-1920s rent strike that Pa recounted as an important formative childhood experience. Pa spoke of it to oral historians decades later:

At a certain point after the war [World War I] in the large tenement buildings we lived in, the landlords began to introduce electricity. They wired all these buildings. Along with that, they started raising everybody's rents. So the people in the community organized a tenants' organization. I remember in my building, my best friend's father's apartment was where a meeting occurred to form an organization of all the tenants. They decided they would go on a rent strike until an agreement could be arrived at for fair rental. All through the community the rent strikes were widespread. Whoever was on strike would put a sign in his window that said, "Don't Scab." We had the whole neighborhood full of "Don't Scab" signs and the landlords had a rough time.

I remember our landlord used to come once a month to collect rent and he had a big open limousine. Well, all of us kids got ready for him. You used to have to pile your ashes in ash barrels that were in front of the building. So, all of us kids decided that we would make our contribution. We lined up there and that landlord's open touring car got a load of clinkers [cinders] when he drove up. That really was a sight! This whole struggle around the rents was something that affected us and involved all the kids. There was a settlement arrived at and there was a rent increase but it was less than what the landlord had demanded.

During Pa's boyhood in the teens and twenties, Brownsville was widely known as a "Red district," a beehive of political and cultural activity and strong community-supported social services. A coalition of labor and socialist groups built the Labor Lyceum, a hall noted for outstanding lectures and artistic programs. The Lyceum manager was Sol Hurok, who later became a famed concert impresario and manager of world-renowned performers like Andres Segovia, Isadora Duncan, David Oistrakh and Arthur Rubenstein.

The Brownsville Home Relief Hebrew Charity was founded in 1904 to supply coal, food, shoes and loans to those in need, often new immigrants. The United Jewish Aid Society dispensary, opened in 1895, served 20,000-30,000 patients annually by 1909, with 30 physicians on staff. My great-grandparents could be seen by a doctor, an unheard of luxury in the Old World *shtetl* where people relied on home remedies or magical folk cures. My athletically oriented father used the gymnasium at the Hebrew Educational Society (HES). The HES, founded in 1899, still operates and serves all people of the community regardless of racial, ethnic or religious affiliation.

From the historical record it is easy to gain a sense of the community life in which Pa was raised, but we know little about his own family due to his reticence. Pa rarely spoke about his forebears, though in one story he did stress his grandfather's militant unionist orientation:

My maternal grandfather [Max Haber] was once charged with murder in connection with some strike [likely the 1894 tailors' strike]. They tried to frame him for the murder of his boss. The whole basis of the charge was that when talking about the boss he had made the public statement "that son-of-a-bitch ought to drop dead!" Later on the boss got murdered and they charged him with the murder. Some civil liberties lawyer handled this case and they got the charges dismissed.

My grandmother Rose worked as a neckware sales clerk. Around 1910 Rose and my grandfather Benjamin met, perhaps when he was buying a tie. They married in 1911. Ben had worked for a decade at what Pa called "all kinds of labors." Now married and about to become a father, Benjamin sought stable employment. Rose's brother Michael was a postal worker. Despite having quit school in the 7th grade, Ben passed the postal clerks civil service exam and like his brother-in-law, worked for the postal service. Maybe Michael put in a good word for him.

Ben, too, was crafting his American identity. When applying for work with the Post Office, he decided to change his surname. According to Pa, Ben didn't like Falk, the surname assigned to his father at Ellis Island. In Brooklynese it was pronounced "fahk," too close to the local pronunciation of fuck. Because there were a lot of Irish ethnics working at the Post Office, Ben chose the name Fink, which he correctly figured was Irish—even though there are more Germans (and Ashkenazi Jews) who have that name. In German it means "finch," a small bird.

When my father was born in 1912, he was Herbert Fink. In 1915, his brother Morton Fink was born. But Ben became disenchanted with his surname again. To emphasize his Jewish roots he began to use Finkelstein. That name shows up on his 1917 draft registration card.

In 1930, my father changed his name to March. I asked him why he did it. He replied, "I was becoming a union organizer, and the slang meaning of fink was an informer, not so good for an organizer, so I changed it." But why did he pick March? Pa replied, "Well, I got it off the calendar. It was March. I suppose if it had been September, you'd be Richard September now." Pa's youngest brother Irving, over ten years his junior, also adopted March. Morton retained Fink, as have most of his offspring. The Finkelstein name died out with Grandfather Ben.

Coming of Age in Brownsville

When he spoke of his early years, Pa did so in passing, giving out little tidbits about his boyhood in Brooklyn to amuse me or to point out how life was different for kids back then. Though short and disconnected, these anecdotes helped me piece together a portrait of Pa's boyhood.

The city streets and sidewalks outside their tenements were playgrounds for the Brownsville kids. Pa was in a "gang," but to him that had no criminal implications. The kids on his Howard Avenue block were mostly honest. They assembled in their "gang" to play sports. Moreover, a gang was needed for self-protection. Brooklyn kids were territorial. They defended their block from outsiders, occasionally fighting with kids from another street. Sometimes the fights had an ethnic character, with Jewish kids against Italian or Irish kids who lived nearby.

That didn't mean inter-ethnic relations were always hostile. Pa was invited once to an Italian kid's house. They served him a strange food. "That's Sicilian rubber pie," his friend said, "Try it, it's good." Later, in the 1950s, when pizza was becoming a well-known American food, Pa remarked, "Oh look, it's Sicilian rubber pie!"

When it came to food, Pa had an oft-repeated story about a special childhood treat—a slice of bread smeared with lard and sprinkled with sugar! "It's better than cake!" he'd remark. Well, cake frosting is basically made from sugar and lard. And my father loved bread. He commented that when he first heard about prisoners being punished by being put on bread and water, he said, "That was no punishment at all!" He liked plain water, too.

Like all kids in his day, Pa had household chores. Their apartment had a coal stove for cooking and heating. He had to fetch coal and haul away ashes with a little wagon. The gray powdery coal ash always contained "clinkers," coarse, prickly cinders that the boys tossed at the landlord during the rent strike. On Halloween, debris from coal stoves figured in the boys' play. Packing ashes into the long stockings they regularly wore with their knee-length knickers, they went outside to whale away at other boys who were similarly armed. The stocking emitted a cloud of gray powdery dust when it clunked into a playmate's head or body. It was discretionary, depending on how mean you wanted to be, how many clinkers you put in the ash in your stocking. When the boys came home filthy, their mothers spirited them down to washtubs in the basement for a bath.

Pa mentioned he also had to fetch ice for the ice box. He would take a little covered bucket in his wagon to the corner tavern, have the bartender fill it with beer, then bring it home for his father. Transporting things in wagons was considered suitable work for boys in Brooklyn. His father Benjamin had to use one to haul printer's type, but to Pa, a couple decades later, he was just doing family chores. A son of immigrant parents, Pa was able to finish high school and even attend a year of college thanks to the steady work his postal worker father had secured. Ben earned that bucket of beer.

Pa loved reciting poems and songs. Without warning he would quote lines from well-known poems like "Abou Ben-Adhem" or "The Village Smithy," or burst out singing snatches from Gilbert and Sullivan songs. Children's rhymes and songs were a window into Pa's vanished boyhood world in Brooklyn. There were horse-drawn milk wagons, boarders who ate bread and gravy, and old drunks who went pantless looking for buckets of beer.

Pa loved sports. The Howard Avenue boys played stickball and punchball on the street and stoopball against the front steps. Pa mentioned one neighborhood girl who was good at stickball, defying gender conventions. All the street games were conceptually grounded on baseball rules. Using a broomstick as a bat, a boy would throw a rubber ball in the air and whack it with the stick as it descended. Curbs, cracks on the pavement or man-hole covers were designated as bases. The ground rules varied by location, the number and preferences of the players. Punchball was basically the same game, except there was no stick. You tossed the ball up and whacked it with your fist. In the winter Pa frequented the gymnasiums of the Hebrew Educational Society or his schools to play handball and basketball.

Though Pa and the majority in his neighborhood were Jewish, he didn't embrace Jewish identity. He felt "Jewish" was a religion and became a confirmed atheist. But there may have been more to it. He probably found Jewish to be an inconvenient heritage when he pursued the occupation that was his true passion—union organizer. As it turned out, he did not become an organizer among the Jewish working class he grew up with in Brooklyn. A twist of fate in 1930 took him to Kansas City, where he worked on civil rights issues among African-Americans. He also organized workers and the unemployed, who, in ethnic terms, were a cross section of the American Midwest. It was enough for him to be castigated as a radical, a Red, an agitator or a damned IWW. He didn't want to add being a Jew to all that in an anti-Semitic world.

Later, in Chicago's packinghouses, he was chiefly organizing African-Americans, Mexicans and Eastern Europeans, Polish and Lithuanians prominent among them. He usually said he was part Lithuanian and part Polish. That was a bit of obfuscation. In fact, "Lithuanian and Polish" was his English translation of "Litvak and Galitzianer," the backgrounds of his father Benjamin Finkelstein, a Litvak, and his mother Rose Haber, a Galitzianer.

Galitzianers were from Austrian Galicia. The term Litvak is a bit more complicated. For several centuries the home district of my ancestors in Minsk was under Lithuanian dominion. This multi-ethnic realm encouraged Jewish settlement and developed a substantial Jewish population. These Jews kept the name Litvak centuries after Lithuania shrunk to a fraction of its former expanse.

A good-natured rivalry existed between the two groups. The Litvaks claimed the Galitzianers were flighty, emotional and prone to religious mysticism. They pointed out that most of the Hasidim were Galitzianers, an old-fashioned and unlettered bunch. The Galitzianers declared they had educational and advancement opportunities in Austria that the bumpkin Litvaks never had in the Tsars' Pale of Settlement. They contended they were more cosmopolitan, referring to Galitzianer doctors, lawyers, musicians and artists, many of them living in cultured Vienna. The Litvaks countered that they are actually more intellectual and studious, and certain their opinion is always right.

Pa joked that being half Litvak and half Galitzianer made him such an undesirable mongrel in Brownsville, he had to go somewhere else and marry a *shiksa*, a Christian girl, because no pedigreed Jewish woman would have him.

Pa was bi-polar between stereotypical Litvak and Galitzianer personality traits. According to the Yivo Jewish Encyclopedia, "the stereotypical Litvak is portrayed as unemotional, withdrawn, intellectual and mercilessly critical; he challenges authority and is by nature skeptical, stubborn, and impatient with, and suspicious of, others." Pa could be all of that, plus austere, single-minded and dogmatic, also Litvak traits. He and his father, with whom he had a severe falling out at age 17, were two stubborn, unforgiving Litvaks who never patched up their relationship as long as they lived.

Pa's self-discipline and single-mindedness were amazing. From his teens into his 40s, he devoted himself to "saving the world," scarcely distracted from his mission even by threats to his life. Then in his later 40s, he began to study law at night school, thinking becoming an attorney might provide another path to serving the causes he held dear. He spent every possible moment poring over law books at a small desk in his bedroom. To drown out commotion from other household members, he kept a radio near him tuned to his beloved Dodgers' ballgame. But he didn't let Vin Scully's play-by-play distract him from learning law. He graduated *cum laude* and easily passed the difficult California bar exam on his first attempt.

Although he had this rigorous side to his personality, all at once, the austere, serious Litvak could disappear and Pa became a fun-loving Galitzianer—cooking sweetened foods, ready to kid around, spouting poetry and songs, fond of absurd jokes.

By the 1950s, after I had a chance to hear some "Dead End Kids" speak Brooklynese in movies on television, I wondered why Pa didn't speak like that. He claimed most of his chums did. Everybody called him "Hoiby." He maintained that because he was a good student, he emulated the diction of his teachers whose New York accents were more subtle.

He had a few stories about his schooling. There was an elderly male teacher who was an expert shot, flinging pieces of chalk or blackboard erasers at misbehaving boys. "When that eraser hit a kid, it looked like a bomb went off," Pa said, referring to the cloud of chalk dust. But Pa, a good student, probably wasn't ever the target of an eraser. He was a quick learner and skipped through the elementary grades. Rejecting his local high school, he was accepted early into an exclusive program at Boys High School in the Bedford-Stuyvesant neighborhood, graduating in 1928. This from his oral history:

When I was young, at a very young age I started to read, long before I went to school. I started at about the age of four. I imagine I got a library card when I was about six or seven.

(Who taught you to read?)

My father. I wasn't getting very much that interested me at school because I had read SO much. I must have carried cards in about four different public libraries.

I couldn't get my fill of books. My spare time was divided evenly between athletics and reading, about 50-50. I'd read a while and go out to play ball a while. The two things both intrigued me a good deal. And of course I sought out friends who thought along the same lines.

At that time the schools were, as now, overcrowded. And a solution for crowded conditions in the New York schools was to take the brightest kids and push them ahead so they could get them out of there as quickly as possible. Just to give you an idea of how fast they pushed us ahead, I graduated from high school at the age of fifteen.

His favorite anecdote from Boys High concerned their production of Gilbert and Sullivan's "The Mikado." Since it was a male-only school, all the female parts were played by boys. Pa was one of the "three little maids in school." The production hit a crisis a couple days before opening night. The voice of his pubescent classmate, the leading soprano, suddenly changed to a raspy baritone. The music teacher salvaged the situation by teaching the boy to sing in falsetto, and the show went on.

Oral history researchers were most interested in the political aspects of his early life. In 1970 an historian asked about his evolution from Brooklyn neighborhood kid to crusading labor organizer:

(Was your father in the union movement?)

My father belonged to the union among postal employees. Matter of fact, he was a steward in his station.

The neighborhood which I lived in had a strong Socialist sentiment and, as a matter of fact, they elected various Socialists to public office. The first election I remember was the time Debs ran for the presidency from prison. My old man, because he was employed in the post office, didn't want to let people know he was voting for Debs and so he told me that he was voting Republican, which didn't do me much good among my friends in the neighborhood. I ran into a lot of antagonism because most of the kids' parents were voting Socialist and voting for Debs. Well, my father actually did vote for Debs, he told me later.

Pa disdained his father's caution about expressing political beliefs for fear of losing his job, a tactic Pa never adopted in his own life. Pa resented that he had to fight with friends due to his dad's apprehension. Pa always insisted he had a right to his opinions and soundly rejected the notion that he should conceal them, even at the expense of security, financial or physical.

Through several years of his childhood, the case of Sacco and Vanzetti was an ongoing concern. Nicola Sacco and Bartolomeo Vanzetti were Italian immigrants, proponents of anarchism, who were convicted of murdering a paymaster and a security guard in Braintree, Massachusetts. There was contradictory evidence and many felt they did not receive a fair trial because they were immigrants with radical beliefs. During the lengthy appeals process, there developed an international movement calling for their freedom. Pa described the night in August, 1927 when the two men were executed.

I remember the campaign around the fight for Sacco and Vanzetti, which was an issue that moved the whole community. Everyone was concerned about the case and I remember many street corner meetings where it was discussed. I most distinctly remember how on the day that Sacco and Vanzetti were executed there was a corner a few blocks away at which the early morning paper was delivered around eleven o'clock at night. There were just thousands of people gathered very spontaneously--this wasn't organized--around that corner to wait for the newspaper delivery to see whether Sacco and Vanzetti actually had been executed. It was sort of like a wake and I remember the silent crowd, the gasp of shock when the newspaper appeared. I still remember that front page picture of Sacco and Vanzetti covering the whole page, with the banner headline that they had been executed. I must have been about thirteen or fourteen when that occurred.

After graduating from Boys High, Pa got a summer job at a factory that made rulers, but at 15, he was too young for a permanent job. In 1928 he enrolled in the Brooklyn Branch of the College of the City of New York. From the Pitkin Avenue soapbox speakers, he developed an interest in Marxism. Ever the voracious reader, he began to study the subject.

There was a severe internal fight going on in the communist movement then between the [Jay] Lovestone supporters and the [Alexander] Bittleman supporters and this fascinated me because it was on a highly theoretical level. It resulted in my reading a lot, trying to figure out who was right and who was wrong.

Pa's comment about this split was a portent of things to come in the Communist Party: "I couldn't quite understand why they were so vicious with one another."

At his college he tried to organize a Marxist study group. He had to settle for an economics club that discussed the classics, Adam Smith, Marx and others. He said it didn't amount to much, but through it he met a lifelong friend, "Kappy" Kaplan, another bright Jewish boy who also was becoming a radical.

Pa and Kappy climbed up to a platform on a water tower near their college, enjoying the secluded spot to discuss Marxism. They carried on the kind of discussion I remember having decades later, at the family dinner table, which gave me a basic knowledge of Marx's theories. The two teenagers were awash in a world of ideas, idealistically seeking to remedy the social inequities that surrounded them: the fabulous fortunes of the super-rich and the poverty endured by tenement-dwelling workers. "I just didn't think it was right for some people to be so poor, half-starved, while others were so damn rich," Pa said.

But how could the transformation to socialism take place? They knew that with the existing political system set up to perpetuate capitalist rule, the elected Socialist representatives from their community were excluded from holding office. There would need to be a second American revolution, hopefully not as violent, to bring about economic justice. Operating in the economic realm, American workers would come to understand their interests and their ultimate power. They could organize unions, break the power of the capitalists and usher in a democratic, egalitarian socialist society.

Imbued with this vision, at age 16, still in college, Pa and Kappy joined the Young Workers League, which later became the Young Communist League (YCL).

I became a member of the Young Workers League. I joined shortly after I got into college. My family moved out to Ozone Park, Queens. And of course I missed the old gang I'd run around with. Although I made friends with the guys in Ozone Park, I still liked my old gang. I used to go back to Brownsville to see the old bunch a couple times a week at least. And after spending the day there, in the evening I would head out toward the El station. It was a long walk. I used to go along Pitkin Avenue and listened to political speeches being made. A lot of radical organizations had street corner speakers. I started to attend meetings of the Young Workers League.

He discovered the YCL had little interest in organizing college students. Their focus was on industry.

Their tactic was for young people to become active in unions, to bore from within, as it was called, to make the labor movement, which was quite staid and conservative, more progressive, and also to organize the unorganized.

Pa attributed his decision to quit college and go to work at the end of the 1929 school year to a "rough situation" at home. His mother was ill. But clearly the passionate, newly minted revolutionary was chomping at the bit to organize young workers. The "rough situation" may have had more to do with a growing conflict with his father. As a postal clerk, Ben had worked for over 15 years in a secure, decent-paying job. He managed to get out of the Brownsville tenement and become owner of a single-family home in Ozone Park, a newer, better neighborhood a few miles east.

My grandfather now had three healthy young sons. Although he only managed to get to the 7th grade, Ben had already enabled his brilliant son Herbert to graduate from a prestigious high school and to begin college. But the recalcitrant teenager was developing crazy notions. First of all, Herb rejected their move to a nicer house in a better location. He hung around with a gang in the old declining neighborhood. And now he wanted to quit college! Did he realize what a rare opportunity it was that he wanted to throw away! He had the brains to become anything he wanted, a top lawyer, doctor---anything. And for what?! To be a revolutionary! It's fine to advocate for socialism and for unions. Most people around here believe in that. But to throw everything away to become a despised radical, probably wind up in prison, maybe even the electric chair. Ben must have been nearly mad with frustration, anger and grief.

At the same time, the illness of Ben's wife Rose worsened. She had developed "female problems" from complications after the birth of her youngest son. It was the kind of gynecological ailment about which people like them felt a sense of embarrassment. They could have sought up-to-date medical treatment. But instead, Rose opted to rely on patent medicines. In the 1920s, these nostrums contained mainly alcohol and opiates. So in spite of his improved material situation, Ben had a wife whose improperly-treated illness was worsening, along with an out-of-control son who was about to wreck his own life.

Samuel Edward Haber now came into the picture. Sam Haber was my grandmother's younger brother, Pa's Uncle Sam. Sam was a smart kid who quickly became the most ambitious, if sometimes ethically challenged member of the family. Ultimately he made a lot of money in business dealings that my parents intimated were shady—maybe mob connected. The only way he is represented in family stories is as an evil tempter trying to lure his relatives' sons to the dark side. In Census and public records, I found his occupation listed as lawyer or a real estate developer. His 1917 draft registration card noted he was a shipping clerk, single, stout, with flat feet and rheumatism, clearly not good stock for a soldier. By 1920, he lived in Queens, married to a woman whose parents were born in Italy.

It might have been the idea of Rose or Ben, or perhaps Uncle Sam himself to approach his brilliant but unruly nephew Herbert with a lucrative proposition. Sam picked up Pa in his late-model car and took him to view suburban properties his company was developing. Sam offered to finance his education if he would become a lawyer and promise to work for Sam's expanding company. Sam was childless and would treat him like his own son. It's easy to imagine where this conversation went. No doubt the young revolutionary gave a vociferous "No!" to his uncle's offer to join the exploiting class.

Ten years later Uncle Sam, ever persistent, offered to adopt my brother Bob in exchange for paying the young man's way through law school. Bob would have to work for his rich uncle's business in Florida.

Same type of offer, same type of answer!

Getting back to 1929, Pa, firm in his conviction to become a revolutionary, quit college and went to work.

The very first job I got was in a freight yard unloading silica from box cars. It's used in sand blasting. I worked with a shovel. Then I went to work in a furniture factory for a while. I worked in a doll factory, I worked for some months in a printing plant, Street and Smith. They used to print those pulp magazines, like *Argosy* and *Western Stories*, all that stuff. I worked there in the shipping crew. Where I could, I attempted to organize.

Then came the stock market crash and the onset of the Great Depression. As far as Pa and many others were concerned, Karl Marx was looking prophetic. Capitalism seemed to be falling apart under the weight of its own internal contradictions.

Richard March

A few months after the Wall Street crash of October, 1929, I lost my job. I became active in the YCL then, while I was unemployed, because I had a lot of time on my hands. I helped to organize the unemployed and began to speak at street corner meetings, all sorts of meetings. I developed some talent as a public speaker.

(What did you do with the unemployed?)

Well, one of the biggest things was organization of a big demonstration of unemployed in New York on March 6, 1930. This was a peculiar thing. The press became all alarmed about the Communist Party and the Unemployed Councils organizing a demonstration, for the slogan was, "We want work or wages." There wasn't any relief or any unemployment insurance, which was central to our campaign. And the press gave the demonstration so much publicity they inadvertently helped build the thing up. I remember the morning headlines, "Red Day Dawns" that helped attract a bigger crowd to Union Square. There was a tremendous demonstration and the police broke it up, arrested a lot of people.

(Were you arrested then?)

No, I might have been had not somebody fouled up on bringing me the message that I was expected to be one of the speakers. I never got the message and they grabbed some kid to speak in my place. He ended up with six months in jail.

Shortly after that 1930 Union Square rally Herb symbolically reinvented himself with a new surname: Herbert Fink became Herb March. He was a good-looking teenager with a thick crop of wavy black hair, penetrating blue eyes and handsome features. He had a barrel chest and a muscular upper body. His legs, however were thin and bowed because he had rickets as a boy.

Herb had found his calling. He and the rising masses would transform American society. They would help usher in a new day of democracy and economic justice. An effective extemporaneous speaker, he was a rising star in the YCL, with a loud, resonant voice and a charismatic personality. Herb had "studied" the oratorical techniques of Pitkin Avenue soapbox speakers. He understood how to draw in an audience, the importance of timing and a key turn of phrase. Soon an opportunity arose for him to get away from the "rough situation" at home.

63

Before that [Union Square rally] I had been asked to go to New Jersey to help build up the Young Communist League and the Unemployed Councils. I went to Perth Amboy, where I was active in the area of New Jersey immediately adjacent to New York, organizing meetings, demonstrations, fights for relief. We'd call a demonstration, set up an organization, send a committee in to meet with the City Council, the City Fathers, and ask for something like five dollars a week for an unemployed family so that they could sustain themselves.

At the same time, I was active in trying to organize workers in various industries. We would organize small groups of workers in plants and distribute leaflets. We urged people to organize but had no great howling success. We developed, at least, a little nucleus of people who were interested in unions in their plants.

Nearby was Paterson, New Jersey, a famed hotbed of labor unrest, the site of a storied 1913 silk workers strike led by the IWW.

Then a silk strike started in Paterson, New Jersey, a famed hotbed of labor unrest. The strike was organized by the National Textile Workers Union, which was a newly organized affiliate of the Trade Union Unity League. I participated in it and was active as a volunteer organizer in connection with the strike. What I did was live with a striking textile worker's family. I ate in the strike kitchen and helped picket and organize strike activity, particularly with the young people.

Pa was away from home for the first time, contributing to what he was certain would be the coming revolution. On a personal level, it was in Paterson that he lost his sexual innocence with a daughter in the silk worker's family he was boarding with. He must have told Mom about it, because I remember her teasing him about the incident. His rejoinder was, "Well, she crawled into my bed and attacked me....and I let her!"

He had his first run-in with the law in New Jersey, too.

One funny thing that occurred while I was in New Jersey in the fall of '29, the state elections came along and the Communists had candidates. We decided that we would make up little stencils that said,

"Don't starve-- Fight! Vote Communist." We got some red paint and went out late at night stenciling street corners. Then it struck us it would be a good idea-- here was a beautiful white cement railroad viaduct-- and that would be a better place to paint it because it would stand out. While we did manage to paint a few signs there, somehow or other, the police found out and I got pinched. I was brought before a judge and he looked at me. I was a beardless youth, a young kid. The judge lectured me about how I defaced private property. Then he said, "Well, you seem to be a nice young fellow. I'll tell you what, I'll get you a bucket and I'll get you a brush and you can just clean that thing off." I drew myself up in indignation and said to him, "Your honor, never!" Now that annoyed him. "Ninety days in the county workhouse for malicious mischief."

(How was that jail?)

An awful place. I was there for a couple of weeks. The place was overpopulated. It was loaded with people who were just unemployed, who had been thrown in jail for vagrancy. Some of them had been taken off freight trains or arrested while hitchhiking or trying to bum meals. And then, of course, there were petty criminals. You had that mixture. I tried preaching communism to a couple of the crooks. They thought, "Hmmm, what's yours is mine and what's mine is mine. Sounds pretty good to me."

Along toward Christmas they declared a holiday amnesty and got rid of a whole bunch of people because the place was overpopulated and Middlesex County was broke. At least you got something to eat there.

There was one young kid in there about my age, a Polish kid named Frankie Dziubana. I'll never forget the way he got into jail. He had gotten into a fight with his father about the fact he was unemployed. The old man worked in one of the copper smelters; he just couldn't understand why a young, husky, strong boy like Frankie couldn't get a job. Apparently the old man was a big, gruff sort of character. As a matter of fact, he was famous in the community as a weight lifter. And Frankie was no slouch himself, a very powerful young man. We became very fast friends in the two weeks in jail. And the funny thing about it was that later on, when we organized an unemployed organization in Perth Amboy, Frankie was in the crowd and Frankie became the chairman of this unemployed organization, even though he was only about eighteen or nineteen.

Pa was proud of his jailhouse organizing success. He covered a lot of territory in the oral history interview quoted above. However, he didn't mention the most wrenching occurrence during that time: hard upon his release from the New Jersey jail, his mother Rose, succumbed to her chronic illness. There was anything but calm in the bereaved household. Married for two decades, Ben had trouble coping with her death. In its immediate aftermath, he wound up estranged from his eldest son.

In an argument with Herb he said, "You put a knife in your mother's heart. In her grave illness you were in jail like a common criminal." Herb walked out and returned to his YCL comrades in New Jersey. Soon he took an opportunity to go even farther away. The YCL asked him to be an organizer in Kansas City.

Sweet Home Chicago

The Chicago neighborhood where my maternal grandfather Ivan Grbac settled in 1914 is known as West Englewood, located eight miles southwest of Chicago's downtown. The original European settlers were German and Swedish farmers who came in the late 1840s. A few years later, as rail connections to Chicago were established, more Irish and German immigrants arrived seeking job opportunities with the railroads and in the nearby Chicago stockyards. Notably, a small community of African-American railroad workers was established early in the 1860s only a few blocks southeast of 59th Street where Ivan settled.

In 1871 Chicago was devastated by the Great Chicago Fire. Survivors needed housing, prompting a building boom in the area. In 1889 the City of Chicago annexed the district and integrated it into the city's transportation network: street car lines came in and an "El" station opened.

In the early 20th century, an influx of Italian immigrants arrived, along with Slovenians, Croatians and other Eastern Europeans. Chicago's first Croatian Catholic parish, Assumption Church, was founded in West Englewood in 1903. When Ivan and son John arrived in the neighborhood, they joined a thriving immigrant community. In 1930, eight years after Nona and the younger Grbac children arrived, the Census showed fully two-thirds of West Englewood residents were either immigrants or their American-born children.

Within days of their arrival in December, 1921, the Grbac youngsters enrolled in nearby Earle Elementary, a Chicago public school. There was no provision for teaching English as a second language. The newcomers were simply put in the first grade classroom with the six and seven-year-olds. Even though they brought in a larger desk for him, thirteen-year-old Joe couldn't stand the indignity of it. He walked out of the schoolroom and ran home.

67

"They put me in with the little babies," he moaned to his mother. Nona had to give firm orders—he had no choice but to attend school.

The girls' initial reaction to school was less tumultuous. After having her eyesight examined by the school nurse, Jacinta soon was fitted with glasses and for the first time she saw the sharp edges of everything around her. Joe got glasses, too. As they mastered English, the Grbac kids moved ahead to higher grades during the course of the school year, eventually catching up with their age groups. Joe and Agata learned to speak English with a slight but noticeable foreign accent which stayed with them, while Jacinta struggled to eliminate all trace of an accent.

She was humiliated by a cruel teacher who sat her in the "dunce's seat" and made her repeat attempts to pronounce the words "shoulder" and "soldier." She conflated them into "shouldier," to the hoots and ridicule of her classmates. Mom spent hours at home staring at her lips in the mirror practicing English pronunciation. She eventually achieved her goal. By the time she was grown, no one would take her for anything but a native English-speaker. Except when she said "shouldier," her lifelong linguistic Achilles heel.

After Nona's shock on the day she arrived in Chicago, she laid down the law for husband Ivan and sons to clean up their acts. In pictures from the 1920s, Ivan and the Grbac boys appear well groomed and well dressed. Nona wouldn't stand for the grime and lice that had resulted from years of neglecting cleanliness in their "bachelor pad." Having been accustomed to lots of space in the roomy house in Nerezine, she pushed for bigger and better quarters. Before long, the Grbacs acquired improved housing to replace the crude digs over the shoe store. Ivan got a good deal on a house that had to be moved or else torn down. He and the five Grbac brothers undertook the house-moving themselves, bringing it to a lot on 59th Street near the corner of Ashland Avenue, just around the corner from his shoe shop. The house was tall, a two story duplex with a high, roomy attic.

During the moving process, they had quite a scare. Brother Dan nearly was electrocuted. From his post on the roof, he had the task of raising utility wires enough so the house could pass under them. There was a noisy spark from a wire that shocked him but fortunately, not fatally.

The eldest son John returned to Chicago with his bride Katarina. They bought a house just two blocks away. Two Croatian boarders helped household income and kept Kata busy with cooking and housework for three working men. In his youth, John had learned the cooper's trade, and there was work for him making barrels in local factories—first in meat packing plants and later in breweries, where the pay was better. He also made large wine casks for his father. In their basement they made all the wine they needed for their own consumption, which in the 1920s was legal, and for their speakeasy *ošterija*, which was not. Ivan, together with other members of the Croatian community, would order a boxcar of grapes each summer, purchased from Croatian vineyard growers in Michigan. When it came in, the West Englewood Croats assembled at the railroad yard with wheelbarrows to unload each family's share of grapes. All the Grbac kids' toes were stained purple from stomping grapes that became their family's wine.

Ivan kept firm control of household finances and was reputed to be very "tight." Stinginess was considered a common trait of Nerezinci. A fellow from Unije, a small island near Lošinj, once told me, "If you were lying on your back in Nerezine, dying of thirst, they won't even spit on you!" Nerezinci, of course, consider frugality to be common sense.

As the head of the household, Ivan insisted that all his children, including his grown sons still living at home, hand over their entire earnings to him each week. He would return an allowance to them. Mom remembered an occasion when Dick (Gavde) challenged his father about the miserable two dollars of their pay that he would return to each son weekly.

"Can't you give us a little more money? You know what we're going to spend the two dollars on, don't you?" They would spend two dollars at a brothel was the implication. A big argument ensued. Eventually Ivan increased his sons' allowances a bit.

The only Grbac brother who remained in the "Old Country" through the early 1920s was Krešo. The family was supporting him to study medicine at Zagreb University. Deciding the future of the whole family was in America, the Grbacs decided not to support

Krešo to become a doctor in Yugoslavia. He should join them in Chicago.

By this time, the US had enacted the National Origins and Quota Act, which severely restricted immigration. Through the immigrant grapevine, the brothers learned how to bring Krešo into the country. He traveled first to Central America, and then was smuggled to New Orleans aboard a banana boat. Brothers John and Dick traveled by train to New Orleans with the bribe money for the ship's captain, bringing Krešo up to Chicago on the next day's train.

To everyone's dismay, they discovered that learned institutions in the US would not recognize Krešo's years of medical education in Zagreb. Entering medical school in the US would be too costly and would require several years to complete. As an alternative, Krešo entered the pharmacy program at Valparaiso University in nearby Indiana, where in 1927 he became qualified to be a pharmacist. Mom remembered the family outing to Valparaiso to attend Krešo's graduation. Proudly seeing her poised, sophisticated brother in a cap and gown instilled a desire in her to pursue higher education herself.

Krešo was the most cosmopolitan and "European" of my aunts and uncles. He wore a neatly trimmed moustache in an era when most American men did not, and was always well attired in tailored suits. Krešo's wife Eva was of Austrian Jewish background, making him the first Grbac to marry a non-Croatian. He shared our family's leftist views, but wasn't active politically. His contribution to our vision for a better world came in the highly ethical way he practiced pharmacy, a healing profession. In his compact corner drug store, aside from the pharmacy counter, there were just a few shelves stocking over-the-counter remedies, scarcely any non-curative products and no liquor or cigarettes. When I visited it, Krešo always gave me a box of Smith Brothers cherry cough drops, the closest thing to candy in his drug store.

The Grbacs Prosper

In the 1920s, the Grbac clan made economic headway in Chicago's West Englewood neighborhood. Ivan the shoemaker had a significant business. In a 1920s photo of his high-ceilinged, old fashioned shop, Ivan sits behind the counter facing an electric machine, working on a shoe repair. In a glass display case several pairs of boots are visible—perhaps the same fancy type of boots that Ivan learned to make in the Hungarian Navy. Shelves cover the walls nearly to the ceiling stocked with dozens of shoe boxes, a considerable inventory. In addition to repairs he had significant business in new shoe sales.

Ivan's multi-lingual abilities were an asset. He could easily discuss a shoe repair in Italian with a customer, while for various Eastern Europeans, his German, Hungarian or Croatian came in handy.

Ivan Grbac shoe shop, Chicago, 1920s

Ivan wouldn't take any guff from prejudiced white customers if they reproached him for serving members of the nearby African-American community. "Their money is just as good as yours, and what's more, they never complain about the shoe repair jobs that I do for them!" To reinforce his lack of prejudice, he was known to declare, "No Jew has ever tried to cheat me!"

The spacious shop was quite an improvement from the original sheet metal shack he and son John occupied when they first came to Chicago. That dismal hovel had a small commercial space in the front and a cramped, primitive back room with barely enough space for the coal stove and the cots they slept on. When the Great War broke out in 1914, communications with Nerezine were cut. They worried constantly about the fate of their family, cut off in Nerezine.

They scrimped and saved money from the shoe business and John's earnings as a cooper until they were able to purchase a two-story storefront building nearby. America's entry into the World War in 1917 proved a boon to Ivan's business, with a contract to produce boots for the US Army.

By the early 1920s, Ivan had managed to reunite most of the family in Chicago and acquired more real estate. He arrived from his home village, a penniless political refugee, but through the 1920s he became a successful businessman, with five sons who were skilled tradesmen—a cooper, boilermaker, mechanic, plumber and carpenter. A sixth son graduated from college to become a pharmacist.

Four of the brothers were active in the construction business, subcontracting on major carpentry and plumbing jobs. They were an up-and-coming force in the community. Posing for pictures, all of them attired in suits and hats, the six Grbac brothers, John, Dick, Tony, Krešo, Dan and Joe look the part of the "pack of wolves" a pro-Italian Nerezin had once called them. But now they were wolves in Chicago's urban jungle.

Toward the end of the '20s, Ivan's health began to fail. Knowing he wouldn't live much longer, Ivan was grateful to have six sons to carry on the family name.

His three elder daughters were far away. The two eldest, Christina and Lena, lived in Portland, Oregon with their shipyards worker husbands, Maritza and Celestin were holding on in Nerezine in the family homestead. But his two youngest daughters, his babies, were still at home and were a joy to him. Because of the appreciation of opera he developed as a young man in Budapest, he realized that daughter Agnes had a good voice and potential to become a fine singer. She wasn't as studious and intellectual as her younger sister Jacinta, but Agata had talent and a lot of verve. She was a social butterfly, and young men flocked around her. Agnes listened to her father's recordings of Enrico Caruso on their Victrola and hearing her promising attempts to sing along, the usually parsimonious Ivan paid for her to take private voice lessons. Unfortunately Ivan died before Agnes had the opportunity to sing in Croatian community operettas and make a self-produced recording.

Circumstances in Nerezine had deprived my mother Jacinta (Jane) of schooling, so in Chicago she craved, embraced and appreciated learning like a starveling craves food. Like her future husband, she was an avid reader. Because she already needed glasses, Ivan chastised her not to read too much, especially when she became engrossed in a book until late at night. She would turn off the lamp in her bedroom on her father's order, but then hold the book by the windowsill and read by the streetlight outside.

Owing to Ivan's active involvement in the parish, nearby Assumption Church became the family's core community. In addition to church services, Jacinta attended dances, dinners and other social events at Assumption where the Croatian language and culture were dominant. At church dances, one or more of her brothers always kept an eye on Mom and sister Agnes. At the girls' curfew, 10 o'clock, the brothers walked them home, then returned to the dance to spend more time with their girlfriends.

At age 14, while going through puberty, Jacinta confided to her confessor that she had sexual thoughts and feelings. The priest advised her that these "unclean" thoughts could be turned into something virtuous and holy if she were to become a nun. Still carrying guilt about her traumatic first communion, Jacinta seized on the notion that entering a convent might be a way finally to expiate her sin. After school, she began visiting nuns at a nearby convent of the Franciscan order known as the Poor Clares. The nuns were friendly and solicitous.

She revealed to her father she was considering becoming a Poor Clare. He pondered the notion a bit, then delivered an ego-crushing comment. "Maybe it is a good idea for you. You are tall and skinny. You might not be able to get married anyway." But my oldest brother Bob had another seemingly contradictory story about Mom's flirtation with monastic life. "Didn't you hear about what happened when the Mother Superior came over to visit the house? Our grandfather told her, 'No, you're not going to get this girl. She's too smart and too beautiful.'" Perhaps Ivan had rethought his initial idea.

Her arrival in the US at age nine helped Jacinta become the most fully Americanized Grbac sibling. She had no trace of foreign accent and despite her (to Americans) unpronounceable name, she developed a coterie of American-born girlfriends. Her school mates called her Jackie. The gang of girlfriends took playful snapshots of their summer frolics, swimming at Lake Michigan beaches and canoeing at rural lakes.

Her high school teachers, mostly females, recognized Jacinta's intelligence and talents, especially her art teacher and Miss Conrad, her English teacher. As she approached graduation, the teachers encouraged her to seek a scholarship to Grinell College in Iowa, a small liberal arts school with a tradition of social activism. She began to envision attending college and eventually becoming an artist or a journalist. When she brought up the idea to her father, Ivan was against it. "Women who go to college just become prostitutes," he proclaimed.

But as it turned out, it wasn't her father's opposition that prevented Jacinta from attending college. Little could she imagine the disasters that soon were to befall her family and dash those fond hopes.

Despite Ivan's satisfaction with his family's success in Chicago, unfinished business in Nerezine weighed on his mind. Although the political situation for Croatians remained bleak there, he needed to deal with issues concerning his properties in Nerezine. Knowing he hadn't much time, he wanted to see his birthplace once more. His legs were painfully swollen due to diabetes and he had a lot of difficulty breathing due to worsening asthma. After seventeen years away, he wanted to stand on his native soil. He wrote to relatives back home, asking them to inquire discreetly how the local fascist authorities might react to his return. He received assurances that he would be left in peace, as long as he didn't create a stir. So Ivan applied for a US passport and made plans for the trip.

When he received the passport in the fall of 1929, it galled him to have to write his European address on the passport's inside cover using the Italian spelling: Neresine and to indicate that his birthplace was Italy. Late in September he traveled to New York, stopped off at the home of his brother-in-law Luka and at the beginning of October retraced his 1912 voyage in the opposite direction; he sailed for Trieste, arriving on October 7.

It seemed strange to return to the Nerezine house where he had lived for more than twenty years with his wife and kids, the former location of his business enterprises and the Croatian reading room. Now the town was totally under Italian domination. The house was the home of daughter Maritza and her husband Celestin. There had been changes but also much that was familiar. Furniture and items he remembered still were in the house seventeen years later.

When he had been in Nerezine about two weeks, Ivan read in the Italian newspapers about the great stock market crash in New York. In the course of a few days, the value of stocks plummeted, foretelling the Great Depression, which would soon mean calamity to his family's fortunes.

Ivan wound up staying in Nerezine nearly a full year. In the 1970s an elderly relative told me, "You know your grandfather came back here before he died. But he was really sick. His legs were swollen and his asthma was bad; he had to sleep sitting up in a chair in order to breathe."

I found a postcard he sent to Nona in September, 1930. "Dear Wife and cherished children, I want to notify you that I have decided to travel back there on the steamship Vulcanna. It leaves Trieste on September 23. Rosić, the son of Aunt Urbina is coming with me. He will stay in Chicago for a while. Everybody here is fine. I am also feeling much better, so I am returning while I do. On the return I will stay for a few days in NY. Be happy, Your father, Farewell."

Only two months after the Vulcanna departed from Trieste, Ivan died in Chicago on November 23, 1930.

#

Ivan Grbac was known to say, "No Jew ever tried to cheat

me." He died in 1930 not knowing that in 1931 his family would be cheated catastrophically not by a Jew but by Christian banker John Bain. In one of the most sensational financial scandals of the Depression era, Bain, his sons and a son-in-law were convicted of massive embezzlement and fraud.

John Bain came to Chicago in 1887, a 19-year-old immigrant from Scotland. He settled in West Englewood, working as a plumber before starting a realty company. In highly leveraged deals, Bain built over 300 cottages, selling them to the immigrants streaming into the neighborhood.

Using extreme tactics, even for Chicago's notorious corruption, Bain and his family members funneled millions from the Bain banks to themselves and their cronies, to the detriment of over 150,000 depositors and investors, who lost millions, huge sums in 1930s dollars. Most of his victims, like the Grbacs, lost everything they had.

When Ivan Grbac arrived in West Englewood, John Bain was the community's most prominent financier, the obvious banker to deal with. Bain seemed respectable. He lived right in the neighborhood in a fourteen-room mansion. Bain promoted a reputation for honesty—"Honest" John Bain, a slogan that a seasoned Chicagoan should have taken as a sign of its opposite.

Bain used highly leveraged pyramid schemes to start or control twelve neighborhood banks, placing an overlapping set of cronies on the boards and hiring his sons and sons-in-law for highly paid bank positions. He bought the favor of local politicians, making large contributions to the ruling Republican Party, especially to the faction headed by Charles S. Deneen, a former Governor and US Senator. The Deneen faction touted themselves as the "reform" wing, but they were equally corrupt.

In 1929 Bain acquired land at 87th and Stony Island and announced plans to erect a ten story building there. The Grbac brothers were known to Bain as skilled construction workers from his neighborhood. He offered them a big deal to do the plumbing and carpentry work, offering a loan to obtain the needed building materials. After Ivan's death, Bain insisted that the life insurance benefit the family received be put in his bank as security on the loan.

The Grbacs didn't know Bain's financial empire was on the verge of collapse. Bain suffered severe losses even before the stock market crash due to a downturn in real estate values. Pyramid schemes only work in a rising market. Bain was scrambling for funds to cover his losses and the outflow of deposits from his banks. Some prescient depositors began to withdraw their savings. To raise money he used outright fraud, soliciting deposits and continuing to sell shares in the banks and real estate company.

By the time Bain lured the Grbacs into the fateful deal, there was an omen of things to come. In May, 1930 Bain suddenly sold his mansion and moved to the suburb of Oak Park, far from the depositors who'd soon lose their savings.

On June 9, 1931, unable to obtain any more credit, Bain closed all twelve banks in his chain, generating banner headlines in the Chicago newspapers. Before closing them, the Bains pillaged the banks, salting away assets. Perhaps the most poignant incident occurred only hours before the Bain banks closed forever. Mrs. Anna Nolan entered the Stony Island State Bank with a $2,500 insurance settlement from a crippling accident her husband had suffered. Before depositing the money, she inquired about rumors that the bank wasn't in good shape. Robert Bain, the head cashier, assured that her money would be absolutely safe. She made the deposit. When the bank closed that afternoon, Robert Bain took the $2,500 home.

In December a grand jury issued indictments for embezzlement and fraud against Bain, his two sons, a son-in-law, and two partners. The partners turned state's evidence. Mobs of defrauded Bain depositors attended every court session. The judge often had to admonish spectators to remain silent. At the close of one session, a woman confronted Bain and loudly exclaimed, "God will punish you!" As it turned out, she indeed had to rely on God to do it. When the judge pronounced the defendants guilty, he sentenced John Bain leniently to 1-5 years in the penitentiary, and slapped the three younger men with fines of only $1,000.

Bain remained free on an appeal bond until his political allies on the Illinois state Supreme Court overturned the convictions on narrow technical grounds. Although the ruling had nothing to do with the evidence against him, Bain was quoted exclaiming, "See, I always said that I have done nothing wrong!"

Bain's theft of the family's funds was a major cause of three Grbac sons making the fateful decision to go to the USSR, where they all perished.

Uncle Dick

I often wonder how much my deceased namesake Dick Grbac influenced my life. Named after all three of my "Russian uncles," my first name, Richard was the "American" name of the brother whom my mother admired the most.

He went by a number of names: Gavde, Rade, Richard and Dick. He was physically fit, an enthusiastic soccer player. He had a brilliant mind, although largely self-educated. He was an avid reader who encouraged her to read. He took plenty of books on his frequent ocean voyages. He sailed, but was more than just a sailor. He was a skilled mechanic, not only of ships' engines, but automobiles, too, from work in three auto factories, in Chicago, Portland, Oregon, and Moscow.

From the time he left home in Nerezine at age 12, he was a traveling man, never living anyplace long. As a maritime worker or mechanic, the whole world was his home and he didn't hesitate to navigate it. But the most important thing about him, Mom said, was that he was a committed idealist. He fervently devoted his life to the causes he believed in.

His first cause was Croatian nationalism, which he got with his mother's milk. As teenagers in Nerezine, he and his brothers formed a tamburitza orchestra, an ensemble featuring the Croatian national instrument. The Grbac boys sang patriotic songs but even their love songs in Croatian were implicit political statements. Their music, performed in the big *sala* of the Grbac house, was the highlight of Croatian gatherings in Nerezine.

The brothers resumed musical activity in Chicago, playing at dances in Assumption Church hall and at Croatian lamb roasts in Dan Ryan Woods, a nature conservancy. It was one of many Chicago forest preserves that provided city residents green parkland and were a locale for ethnic picnics.

Much as playing tamburitza in Nerezine symbolized resistance to the Italianizing elite, in Chicago the music likewise affirmed the worth of Croatian culture, a message to the dominant English-speaking elite—we immigrants are equal to native-born Americans.

Other Grbac siblings found cultural and political affirmation in music. In the 1930s Agnes and her brother Joe sang in Chicago's "Crvena zvijezda" (Red star) Croatian choir, performing folk songs, patriotic and socialist hymns. In the 1940s, when Agnes lived in Detroit, she performed in operettas produced by the local Croatian community. In Detroit she became the on-air host of the weekly "Croatian Radio Hour." She aired tamburitza recordings, announced community events and read the news in Croatian. During the mid-1940s when Krešo lived in Detroit, he took over the newscasts using his good Zagreb University diction.

As in Nerezine, in America the Grbacs endeavored to become a middle-class family. But historic events, the Depression, wars and fascism, thwarted their best efforts. Like the worthless Austrian *kroner* banknotes that Nona burned in anger on the hearth, thousands of hard-earned dollars disappeared into Bain's crooked money maelstrom. The Grbacs were among millions of Americans betrayed by capitalism's failure, stripped of assets, hungry and turned out of homes. Many began to ponder whether a different economic system was needed to end their misery. In the United States the Grbac family and many Croatian immigrants became devotees of a new cause, socialism. Dick was the person who brought socialist ideas into the family, ideas that six siblings espoused, while two more were sympathizers.

Socialist ideas had been percolating for decades among the workers and intellectuals of industrial states. Excitement about socialism peaked following the 1917 October Revolution in Russia. Bolshevik abuses of power and Stalin's crimes were still unknown. There was genuine hope among workers, many who had recently survived serving as cannon fodder in World War 1, that the Russian Revolution represented the dawning of a new age of economic justice and democracy. In 1919 there emerged Bela Kun's short-lived Hungarian Soviet Republic. There was the ill-fated Sparticist revolt in Berlin led by Rosa Luxemburg and Karl Liebkneckt, and in China, Sun Yat Sen's revolutionary Kuomingtang allied with the

Bolsheviks. In the United States, the city of Seattle was paralyzed by a general strike. A world-wide revolution seemed possible.

During the 1910s Dick worked as a seaman starting at age 12, surviving a shipwreck on the east coast of Italy at age 15. As a youthful seaman he learned about socialism in Trieste, a city with a strong leftist movement since the early 20th Century. In many countries the radical ideas of anarchism, syndicalism and communism were rife in port cities among dock workers and seamen. The idea of class struggle had resonance among common sailors who were subjected to rigid, semi-military control by their privileged ships' officers.

In 1919 in Trieste, Dick hired on as a crew member of the ocean liner Martha Washington, sailed to New York where he jumped ship, and traveled to Chicago to join his father. He found work, sailing out of Chicago on Great Lakes ore boats. During the winter, when shipping stopped on the ice-choked lakes, Dick found other jobs—taxi driver, factory worker. As an immigrant proletarian, he continued to be exposed to leftist politics. Radical organizers targeted the Ford Motor factory in South Chicago where Dick worked. Communists and other radicals recruited workers from Chicago's industrial plants and working class neighborhoods, areas with large numbers of the foreign-born.

Dick's own Croatian ethnic group became a hotbed of communist sentiment in Chicago. Statistics from 1930-31 show that South Slavs (Croatians, Slovenians and Serbs) constituted a little less than 2 percent of the total foreign-born population of Chicago. They constituted, however, more than 10 percent of the Chicago Communist Party's foreign-born membership—more than five times their proportion in the population. Only Chicago's tiny Finnish immigrant group exceeded this ratio with six times their proportion being Party members.

Dick embodied the rambling, thinking, radical proletarian that Woody Guthrie, a decade Dick's junior, symbolized for many Americans. Both were musicians and, like Guthrie, Dick seemed to have "itching heels." In America he sailed the Great Lakes, or headed to New York where he had relatives in Hell's Kitchen and a large community of fellow Nerezinci in Astoria, Queens. He played soccer in Astoria and skated on the lagoon below the Hell's

Gate Bridge. He worked in the heart of Manhattan at Schrafft's Candy, and from New York's harbor, he shipped out on ocean voyages. He sent snapshots to the family from Liverpool, England, Bremen, Germany, pictures of Norwegian glaciers and of himself on deck in the mid-Atlantic.

These photos excited the imaginations of his younger siblings, especially my mother. Dick had a swaggering style. He posed for a photo in a dress shirt and tie, wearing a straw boater hat, brashly grasping the wheel at the helm of a real ship, or in another picture taken at Coney Island, perched on an ersatz boat in front of a painted maritime backdrop. He exuded poise, confidence and adventurousness. His little sister Jacinta idolized him.

Dick at helm with boater hat at wheel.

His sojourns with the family in Chicago, never lasted long. Dick was loath to accept the patriarchal domination of his father, especially Ivan's control of the purse strings.

In 1926 Dick's itching heels took him west. He worked his way across the continent, ending up in Portland, Oregon, where his older sisters lived. In Portland he found work at the Ford Assembly Plant on the city's southeast side. He connected with local leftists, some of whom had been cohorts of Portland native John Reed, the famed radical journalist.

During that period, Dick fell in love and became engaged to a Portland woman. But in 1929, differences arose and the engagement was broken. Disappointed, Dick's itching heels yearned to hit the road. Soon he found a place to go. On January 1, 1930, in the Imperial Valley, in the far southeastern corner of California, aggrieved Mexican and Filipino lettuce workers spontaneously went on strike. Their union was only loosely organized but communist organizers voluntarily came to the valley to bolster the faltering strike.

The Imperial Valley was (and remains) corporate agriculture in its most extreme. Massive federally-supported irrigation projects transformed it from an arid desert into a prolific vegetable and melon growing area. Right across the border, an army of impoverished Mexican farm workers provided cheap labor, toiling stooped in the scorching heat. Two years earlier a spontaneous strike had broken out during the cantaloupe harvest and was brutally crushed by local and state lawmen acting as the growers' Cossacks, under the leadership of Charles Gillett, the county sheriff.

Gillett intensified repressive actions during the 1930 strike, arresting strikers, organizers and even journalists who dared to report on it. At one point, Gillett's deputies surrounded a hall where a union meeting was taking place, arresting more than 100. Dick managed to avoid Gillett's dragnet but when strike leaders learned he was undocumented, an "illegal alien," they advised him to get out of the Valley. "You'll just get pinched and deported," they said. So early in 1930, Dick made his way back to Chicago.

Chicago was in turmoil. A growing communist-led movement of unemployed workers staged a large demonstration to demand relief on March 6, the same day as Pa's Union Square rally in New York. Efforts were under way to organize militant unions through the Trade Union Unity League (TUUL). Dick didn't stay in Chicago long. The organizing bug had bitten him, and feeling he was first and foremost a seaman, he headed for New York, where he became an organizer for the TUUL-affiliated National Maritime Workers Union.

Soon Dick was one of several American trade unionists invited to tour the USSR by the Friends of the Soviet Union, a group that had arranged such tours since the mid-1920s. They were taken to see model facilities: factories, hospitals, and workers' resorts. The tour was paraded through the best of the best "Potemkin village" sites, greeted by hand-picked workers, enthusiastic supporters of the regime.

Back in New York, Dick learned of his family's unemployment and financial ruin. Moreover his younger brother Dan experienced a "nervous breakdown." In a paranoid panic attack, Dan leaped off a moving Illinois Central commuter train, miraculously managing to avoid serious injury. Dick hurriedly traveled to Chicago to see about Dan's condition. Dick found him confined to an insane asylum where he was subjected to the typical mistreatment of the mentally ill practiced then. He was strapped down and bruised from beatings.

Dick, the seaman used to ranging across the entire globe, made a snap decision. On his tour of the Soviet Union, he had seen a mental hospital in Rostov, a model facility. The psychiatrists had explained their humane up-to-date treatment of patients. Much as Krešo rescued Dan from the clutches of the cruel pig farmer in Croatia, now Dick would get him out of this hell hole. He became determined to take his brother to Russia for suitable treatment in the Workers' State.

The Grbac family in Chicago was reeling from the death of their patriarch only months earlier. Agnes became ill with tuberculosis of the spine and was confined in a full body cast. There followed the crushing loss of their savings in June, followed shortly by Dan's mental breakdown. Amid all that turmoil Dick proved persuasive. He proposed to take Dan to Russia for treatment. Capitalism had crashed. They were unemployed, facing hunger and uncertainty. Dick declared there was plenty of work for everyone in the Soviet Union. When he was in Oregon, he heard about Seattle Commune, a utopian farming settlement in southern Russia, about 100 miles southeast of Rostov. The commune had been founded in 1922 by Finnish- and Russian-Americans from the Pacific Northwest. A peaceful life on the farm might be all Dan needed to get well, and if he worsened, there was always the model mental hospital in Rostov.

The expected construction job on the Bain building was off, so Tony, the boiler-maker was unemployed and unencumbered. He had no wife or kids. "What the hell," he said, "If you're going, I'll go too. You say there is plenty of work there."

By the end of August, 1931, three Grbac brothers were ready to depart for Russia to join Seattle Commune. Dick had been recommended by comrades from the Northwest known to the communards. Moreover, they wouldn't arrive empty-handed. They were skilled tradesman bringing the tools of their trades, Dick a mechanic, Dan a carpenter and Tony a boilermaker and plumber.

They traveled to New York in Dan's car; my mother and Uncle Joe went along in the jam-packed vehicle to drive it back to Chicago after the brothers' departure. With heartfelt farewells, Dick, Tony and Dan sailed away. Jacinta and Joe decided to take a longer return route, via Niagara Falls to see the world-famous cascade. While driving through upstate New York, they found the highway blocked by state patrol cars as they approached a bridge over a small river. Curious, they ventured on foot to the bridge to see what was happening. To their horror, protesting dairy farmers were dumping barrels of milk into the river. As victims of starvation during World War 1, and now enduring new privations in the Depression, this was a horror beyond comprehension. They could not accept as justification that the market price of milk was too low for the farmers to cover costs. Milk was being dumped while children were starving. They returned to the car and broke down in uncontrollable sobs.

The cascade of milk spilling into the river overwhelmed their recollection of seeing the mighty falls at Niagara. I heard the story of the dumped milk from both my mother and Uncle Joe, without ever a word about their impressions of Niagara Falls.

A Teenage Revolutionary

In 1930, seventeen-year-old Herb March left the nest and was ready to change the world. His mother died, he and his father were at loggerheads; his YCL comrades became a surrogate family. That summer, YCL leaders offered him the job of organizer for a seven-state district: Iowa, Missouri, Kansas, Nebraska, Oklahoma, Arkansas and Texas. Pa said an optimistic estimate would be about 150 YCL members in the seven states then, mostly in Kansas City and Houston. A hotel manager in Kansas City was a movement sympathizer. He could surreptitiously provide lodgings. Herb was promised a salary, $5 a week. Pa said, "I received that $5 for one week, the first week and never got any salary thereafter."

Pa's move from the New York City area, the nation's hotbed of radicalism, to the dusty Great Plains might seem like an exile, being sent to Siberia. And perhaps some higher-ups in the YCL or Party thought it best to send this unruly, ideologically eclectic teenager to the hinterlands, where his political career would likely wither on the vine. But in fact it had the opposite effect.

While nowadays the central and southern plains are a region where conservative politics dominate, in the 1880s and 1890s, the area was a breeding ground of populist politics and the most significant agrarian upheaval in American history. After the Civil War, southern farmers, both whites and freed slaves, were forced into debtors' servitude in the crop lien system. With no other sources of credit, farmers borrowed directly from local merchants who provided basic foodstuffs and supplies until "settling up time" in fall when the farmers' cash crops, frequently cotton, would be sold. The tight money, gold standard policies coerced on the nation by the big bankers led to a constant drop in farm commodity prices, so the indebted farmers year by year fell further into debt. Those that owned land often lost it to settle the debt, joining the ranks of landless tenant farmers, even more impoverished. Many moved west to the plains, where cheap homestead land was available, but the oppressive crop lien system followed them to the new territories.

In the 1880s a cooperative movement, the Farmers Alliance, sprang up, attracting thousands of farmers who pooled resources to mutually support production and marketing of their crops. They were fiercely opposed and eventually smashed by business interests who refused to engage in commerce with the cooperatives. By the 1890s the political dimension of the agrarian movement reached its zenith with the formation of the Peoples (Populist) Party. Their presidential candidate in 1892, Iowan James B. Weaver, carried four states, Kansas, Colorado, Idaho and Nevada, the greatest success a third-party candidate ever achieved.

Twenty years later, the Industrial Workers of the World (IWW) attained considerable success among itinerant harvest workers. From 1913 to 1917 they organized the Agricultural Workers Organization (AWO), headquartered in Kansas City. Calling strikes just as perishable crops were ready for harvest, they succeeded in raising the pay and reducing work hours for thousands of farm hands. The AWO's membership reached 18,000 by the end of 1916.

Persecution of the union intensified with the entry of the US into World War 1 and the Red Scare that followed. By 1919 the IWW was decimated by lynchings of organizers and show trials of its leaders and even many rank-and-file members. Nonetheless, in 1930 there were still many veterans of the AWO and other IWW unions abroad in the plains states.

For nearly thirty years prior to Pa's arrival, socialist advocates had been active on the Great Plains, such as Kansan Kate Richards-O'Hare, a passionate writer and lecturer on socialist and women's causes who was imprisoned for speaking against US participation in World War 1. Richards-O'Hare, a tall woman who customarily dressed in white, "spoke with such fervor that she would be wringing wet with perspiration at the end of each performance," according to Elizabeth Gurley Flynn, another famed leftist orator.

By a remarkable coincidence, the diminutive town of Girard, Kansas, where Pa had a memorable experience speaking to the Crawford County hunger marchers, also happened to be a major hub of socialist publishing. Socialist publisher Julius Wayland moved his operations there in 1897, because he viewed Kansas as "ripe for socialism."

Wayland's newspaper *Appeal to Reason* became the most widely circulated socialist publication in the United States through close association with Eugene V. Debs, the railroad workers union leader who became the Socialist Party standard-bearer in four presidential elections. In 1900 when Debs was making his initial run for President, Wayland made *Appeal to Reason* an unabashed supporter of the campaign. Debs was one of the great orators of his generation. He crisscrossed the country delivering hundreds of speeches, travelling on behalf of the *Appeal*'s Lecture Bureau. For their 25¢ admission, attendees received a year's subscription to *Appeal to Reason*. With thousands attending lectures, circulation grew every week of the four years Debs was on the road. From 1900 to 1917, the *Appeal to Reason* staff expanded to nearly 100 employees, producing weekly print runs ranging from 500,000 to 750,000.

In 1917, the editors of the paper broke with the Socialist Party over its opposition to US entry into the World War. It was a pragmatic capitulation. Had they not done so, the government would have prosecuted the editors under the Espionage Act and prohibited use of the Postal Service to distribute *The Appeal*.

In 1919, staff members Emanuel and Marcet Haldeman-Julius purchased a controlling interest and phased out *Appeal to Reason*. For decades they published "Little Blue Books," inexpensive tracts on science, hygiene, atheism, sexuality, birth control and various schools of socialist thought.

The region Pa entered in 1930 had been a cauldron of dissent for decades, thwarted and stilled at times, but reemerging in new ways. The desperate people of the Great Plains were again spurred to act by the privations of the Great Depression.

Pa described his journey to the middle of the continent:

They gave me a bus ticket to Pittsburgh. They said, "You get yourself out to Kansas City, the rest of the way." So I shipped a suitcase to Kansas City, the Chrysler Hotel, and hitch-hiked.

When I got to Pittsburgh, there was a strike going on by a miners union, the NMU [National Miners Union], a left-wing union, and one of the organizers had a return ticket to Cincinnati. He said, "You take this. It'll get you to Cincinnati." From there I started to hitch-hike. In a couple of days I only got as far as Terre Haute, Indiana. I wasn't making much headway. Then I ran into some kids about my age who were going to work shucking broom corn. "Take the freight train with us. That'll get you to Kansas City." So I went with them. They showed me how to hop a freight. I got as far as St. Louis where we were thrown off the train by railroad dicks, so I hitch-hiked the rest of the way to Kansas City.

Thus Pa learned to ride freight trains. During the next couple years, if he needed to go to a meeting in Omaha, Sioux City or elsewhere in his district, he headed to a "hobo jungle," an encampment of homeless people, and inquired when a train might be heading his way.

I met Bob Long, the manager of the Chrysler Hotel, which became Pa's residence, when I was 13. In 1960 my parents and I were driving cross country from Los Angeles to Madison, Wisconsin, on our way to see their new-born first grandchild. Passing through Kansas City, Mom had the brainstorm to look up their old friend. Twenty-eight years earlier he was the best man at their humble wedding. She found him in the KC phone book. We met him, a slim gray-haired man, in front of the vacant Chrysler Hotel building on Wyandotte Avenue. I could scarcely believe the decaying three-story brick building was big enough to have once been a hotel.

The neighborhood had become a crumbling, half-abandoned warehouse district on a hill commanding a view of the Missouri River, a large suspension bridge visible in the distance. For 2½ years in the hungry early '30s this was Pa's home base and the first residence of my newlywed mother and father.

Pa was assigned a fictitious job as "night clerk" at the hotel for which he received lodgings and occasional meals. But he spent little time hanging around the hotel. With only the vaguest instructions from the YCL, he wasted no time to swing into action. He had experience in New Jersey organizing the unemployed, then an emphasis of the Communists. Freshly arrived in Kansas City,

Richard March

Pa set out to develop an Unemployed Council:

I met with a group of unemployed people in the Rosedale section of Kansas City, Kansas. That's a poor working class area, right adjacent to the packinghouses. The group was about 1/3 Anglo, 1/3 Mexican and 1/3 Black. People were out of work. This was September, 1930. School was about to open. The kids were required to wear shoes to school. And women at the unemployed meeting said, "Our kids haven't got shoes, they've gotta go to school and we oughta get 'em some shoes." They were barefoot, y'know.

Well I made a motion. "Tomorrow let's go down to the relief station as a committee and we'll ask 'em to give shoes to the kids so they can go to school. Everybody thought that was a great idea and they asked me if I would be the spokesman.

So they passed the word and the next morning we came down to the relief station in Rosedale. No one had told me that it was on the second floor above the police station. Well we got out there, about 100 to 150 women and kids. It was early. We were waiting for the relief station to open up. And the police were there, looking at us as they went in and out of the station. One of 'em asked me what we were doing, and I told him.

Just before 9 o'clock, a whole squad of policemen rushed out with clubs and sawed-off shotguns. They grabbed me, arrested me and chased the women and kids down the street, waving their clubs and guns at them. They took me in the cell block and the sergeant says, "You're one of those goddamn IWWs. I took care of them before."

So the sergeant "questioned" me, with two other policemen holding guns on me. He had a club in one hand. He'd ask me a question, about anything, "What's your name?" and before I could answer, whop, he hit me, knocked me down, sort of to punctuate the question, one time with his fist, next question with the club. After his fist got sore, he used the club exclusively.

This kept up, I'd get a slug, he'd knock me down and I'd turn my head and look at him with a smile as if to say, "You old son-of-a-bitch, if it was just me and you, I'd take care of you." I was a pretty husky young fellow.

When they finally got tired of this, they left me in a cell. The next morning, they charged me with Inciting to Riot and I got bailed out.

91

There was a series of mass meetings stemming from that incident which resulted in organizing the unemployed. Tremendous sentiment swept the whole area. Kids ask for shoes and somebody gets beat up for it! They ended up with a big mass meeting in a ballpark in Kansas City, Kansas. Five or six thousand people, unemployed, showed up at the protest and the police captain, I think his name was Beady broke it up with tear gas and clubs, and of course, shotguns always were present as a threat. And Jeez, we had a hell of a time convincing these young Kansas City kids that they shouldn't go home and get their shotguns. They were ready for a fight. A hell of a big unemployed movement developed in Kansas City, Kansas, and by the way, the kids got the shoes.

Pa became the "lightning rod," the guy up in front who was willing if need be to take a beating or a bullet, if that was what the movement required. Pa wasn't a masochist. Though he intensely disliked pain and discomfort, he was proud that he could take it. He felt he should be free to pursue the legal activity of organizing people to demand their rights. He refused to be dissuaded by illegitimate, unconstitutional actions of authorities.

Pa followed his own judgment about organizing efforts. When asked by historians about how much he was instructed by Party or YCL leaders, he replied,

Well, I was a maverick. I'd just go out and do what I thought was the right thing. There were people in the Party who felt I was hard to control. In all the time I was out in Kansas City, no one from the YCL ever came to meet with me. I'd send them a letter about every two weeks to let them know what I was doing. Sometimes I'd get a letter back saying 'That's fine.' or suggesting something. Essentially we were on our own, so we did what we could.

Pa worked on three fronts: organizing protests by unemployed councils to demand relief, union organizing in the Kansas City packinghouses, and efforts to oppose "legal lynchings," frame-ups and executions of African-Americans, usually on trumped-up rape charges. He worked on the racial justice issues with a young African-American from Kansas City, Henry Winston, who later became a major CP official among the Party leaders persecuted in the infamous Smith Act trials.

One of the first guys we recruited was Henry Winston. We got involved in fighting "legal lynchings." Winnie would follow the press very closely. We discovered in 1930 a case of a man in Daingerfield, Texas named Bonnie Lee Ross who was charged with rape and sentenced to die in the electric chair. We had a branch of the YCL in Houston that we contacted and they sent a young lawyer to Daingerfield and he started investigating. He discovered that the woman who alleged rape wasn't quite sure who did it. What they did was pick up this fellow Bonnie Lee Ross who was a transient coming through town. He wasn't local so they agreed to blame him. This would make less hard feelings in the town than charging someone from the local Negro community...He had some local whites tell him, "Well, he's not from this town. Maybe it's for the best."

When the locals found out what the lawyer was doing, they threatened to whip him with trace chains. He left town. He had to. But he filed this report and made it available to us. So in Kansas City we held meetings on the streets protesting this case. We were getting organizations to send telegrams to the governor of Texas and we got it in the press as much as we could, which was limited. We got into the press by getting arrested. We held a mass meeting, the KC police came down. They arrested me and a whole bunch of us, beat us up. So it got some publicity.

On the day before the execution date, because of all these protest letters, the Texas governor issued a statement. He said, "It may be that this "nigra" is innocent, but sometimes you have to burn a house in order to save a village." He actually made that statement, and the guy was executed.

These efforts by Pa and Winston, protesting racial injustices through rallies, arrests and civil disobedience, presaged the Civil Rights Movement by 25 years. Their efforts also preceded the cases of the Scottsboro "Boys," nine African-American teenagers arrested on rape charges in Alabama. By 1932 their cases became an international cause supported by the CP and the NAACP. Unfortunately, there was no shortage of legal lynchings to be concerned about. Pa continued:

About six months after the Bonnie Lee Ross case, another case arose in Slick, Oklahoma involving a man by the name of Jess Hollins. It was another case of rape. We saw an article in the paper that this Jess Hollins was accused of rape. The trial lasted twenty minutes and they sentenced him to death. Well, that looked like a frame-up. So we investigated and found out that the man was told, "Look, if you plead innocent, we'll turn you over to the mob, but if you plead guilty we'll spare you." So he pleads guilty and they sentenced him to death anyway.

So we got two of our members to go to Slick and find out what was happening. They found Hollins had a wife, Irene. They were being watched very closely. But they managed to bring Hollins' wife out of there to Kansas City, tearing through Oklahoma pursued by a couple cars full of Ku-Kluxers.

After that I went down to Oklahoma City to organize a protest movement. First I contacted the black American Legion post. They were interested. I spoke before the post and they went on record to support the fight for freedom for Hollins. They set up a defense committee and organized a fundraising banquet for Hollins' defense. The banquet was inter-racial, which was quite a new thing for Oklahoma City at that time—they were strictly Jim Crow then.

Then I met with Roscoe Dungee, who was head of the NAACP for Oklahoma and editor of a newspaper called the Oklahoma Black Dispatch. Roscoe Dungee agreed to head up the Hollins defense committee and to publicize the case in the Black Dispatch. He put a picture of me and him shaking hands on the front page, identifying me as the organizer for the YCL.

After we had the banquet, we decided to see what we could do to get to the governor of Oklahoma, Alfalfa Bill Murray. We were told that the best approach would be through a lawyer named Lohman Pruitt. Years before, in the early '20s Pruitt had defended the blacks who were arrested in connection with the Tulsa race riot. Well, Pruitt was a character. In Tulsa, he came to court with a pistol, he laid it on the table, said he had been threatened but that he knew how to defend himself.

He was famous for another case that people told stories about.

Pruitt defended a guy who got convicted of murder and he was due to be hanged. So Pruitt appeared at the execution. They asked the guy if he had a last wish. He said, (this was worked out in advance) "Yes, could I have my lawyer pray for me before I'm hanged?" And they said, "Why yes, of course." So Lohman Pruitt got down on his knees and prayed and prayed and prayed, and then finally he looked at his watch and finished his prayer. He got up and said, "One moment please." He pulled a copy of some statute out of his pocket that said if you delay execution beyond a certain point, then the execution is cancelled. He saved the guy's life. So that was Lohman Pruitt. He was fabled around there.

Pruitt had an office in Oklahoma City. He was a pretty old man then and in his cups most of the time it seemed. Our committee went to see him, Dungee, me, Irene Hollins and a couple more people. We told him about the case. All the while he was sipping a little whiskey. So he told his secretary, "Get me Bill, Alfalfa Bill." He knew him personally. He got Murray on the phone, he says, "Hey Bill, you know as well as I, there's no such damn thing as rape." Well we just roared. Pruitt asked him for a stay of execution, and the governor, right then, while we were sitting in the office told him, "Yes, I will grant a stay of execution. See what you can do."

Subsequently this case was handled by the local committee and the NAACP. They found that the woman and Hollins were having an affair. When it was found out, she claimed rape. Hollins ended up with a jail sentence, about eight years, but at least he didn't get executed.

Pa did pioneering civil rights work in the Jim Crow Southwest. Although his Brownsville upbringing offered him few opportunities to encounter African-Americans, in Kansas City his sincerity, fearlessness and passion were convincing. He would become a groundbreaking anti-racist leader, respected and trusted by African Americans as he fought for equality in Chicago in the meat packing industry. Thanks in large part to his decisive role, the United Packinghouse Workers of America, the union he helped found, is noted as one of the most actively anti-racist unions in American history.

Before he relocated to Chicago in 1933, Pa also had some direct experience organizing packinghouse workers in Kansas City.

We decided to work on packinghouses. It was the biggest industry in KC then. We had a group of union-minded people particularly among the Yugoslavs there, and the Russians and some Blacks. We got out a shop paper, a one-page two-sided leaflet called "The Packinghouse Worker." We wrote up why we needed a union, an industrial union. We got info from our people, that in this department they were doing such and such to the workers, and in that department the foreman was a son-of-a-bitch. We stated the need for unionism, all the grievances at Armour, Swift and Wilson.

On Strawberry Hill, or as we liked to call it "Garlic Hill," there was a Croatian Hall and most of the Croatians were left-of-center and a lot of them were packinghouse workers. So I used to meet there, developed a group, kept on making contacts. We had an informal packinghouse workers union, or so we called it, but it was not any real union yet. It didn't dare meet openly. You had to be very careful. They'd fire anybody for talking union. It was done completely like an underground organization. The only thing that surfaced was this bulletin. We got non-packinghouse workers to distribute it in front of the plant. Of course, that shook up the whole management. There was intimate knowledge of details of one or another department written up. They wondered, "Where is this coming from?" It shook 'em up.

Years later, when the unionization drive began in the KC packinghouses, several of the workers active in these early efforts became union leaders, especially the Croatians.

According to his assignment as YCL organizer, Pa was supposed to concentrate only on young workers. But he remained a maverick, bristling at the Party's rigidity.

There were maybe 300 Party members in the Kansas City area. Because I was organizing packinghouse workers, there were people in the Party who felt I was out of control. Organizing the packinghouses should have been done by the Party, but they didn't do it. I was YCL. So I got young guys and I got older guys. It didn't make any difference to me. I was functioning—call it whatever you want.

As the Depression continued, unemployed workers and dispossessed farmers fell into worsening straits, and their demands for relief became ever more urgent. Pa organized people facing starvation to demand at least the aid needed to sustain their lives. One such effort was the Crawford County hunger march.

In Crawford County, down in the southeast corner of Kansas, we had developed unemployed councils among the coal miners who live there. The miners were in bad shape. They were locked out, or only working two, three, four days a month. There was a certain militant tradition of the miners in that area around Pittsburg, Kansas, Joplin, Missouri, all through there.

Wages had been cut. Wages were based on tonnage; you got so much a ton. And the miners had to furnish their own blasting powder. They were working at a starvation level when they were working at all, and winter was approaching. The miners had managed to get along with a little work and the produce from their gardens for a little food, but there was no welfare, no relief, no unemployment insurance then. They were facing starvation that winter.

The unemployed decided to demand some relief from the county commission which was scheduled to meet in November [1931] in Girard, Kansas, the county seat. It was decided to organize a Crawford County hunger march. It would start from Pittsburg and all the little coal camp towns and converge on Girard. A committee from the march planned to go in to the county commission meeting and ask for some form of welfare, or relief as we called it.

Since I had a big mouth and could make a speech, they contacted me. I rode the blind of the finest passenger train from KC down to Pittsburg, Kansas on the night before the march. So we marched. I was not part of the delegation to go into the meeting. I was supposed to be the speaker. We got into Girard and the merchants on the town square had boarded up all the store windows. We must have had 5,000 people there, mostly miners and their families, men, women and kids, a tremendous thing.

Well, the delegation went into the county building and they told me, "Just keep speaking until we come back out." So I did. I had a loud voice then, I was what, 18 years old. At that time the Lindbergh kidnapping had taken place and they were publishing in the newspapers messages to the kidnappers, a menu for the kid's nourishment, urging them to take care of Lindbergh's baby. And they mentioned orange juice and so on. So during the course of the speech, I said, I appreciate the grief of the Lindberghs, worrying that their kid might be suffering and he should have his orange juice, but we have people right here who are almost starving. They're lucky if they have bean juice for their kids. And at that statement, a roar went up.

I had a real loud voice, and my voice was hitting the opposite side of the square and bouncing back, a funny acoustic effect. It was loud enough to be heard upstairs. The guys told me later that the commissioners started shaking, some of them, to hear this loud voice and the roar from the crowd.

The delegation guys came back out and reported that the commissioners told them they would get favorable consideration, a big victory, and the details came out later: $5 a week for a family of such a size and $7 a week for bigger families, etc.

As the meeting was breaking up, a group of about ten deputies and the sheriff grabbed me. Right away, over a hundred miners surrounded them. They said, "Goddamn it, turn that kid loose." The sheriff said, "Oh we just wanted to ask him a question." They asked me how I spelled my name, some goddamn thing and they beat it. Those miners weren't about to let anything happen to me.

The success of county-level marches led to a plan to mount a state-wide hunger march in Missouri to converge on the state capitol in Jefferson City. Pa and his YCL cohorts organized meetings to rouse participants for this march. One foray took him to the town of Independence, Missouri, hometown of Harry Truman, where a local group had booked the town's movie theater for a rally. Pa was asked to speak, so he and an unemployed seaman, Bill McQuistian, came on the inter-urban trolley from Kansas City.

The theater was packed with unemployed, but looking from the stage, Pa noticed something fishy:

In the three back rows there was a large group of robust looking young men who didn't appear to be in the unemployed category. They didn't look hungry. I spoke first and nothing was said by that group. I talked about the hunger march and about why they should organize to get relief from the city authorities. I got a fairly enthusiastic response.

98

Then McQuistian got up to speak. He wore glasses, and with them on, he seemed a very meek sort of character. After he had spoken for about five minutes, several of these young guys from the back rows came charging onto the stage. "That's the Home Guard," somebody yelled. One of them, I suppose the bully boy, shouted, "I believe in God and country and nobody's gonna tear down God and country." And he started moving aggressively toward McQuistian. Well McQuistian very calmly took his glasses off and set them on the rostrum. McQuistian's face without the glasses was enough to scare the daylights out of anybody. He was a seaman who had been in a million fights. He had a flattened nose and scars all over his face. He looked like a pug-ugly if ever there was one. This bully boy was so taken aback, he stopped, said, "Well, all I've got to say is I'm for God and country," and he walked off the platform and they let him finish his speech.

The "Home Guard" accompanied Pa and McQuistian to the street car and warned them never to set foot in Independence again. Pa was pleased, however, they got a delegation of unemployed from Independence to join the state hunger march.

On the day of the march, they set out from Kansas City in a convoy of jalopies and rickety old trucks jam-packed with unemployed, heading east toward the State House in Jefferson City 160 miles away. When they passed through Sedalia, Missouri, their column was attacked by local vigilantes. They fought with fists and clubs. Before managing to get out of town, several people on both sides got "banged up."

Along the route the column passed a grove of persimmon trees. Wild persimmons are a regional specialty, usually baked in a pudding. The cry went up, "'Simmons!!" The column halted and dozens of unemployed charged off the road into the woods. But the persimmons were unripe; the few who tried them got a terrible taste in their mouths. It took a lot of shouting to get the march proceeding onward to the State Capitol, where a delegation went in to present demands for relief.

A story Pa never recounted to oral historians, probably because it didn't provide a positive image of the unemployed, concerned the looting of a Piggly Wiggly grocery in Oklahoma City. A group of unemployed, on the way back from protesting at a relief station, decided they really needed food. They walked into a grocery store and started carrying items out. The police were called. Pa chuckled, recalling that a tall, stocky black woman stood outside the door and fought off the police, walloping them with a hefty ham!

After nearly two years organizing from his base in Kansas City, Pa, now 19 years old, made a long hitch-hiking trip to attend a YCL conference in Chicago in 1932. At the meeting, he pinned on a badge indicating he was from Missouri. A nice looking young woman struck up a conversation. "Oh, you're from Missouri. Does that mean you won't believe anything unless you are shown?" That young woman, who later became my Mom, told me Pa replied, "That was a lousy joke."

Marriage License

In her 70s, Mom wrote a striking piece for the creative writing class about the events that were battering the nation, her city and her family during the Depression. At the very beginning of adult life, she was forced to make an abrupt transition from an ambitious and hopeful daughter in an upwardly-mobile immigrant family to a young woman with her back to the wall, who seized opportunity out of desperation to rapidly become an active fighter for justice. And just as suddenly she encountered the man with whom she was to share a long, eventful life.

Marriage License, 1932

It was a painful decision. In 1932, $3.50 was a lot of money. A loaf of bread cost 5 cents, a chicken cost a quarter, sometimes only 15 cents from a farmer's truck on a side street in Kansas City.

It was just after Labor Day. I had hitch-hiked from Chicago with my intended, a young fiery organizer of the unemployed. We had spent a nickel each for a street car ride to the end of the line near the highway where we could hitch a long distance ride. Ten cents were already gone from the cache sewn into my skirt belt.

In preparation for going to Kansas City to get married, in Marshall Field's basement I bought a silk remnant for one dollar, and for two dollars, a piece of navy blue wool serge. I wanted to look elegant in spite of the terrible two years I had just lived through. The silk was an extravagance, but it was pretty, light blue with darker blue forget-me-nots. I had very romantic feelings about marriage.

My father had died in the fall before my graduation from high school in June, 1931. The Bain banks closed shortly before graduation day. We lost all our savings plus the life insurance benefit money on my father. All our assets were in the Bain bank as security on a loan my brothers John, Tony and Dan were seeking to pay for needed building materials. They had contracted to do plumbing and carpentry on Bain's new ten-story building. Now plans for the building were off, and my brothers were in debt and unemployed. Another brother, Joe, whose wife just had a baby, lost his job at the gas company and they moved in with us. Brother Dan had been working in New York and recently came home sick with mental problems; my older sister Agnes was diagnosed with Pott's disease (bone tuberculosis in the spine). She had to wear a full body brace and was not allowed to lift a finger, not even to wash dishes.

We were left without a cent. The president of the bank, John Bain, absconded with all the assets of his banks, leaving nothing to pay depositors. Here we were, a very successful immigrant family with three paid-up buildings, and we could not even get groceries on credit. The tenant in our rented storefront building, a Greek immigrant who ran a restaurant on the ground floor and lived upstairs with his wife and five children, couldn't pay his rent. His restaurant served single men on weekly meal tickets. Since the 1929 stock market crash, his customers, workers in the packinghouses, on the street car lines, for the gas company, all were laid off.

With all this turmoil in my family, I didn't know who to turn to. My mother (Nona) could scarcely comprehend the economic calamity that had befallen us. She was 50 years old when we came to Chicago from the island of Lošinj in the Adriatic Sea. With the big family to raise, she had little time to learn English and now, after nearly ten years in Chicago, America still remained a mysterious country to her.

As the ravages of the Depression struck, I was finishing my senior year in high school. I had the ambition to go to Grinnell College in Iowa to study journalism. I was working on the Lindblom High School newspaper and the year book, and had expected to get a small scholarship for college. My college ambitions caused a big controversy in the family. Near the beginning of my school year, my father returned to Chicago, deathly ill, after having spent nearly a year back in our home village. He was appalled at the notion that I wanted to attend college. "Women who go to college become prostitutes," he asserted.

With the Depression deepening, my father's death was a crushing blow to the whole family. He had been a successful businessman and a strict patriarch; we all had to adjust to his sudden absence. But it seemed his death removed the obstacle to my college plans. My mother and brothers did not oppose them. Our financial catastrophe now became the new insurmountable obstacle.

As the day of high school graduation approached, we didn't even have money for my class ring or my cap and gown rental. Miss Conrad, my English teacher had been an inspiration. She urged me to take college prep courses even though my father, being practical, had insisted I prepare for an office job. Miss Conrad said I could do both and it was she who advised me to apply to Grinnell and seek a scholarship.

She even paid for the rental fee on the cap and gown so I could proudly march up to receive my diploma and graduate as an honor student. At that time I didn't understand the significance of her generous gesture. The devastating understanding came only a few weeks later. Miss Conrad was a single woman without close family who devoted her life to her students. That summer I was shocked to hear that she committed suicide after the Bain banks closed. She learned that she and the other depositors would never recover their savings. Miss Conrad had just retired. She had told me about her grand plans to travel, but now all the money she had saved through the years was gone. There were no pensions or Social Security. She didn't want to live as a pauper. I was shattered by the realization that she spent some of her very last dollars for my cap and gown. With Miss Conrad's death, there also died for me the world of possibilities she had helped me envision. No bright future, no college, now it was to be a struggle for sheer survival.

Looking for work that summer was futile. I'd answer every advertisement. "High school graduate wanted for promising position." I'd walk for miles to get downtown. There would be two hundred or more girls and women crowding around the door of an employment agency. Someone would come out and ask everyone with prior work experience to form a line over here. I'd get in that line because when I was in high school I had worked as a sales clerk on Saturdays at Goldblatt's Department Store. We'd be given a card to fill out with our education and work data. Then the person would come down the line and ask each of us for $5.00 for them to do a job search. It was a scam! I was disgusted.

One day, walking home I saw about two hundred people listening to a soap box speaker. I stopped to listen. A very earnest young woman was saying how unfair it was that people were being thrown out of their homes for non-payment of rent. No one had any money these days! She asked us to go over to a nearby building to help keep the police from putting a family with two small children and a baby out on the street. Curious, I went along. A crib, an icebox and chairs were standing out on the sidewalk. Two little children were hanging onto a young woman who was sobbing into a bundle clutched to her chest. It was her baby. As about fifteen of us approached the house, a policeman warned, "Stay back!" One of the men spoke to the police officer. He said he was representing the neighborhood unemployed council and that we had come to assist this family. As he was talking to the policeman, two women picked up the crib, two men took the chairs and they walked into the house. The other policeman on the scene did not try to stop them.

A big surly man who had been tossing bags of clothes out on the rickety porch rushed outside yelling, "What are you doing? I have a legal eviction notice here. I can remove these people from my premises. Officer, stop these people!" The policeman shrugged his shoulders and turned away as our group carried the family's possessions back inside. I was electrified.

From that day on I became a volunteer at the unemployed council's center on 48th and Ashland, about a mile from my house. We were accomplishing something! It was much more satisfying than looking for work that did not exist. We got day-old bread from the big bakeries, we scrounged around for clothes and shoes for the children facing a winter in bare feet. We sent delegations to petition the city and county governments to do something to keep people from being thrown out on the frozen wintery streets. Our group assembled baskets of donated food to give to starving families. This was 1931, before any kind of help came from the federal government or President Hoover.

The City of Chicago was broke. They were paying policemen and teachers with scrip that very few merchants accepted. We wanted a moratorium on rents. We wanted unemployment insurance and other programs to help the more than 25% of workers who were unemployed. The wages of people still working had been cut to next to nothing—30 or 35 cents an hour.

In the spring I met Herb March, a young man who came through Chicago for meetings of the organizations that were trying to do something. It was an election year in 1932 and things had to change. President Hoover's campaign slogan, "Prosperity is just around the corner, a chicken in every pot and a car in every garage," was just too much. It drew blank stares and sighs of despair. The two preceding years had destroyed the livelihoods of millions of Americans and the hard times just continued on dreadfully. Roosevelt's slogan, "One third of the nation is ill housed, ill fed and ill clothed," won in November, but it wasn't until the end of March, 1933, when FDR was inaugurated that anything began to be done. The deprivations continued in 1932.

At the meeting, I started talking to Herb, a sparkling young man with the deepest blue eyes I had ever seen. His tanned skin and dark brown hair set off his chiseled, very intense face. He spoke with a deep resonant voice. We went to a little family restaurant where for just ten cents we could get a big bowl of thick beef vegetable soup with all the bread we could eat. He had also recently lost a parent. He told me the story of his mother's death. I cried for him but also for myself as I remembered my father's passing. His father was left with him and his two younger brothers. He had to quit college and go to work. He wound up leaving home at 17 to look for a way to make a life for himself. Now at 19 he had already experienced over two years of life on the road organizing the unemployed, riding freight trains and sleeping in hobo camps.

We found we had similar families, close-knit, with aunts, uncles, cousins getting together for dinners and holiday celebrations. Now all of that was gone. He had found a place to stay at a hotel in Kansas City where the sympathetic manager had given him a room. He was officially listed as the night desk clerk.

Out–of-town participants in the Chicago meeting were offered lodgings in local homes. So he wound up staying for a few days in our attic bedroom and having some meals with my family. By the time he returned to Kansas City a few days later, we were in love.

During the summer of 1932 I found work in the office of **Narodni Glasnik**, a progressive Croatian-language newspaper, filling in for a woman who had taken maternity leave. I greatly admired the editor, Leo Fischer, a very learned man. My pay was supposed to be $15 a week, when the paper had enough money from subscribers to afford it. Many weeks I only received $10 or as little as $7. Still, after giving half of my pay to my mother, I had saved nearly $50.

I got a letter from Herb every day. Occasionally I put a dollar in my letters to him, urging him to buy food when he was on the road. He often skipped eating when away from his "job" at the hotel. It cost 3 cents to send a letter, but sometimes he'd spend 7 cents for air mail, not that it made any difference in the delivery speed from Kansas City to Chicago. His letters began to seem almost frantic as the end of August approached and he knew my job at the *Narodni Glasnik* would be ending. "I want you to come to Kansas City. I will come to Chicago for you and we'll get married," he wrote.

Finally, I told my mother that the young man who had stayed with us in May wanted me to go with him to KC and get married. She was quiet for a long time. My mother was a very thoughtful person. She had lived a hard life rearing 13 children. I was her baby. I would not go against her wishes. Now I was watching her pensive face, fine and strong with caring blue eyes. She gazed into the distance. Then a look of resignation relaxed her features. Softly she asked, "How are you going to live?"

"Oh, Herb wrote he has a promise of a job for me at $5 a week, working mornings for a window washing service." She sighed and looked sharply at me.

"Where will you live?" I told her about the hotel.

"You have everything solved, don't you? Tell me how much do you know about him?" I told her the story of his childhood as he had told it to me, of his family in Brooklyn and the reasons he had left home.

"You really are determined to do this?"

"Yes, yes, I'd like to. What can I do here in Chicago with no job and the house full of people you have to feed?"

There was a long silence again. I felt sure she would say, "No, I won't let you go." Instead, she spoke of how she had observed him while he was with us for those days in spring.

"He's very good with children. Little Gloria took her first steps for him when he was playing with her in the garden. He wouldn't even let me wash his clothes, he did his own. He looks like your brother Dick with his blue eyes and dark hair, and he is almost built like him, slim and muscular. I know Dick is your favorite brother. I don't know what to say."

After some time she asked, "How will you have a child in a hotel room?"

"Oh, I won't have a baby," I said emphatically. "I spoke to a woman who said I can get a diaphragm for birth control, that there is a Margaret Sanger clinic in KC. They are not legal, but they can be found. The women at the "Y" would tell me where it is."

She arched her eyebrows. This was a big surprise to her. She had often told me she had wished not to have so many children under such awful conditions. She had heard of women who used powders, herbs and douches but she never found any such things in our small village.

"Well then, you seem to have solved everything. What can I say?"

Then looking straight into my eyes she said, "You know, this what-cha-ma-call-it may not work. Do promise me then you'll come home to have your baby. There's always room for one more." I promised but I felt very smug. I was sure it wouldn't happen to me.

At the beginning of September Herb came up to Chicago and we traveled to Kansas City. I felt that we had to get married right away. It never entered my mind that we could fool around without having the marriage license. My whole upbringing had made me fear the hell and damnation that would come down on me and my family if I should have a child out of wedlock.

In Kansas City I was staying at the house of a family Herb had befriended. We had to make arrangements for our wedding. There scarcely was any money for anything. We got my ring from a nice jeweler for $2.00. It wasn't very thick but it was 14 carat gold. Herb went to get the license at the Jackson County courthouse. He stood before the clerk in the license bureau who asked him if he wanted to get a dog license.

"No, I want a marriage license."

"Well, who are you marrying? You have to bring her in here, too."

Herb came to fetch me. He had found out the marriage license would cost $3.50. We had hoped it would be only about $2.00. I hadn't gotten the promised window washing job yet and my money stash in my skirt's belt was fast disappearing. We'd used some of it on our trip to KC. Now we'd also need $5.00 to pay the Justice of the Peace. Well, we had to do it.

We arrived in the clerk's office in the basement of the County building.

"Oh here you are. Well, fill out this form," he stated. The clerk asked if we wanted a diploma-like certificate or a book. The book sounded like more for the money so we chose that. The clerk climbed up on a stool to reach a top shelf. As he pulled down a box, a cloud of dust engulfed him.

"Ugh, look at this mess! You know you are getting the first marriage license I've issued in more than 30 days."

Herb and Jane March, newlyweds in Prospect Park, Brooklyn, 1922

We got married the next day, September 20, 1932, in the suite of Bob Long, the hotel manager. He was the best man. His girlfriend Thelma was the maid of honor. He had gotten the Justice of the Peace to come to the hotel as a personal favor.

When the honorable Justice Roach came in, he said, "Well, let's get it over with. Bob, stand right here with your bride-to-be."

"Hey, I'm not getting married, this guy is," Bob said, putting Herb next to me.

"This young whipper-snapper? He can't be old enough! Let me see the license." After inspecting the license, the Justice proceeded with the ceremony in a solemn stentorian voice and pronounced us man and wife. Bob gave him five dollars, saying that was his wedding present. Thelma gave us a pink glass dish she bought at Woolworth's for ten cents.

That same day, in the Kansas City Star right under the cartoon that was a regular feature in the center of the front page, there was a brief item stating that the first marriage license in Jackson County in over a month had been issued to a Herbert March and Jane Gregg, a first page news event in the worst year of the Great Depression.

Mom received accolades from her writing teacher for this story. Notably, she chose not to name the YCL. She called it "organizations that were trying to do something." Nearly forty years after our family's persecution during the McCarthy period, Mom was still hesitant to openly acknowledge her one-time Communist connections. The threat of prosecution under the Smith Act, criminalizing communist viewpoints, faded after the Supreme Court finally declared it unconstitutional, but demonization of Communists continued unabated in every sphere of American life. Mom kept espousing her viewpoints, but she ceased to identify herself as a Communist, for two reasons: to avoid having her viewpoint tarred with the Communist label, but also because she lost faith in the CP after 1939, when she learned her beloved brother Dick was imprisoned in the Soviet Union.

Mom made no mention that when her whirlwind romance began, she was more-or-less engaged to marry a different man several years older named Bert He was a Socialist of Dutch heritage, a farmer living in South Holland, Illinois, then an area of vegetable farms on the outskirts of Chicago.

Mom also omitted writing about their trip to Kansas City. For two days they traveled most of the way with a bootlegger driving a big new sedan. The young couple slept in the car while their host took a room at a motel. During the journey, while they waited in the car, he stopped at various store front buildings and residential looking houses. Mom figured they were speakeasies and he was transacting some business, receiving payments and/or taking orders and using the teenaged couple for cover.

They never went into restaurants to eat. Instead he sent Mom into grocery stores to buy food with a five dollar bill—a tidy sum in 1932. She splurged on high-quality cold cuts, rolls and fruit. They got to Kansas City with relative ease and well fed.

In the period Mom described, Pa had recollections of his earliest interactions with the Grbac family. Pa thought it hilarious that during his sojourn with the family, Nona pointedly commented, "*Nima dupe!*" which means, "He has no ass." Mom always said, despite his barrel chest, he was otherwise quite skinny from a lack of food. The phrase became the first words of Croatian Pa learned.

Pa also recalled that when he returned to Chicago in September, Mom's brother Joe sat down with him at the kitchen table and poured two large glasses of wine. Joe gestured that he should drink and Pa obliged. Joe kept pushing him to drink more, all the while refilling the glass to the brim whenever it was half full. "He wanted to get me drunk so that he could check me out, figure out if I was on the level about marrying his sister. I guess Joe figured that wine would be truth serum, y'know *in vino veritas* is the Latin saying." I asked Uncle Joe about the incident. He readily admitted that Pa had discerned his motive.

"Well, what did you find out?" I asked.

"That he was all right," Uncle Joe replied.

#

The short period from September, 1932 until April, 1933 was Mom's first sojourn away from her beloved mother and close-knit family. She and Pa were teenage newlyweds, madly in love. But Pa's continuing organizing efforts often took him away for days at a time. When he needed to hop a freight train to get to a meeting in Omaha or Sioux City, it wasn't appropriate for her to travel with him. So Mom settled into the routine of living at the hotel. Never acquiring the promised window washing job, she helped with housekeeping, not as a formal job, but a courtesy to their benefactor, Bob the manager.

Since the YCL group in Kansas City was smaller and less active than the cohort she left behind in Chicago, Mom had time on her hands. She took long walks, exploring and observing conditions in the city. In an uncompleted piece for the writing class, Mom described an incident when she was on her own at the hotel.

I was walking to my hotel room in downtown Kansas City one evening. The wind was shoving me, blowing through my jacket, stocking hat pulled low over my head, snowflakes stinging any exposed skin. I was startled by a small dark figure of a girl as she ran out the fire door alcove of the hotel. A man was walking by, coming in my direction. The girl ran out to him. "Please mister, take me for a quarter. I will do anything." The man quickened his pace, the girl fell back into the alcove. Seeing her crying, cold face in the dim light of a street lamp, my heart stopped.

"Come with me. I won't hurt you. Come get warm. I have a room in this hotel." She shambled in, feet wrapped in rags, crying softly as we walked the 100 feet or so to the lobby.

In my room I got a good look at a very pretty, quite mature, girl about 12 years old in a shiny black satin dress. Her body shivering, I wrapped a blanket around her. We hardly spoke. I told her to sit on the side of my bed, the only place there was. I was going to get something warm for her to drink.

I often ate at the manager's suite. He had a fully furnished four room apartment with a big chef's kitchen which, before the Depression hit, was used to cook meals for a coffee shop restaurant on the first floor. The huge refrigerator always had a lot of food. I warmed a pot of water, and put it on a tray with tea and lots of things to eat.

The little girl had huddled against a pillow, hiding her face, still in tears. I took some of the hot water, poured it into the wash basin, took a wash cloth, and gave it to her. "Come wash your hands and face. Then we'll eat." Revived by hot tea and a sandwich, I asked her why she was out on the street. In a voice almost inaudible, in a thick Kansas twang, she simply said, "My grandma said to tell any man to give me a quarter and he could have me." I had heard her say just that to the passing man, but now I was also shaken by the realization of the grandmother's sacrifice. I hugged her and held her, both of us sobbing.

She had two younger brothers and a little sister. Her grandfather and father had lost their farm in a sheriff's sale. The farm had been homesteaded by her great-grandfather in the pioneer days.

They had no place to go except KC, 25 miles from the farm. For a few weeks with the little money they received in the auction, they took a furnished room. The men looking for work, their money gone, the three-generation family of eight was out on the street. The winter of '32 was fierce. They went to a shanty town on the banks of the Kaw River, built a shelter from cardboard boxes, and whatever scrounged materials they could find, as other farmers and evicted working class families of the city had done. The riverbanks in KC became a quagmire of misery, disease, hunger. Most of the men who were still physically fit left to look for work. Now the women and children had to struggle on their own to keep themselves alive.

Her grandmother's sacrifice was so great I could scarcely comprehend it. But I realized, a quarter would buy a chicken, some bread and cabbage in this Depression year of '32. They might survive until the men would come back with something.

They had been religious, law-abiding owners of land, comfortable homes, gardens, with cows, pigs, chickens. The women went to Kansas City on farmers' market days to sell fruit, vegetables, butter, chickens and eggs. Their barns were full of fodder and their storage bins held grain for the kitchen and for sale. In those good times, it seemed God had been very good to them. Now in these desperate Depression years, they were dispossessed and starving.

Mom's handwritten text trailed off. An unstated point in this piece was Mom believed in concrete acts to assist people in need. Pa's narratives stressed he could be a leader, could make a speech or take a beating, and by doing so he could inspire people to fight for their rights, Mom typically acted one-on-one, much as she had seen her mother do.

She most likely had the half-starved child prostitute spend the wintery night in the hotel room and doubtless sent the girl home with food scrounged from the hotel's refrigerator. She helped the girl, but by helping her, Mom also gained from learning about her Midwestern farm family. Their history and circumstances was an enriching experience, especially for a young immigrant woman who'd known few old-stock Americans.

In her own mother, Mom had a strong role model to be principled and charitable. Nona assisted others. Forty years ago in Chicago I heard from Mato Brzovich, a long-time staff member of the *Narodni Glasnik* newspaper, that in the 1930s, Nona willingly bailed out unionists from jail, signing to have her property as collateral.

"We offered her streetcar fare to the police station," Mato said, "but your grandmother would say, 'Don't waste money,' and she would walk all the way. She was a great woman."

When Mom was a teen-aged clerk at the Goldblatt's store, she used her high school Spanish to advise immigrant Mexican women buying their first overcoats for the Chicago winter. "They wanted to get coats with cute little fur collars, fancy buttons and such.

But I showed them, 'This coat isn't warm enough for Chicago. You need one like this, with thick lining.'" As an adult Mom continued to assist Mexican immigrants in Packingtown,

Mom was also a lifelong advocate of women's reproductive rights. In the 1960s she routinely mortified my female friends, taking them aside to discuss birth-control measures. Her passion for reproductive issues stemmed from awareness of her mother's anguish bearing 13 children in adverse circumstances. She herself had a significant trauma with a reproductive choice when in Kansas City she sought out the Sanger health clinic and obtained a diaphragm.

Although they had been distributed underground for decades, in the early 1930s diaphragms were banned in the US. The Comstock Act of 1873 made it illegal to disseminate contraceptives or even information about them. In 1932, Margaret Sanger had a Japanese manufacturer mail a package of diaphragms to a supportive New York physician. US Customs confiscated the package, and Sanger filed a lawsuit. Finally, in 1936, in the case _United States v. One Package of Japanese Pessaries_, a federal court ruled that the package could be delivered.

But in 1932, diaphragms were still contraband, less reliable and less expertly fitted. All sizes might not have been available to the underground clinic, and their staff might not have been well trained. Spermicidal ointments to use with the diaphragm also were illegal, difficult to obtain and Mom and Pa didn't have money for them anyway. So, as Nona presciently predicted, the "what-cha-ma-call-it" did not work and Mom became pregnant.

Mom and Pa discussed the matter and confident as they were about the coming revolution, decided it would be better to wait a few years before having children so they could "raise them under socialism." Mom was referred to a physician who performed abortions. The experience was traumatic. After the procedure, the doctor showed her the embryo, "the little fishy thing" Mom called it. She had terrible nightmares, plagued by the image of "the little fishy thing."

Deciding to become parents and not wait for the revolution, Mom and Pa came home to Chicago to have her baby in the spring of 1933.

The Russia They Found

When the three Grbac brothers departed for Russia in the summer of 1931, it seemed a wise move to them. In the United States the Great Depression was dragging on, with no effective measures to create jobs or counter the misery of unemployed workers. As a seaman accustomed to tramping across the globe, Dick had already been to Russia, and what he was shown looked promising: rapid progress, work for all, an end to capitalist exploitation, and good, modern mental health treatment for brother Dan if needed. As prepared as the Grbacs were to cross oceans, they figured they could just return to America whenever that seemed advisable.

Knowing today the repressive regime the Bolsheviks eventually put in place, relocating to Russia from the United States might seem a foolish choice. At the time, however, the idea seemed logical, and even heroic, to many Americans. Between 1917 and 1939, an estimated 80,000 foreigners—workers, political exiles, and specialists like engineers—worked for a time or permanently settled in the Soviet Union.

The first foreign workers to go there were Russians, Ukrainians and Russian Jews who had emigrated earlier to the United States and Canada. Some returned voluntarily, while others, like anarchists Alexander Berkman and Emma Goldman, were deported to Russia. According to Soviet sources, approximately 10,000 came back between 1920 and 1922.

In 1922, a Soviet commission on foreign immigration was established, directed by Simanis Bergis, a Latvian-American who had immigrated to the US after the failed Russian revolution in 1905. He returned to Russia just as fellow IWW members were being fiercely persecuted. Between 1922 and 1926, the commission established 26 agricultural collectives, nine industrial combines and allowed over 10,000 foreign workers to settle in the USSR.

Bergis' commission steered the foreigners into rural pursuits.

In the 1920s, the agrarian collectives outnumbered industrial nearly three to one. In addition to agriculture, the arrivals went into other rural-based activities, such as fishing. Fishing collectives were formed on the White Sea by Finnish-Americans from Oregon, New York City, and on Sakhalin Island by Japanese. A few thousand Finns and Finnish-Americans worked at logging in Karelia.

After 1926, when Josef Stalin consolidated power, Bergis' commission was dissolved and the influx of foreign workers ceased. But in 1930 he reversed the policy with a strategy of building socialism in one country, as opposed to Trotsky's concept of worldwide revolution. The Party adopted the first 5-Year Plan with the goal of making the Soviet Union self-sufficient. But Russia and the other Soviet Republics were impoverished and economically primitive. This was an ideological as well as a practical problem. Karl Marx predicted socialist revolutions in the most advanced industrial capitalist countries. To build a powerful nation and correct this discrepancy of the Russian Revolution from the Marxist ideal, Stalin accelerated a program already begun by Lenin to rapidly transform the Soviet Union into an industrial country. To do so, Stalin proved willing to employ harsh measures to force urbanization and collectivization and break up the centuries-old institutions of agrarian peasant society.

Though they opposed the American political system, Soviet leaders were impressed by American industry. Stalin extolled Henry Ford, a notorious right-winger, as "one of the world's greatest industrialists." In 1929, before the US diplomatically recognized the USSR, Ford signed a major contract with the Soviets to supervise construction of new automobile factories in Nizhni Novgorod and Moscow. In return, the USSR agreed to buy $30 million worth of unassembled Ford cars and trucks.

To assist rapid industrialization, the 16th Party Congress decided to admit "foreign engineers, foremen and skilled workers" to utilize "their experience and knowledge inside Soviet plants." But the Party did not fully open the floodgates to immigration. Concerned about them destabilizing the country, the Congress set a ceiling of 40,000 foreign workers. Amtorg, the Soviet trade agency in the United States, received over 100,000 requests for permission to work in the USSR during the first eight months of 1931. By the second quarter of 1932, when the peak was reached, 42,230 skilled foreign workers and engineers were in the USSR, including my three uncles.

In the 1930s, most foreigners worked in heavy industry, like the steel mills of Magnitogorsk, or the Nizhni Novgorod Ford Factory, where future UAW-CIO leaders Walter and Victor Reuther were employed.

Some foreigners helping to kick-start Soviet industry had socialist sympathies, others worked solely for financial interest. It was a lucrative place for an engineer when the West was in a severe depression. By 1931, foreigners accounted for 2-3% of the work force in big industrial initiatives. To make life in Russia palatable, they had privileges not provided to Soviet citizens—higher pay in hard currency, better housing and shopping in restricted stores. For English-speaking workers, a newspaper, the *Moscow Daily News*, was published, although it offered little beyond smiley-faced propaganda about glorious Soviet advances.

In 1931, the Grbac brothers, despite their industrial skills and building trades experience, did not go into Russian factories. Heading for the Seattle Commune, the Grbacs oddly bucked the dominant Soviet trend. Except for Dick's wheat harvesting, they hadn't done farm work since their childhoods in Nerezine.

Another trend the Grbacs were bucking was that Soviet authorities had never particularly favored communes. Ironically, they were too communistic for them. While Lenin pushed collectivization of production, he felt consumption still had to be based on work incentive. Most of the communes were formed during the first five years after the 1917 revolution, before there was a clear policy. In the 1920s, Lenin suggested that "artificial false communes" be the lowest priority as a form of collective farm. He stated it was "harmful, even fatal for communism" to put into effect prematurely "purely and narrowly communistic ideals." They were criticized as being "utopian," even "petit-bourgeois."

Despite official disapproval, it may have been precisely the idea of a utopian, communistic life that attracted my idealistic Uncle Dick. In Oregon he had met comrades who knew the Seattle Commune founders. Some had been labor activists in the

1919 Seattle general strike and were deported or threatened with deportation in the "Red Scare" that followed.

The commune was founded in 1922 in the Salsky region of southern Russia by 89 Americans from the Pacific Northwest, mostly Russian- and Finnish-Americans. The Soviet government granted them 5,290 hectares (over 13,000 acres) of virgin steppe land twelve miles from a railway line. The founders invested $500 each as a membership fee. They shipped agricultural equipment, fertilizers, seed and nursery stock to Russia.

Perhaps Dick visited Seattle Commune on his tour with the Friends of the Soviet Union. Until 1933, despite the Soviet government's general disapproval, the agrarian communes were among the showcase locations displayed to foreign visitors, where visitors would meet idealistic, enthusiastic communists. A notable, well-publicized instance occurred in 1931, when British playwright George Bernard Shaw, a Fabian Socialist, and Lady Nancy Astor, a Conservative, the first female Member of Parliament, visited a commune in central Russia.

In letters to his family, Dick expressed enthusiasm for the commune. Encouraged by Dick, the Chicago chapter of the Friends of the Soviet Union organized a benefit party in March, 1932, with each guest donating a hand tool to be shipped to the communards.

Mom saved a few of Dick's letters and more than twenty snapshots of the Seattle Commune. Dick touted the advances they were achieving in the new workers' civilization. In a neat hand he captioned the pictures in English: "Working on Cultivators," "Modern cow barn," "Workers on Ford truck," etc. There were pictures of their communal residences, their windmill, youths playing volleyball, kids herding geese, the commune's office building identified by a sign in Russian and English, groups of communards, and snapshots of the Grbac brothers, plus a young woman Ana, who became Uncle Tony's first wife. There is a picture of Dick outside a spa. On the back, Dick carefully explained "This was taken on Nov. 3, 1932 on our excursion to Zhelesnovodsk in front of one of the villas, formerly belonged to some duke, now workers' sanatorium."

In their 1935 book *Soviet Communism: A New Civilisation?*,

English economists Sidney and Beatrice Webb praised the Seattle Commune. After the hard pioneering years, the "American" Commune had become prosperous, claiming production ten times higher than the peasant average. The Webbs observed that there was "an interesting article by Richard Gerbacy [Grbac], a member of the [Seattle] commune, in the *Moscow Daily News*, October 20, 1933, [which] described the celebration of the tenth anniversary of the settlement."

Dick's journalistic impulse continued even after he left the commune. In a 1937 letter from Moscow, written in Croatian to Nona, Dick added a note to Mom in English. Aware that Mom had worked at the *Narodni Glasnik* newspaper, he suggested: "Hello Jacinta, if you wish, or find it advisable, you may have this letter, full or in part, published in our press. Many, many kisses to Bobby and to all true Pioneers. Yours, Dick." After three years at the commune, Dan left for the mental hospital in Rostov, Tony to Leningrad, Dick to Moscow.

English travel writer E. M. Delafield wrote a detailed description of conditions at Seattle Commune when she visited in 1936, two years after the Grbacs had departed. No lover of socialism, Delafield undertook the visit for her publisher, Houghton Mifflin, who calculated there would be a market for a book that cast her sardonic wit at the Russians. As in her other works, she viewed her surroundings and the people in Russia with snide condescension and scathing wit. But after spending a couple weeks living in Seattle Commune, she was utterly charmed by the communards. With no trace of sarcasm, a chapter in Delafield's book, *Straw Without Bricks: I Visit the Soviets*, provides clear indications of how this small community had put into effect a Marxist ideal.

She traveled there by train from Rostov, arriving late in the evening at a small roach-infested station in Salsky. A Russian youth met her. "He took me to a farm lorry and I climbed into it with my bag, and we drove off–at first over a moderately good road and afterwards across a long tract of prairie-land."

Arriving at night, Delafield described the commune as "something rather like a small hamlet in the middle of a huge farm." The driver showed her the accommodations:

I only saw the dim outline of the single-storied dwelling houses. Into one of these my guide conducted me. It was a brick-built building with a cement floor....The room in which I was to sleep...about twelve feet by fourteen, contained four iron bedsteads, each with a straw pallet, a cushion stuffed with straw, two sheets and a cotton blanket. There were two windows, a table and four wooden stools. Nothing else, except for an unshaded electric light bulb hanging from the ceiling. Neither blinds, curtains, strips of carpeting nor any toilet appliance whatsoever.

Next came her introduction to the toilets. Delafield couldn't make her guide understand what she required, so he found an American communard to translate.

[He was] a tall Armenian who spoke English. He said—with an accent that made me think of a New York taxi driver, "How-d'you-do? what you want?" I replied with equal brevity, "How-d'you-do. I want the W.C."

"Oh, watter-closet! Sure. You see them two buildin's over there? The foist one men, the second one ladies. You'll find electric light, every thin' fine."

The two buildings--little brick erections with what was only too evidently a cess-pit beneath each one—stood about fifty yards apart, and sure enough, an electric-light bulb shone, though rather dimly, in each.

I approached "ladies," and next minute I knew exactly how communal, communal life can be. There was no fastening on the door, and the elementary accommodation was provided for six persons at a time.

Determined not to be squeamish during her stay, Delafield admitted that the first encounter with the toilets was a severe test, and she still had not discovered where to wash. She made her way to her room, slept on the straw pallet, and when she awoke, she recorded her first impressions:

The clanging of a bell–going on, as it seemed, for hours and hours–announced the day. I looked at my watch and saw that it was a quarter-past five. The only punctual thing I ever met in Russia was that bell. Although it was early, it was broad daylight, and I could see people outside. (They could doubtless see me equally well through my uncurtained windows.) Most of the men wore shirts, braces, and trousers that had obviously seen very long service. The women nearly all had shawls or handkerchiefs over their heads, and coarse, shabby blouses and skirts. One or two wore flimsy, faded, printed cotton frocks...Some were barefooted, and a good many wore rubber-soled shoes.

Delafield dressed in the rustic clothes and canvas shoes she brought for commune wear, and like the other women, tied her hair up in a blue kerchief. Still feeling quite inadequately washed, she sought out the dining hall:

It was a very large room, with a stage and curtains at one end, and two open hatches in the wall giving on to the kitchen. A number of wooden tables, with six or seven wooden stools round each, held a corresponding number of tin mugs and tin bowls. In the middle of the tables was a pile of black bread and a large enamel jug containing

Seattle Commune, near Salsky, Russia, 1930s

121

coffee. The bread was made on the farm and was good—the coffee was not real coffee, but made out of barley. It tasted of nothing in particular. The Comrades ate in almost unbroken silence, and nobody took any notice of me, to my great relief, when I also sat down and began to eat black bread. Presently, however, a pleasant girl brought me a mug of boiled milk and smiled very nicely when I thanked her. Every day she brought me the boiled milk, and much as I abominated it, I always drank it gratefully.

As soon as she finished eating, the Secretary of the commune, "a slow and amiable man," introduced himself and "offered to show me all over the farm, and to tell me anything that I wanted to know." As they strolled, the Secretary explained that Seattle was one of only two communes left of many that had been founded after the Revolution. There were nearly 50 lath-and-plaster dwelling-houses, and several brick barns and service buildings. The bricks were made on site. Indeed, nearly everything came from the site. They had their own electric plant, carpenter's shop, garage, repair shed, bakery, and builder's yard. Twenty-one tractors were in use. There were 876 head of cattle, also 56 horses, kept for the Red Army and never worked on the land, "fine-looking animals, and seemed to me to have a much easier life than the people who looked after them," Delafield mused.

She viewed six bulls "of an almost incredible mildness...more like sheep than bulls." There were also pigs kept about ten kilometers away from the main settlement, a chicken yard and bee-hives. There was a flourishing vineyard, but the fruit orchards were not thriving. The heavy soil, black for a depth of about four inches, and under that thick clay, was not suited to them.

The Secretary showed her nearly everything. They went to his small office, furnished with a large typewriter, a table and two stools, a telephone and the customary portraits of Lenin and Stalin on the walls.

The Secretary explained that everything was held in common by the workers. After taxes had been paid to the Soviet government, in cash and in produce, the remaining assets were allotted to the workers. One ruble a day was deducted for each one's food. Only the Secretary and Treasurer handled any actual cash; each person had a book in which to enter credits and debits. A worker requiring money could ask for it, but as most of them never left the settlement, and almost nothing could be bought there, not much money was in circulation.

To manage operations, work plans, and the budget, there was a three-member Controlling Board overseen by a nine-member Executive Board, all elected by general ballot. They held frequent meetings with workers in each particular department, and invited their suggestions and criticisms. Four times a year a General Meeting was convened, which every worker was expected to attend.

Misbehavior by comrades was dealt with by an elected "Comradely Court." The courts apparently were very popular, always crowded with spectators. The principal offences were petty theft, bad or careless work, damage to farm property and refusal to work. Notably in this commune where basic needs were routinely provided, refusal to work or bad work were criminalized. The first part of my family's communist-inspired watchword "from each according to his ability, to each according to his need," had to be made compulsory at Seattle Commune.

The penalties inflicted were usually fines. Asked what the alternatives were, he said offenders might face expulsion from the commune, but only on a two-thirds majority vote.

There were many nationalities at the commune. The majority were Russians, Ukrainians and Caucasians. There were Poles, Finns, Armenians, Lithuanians, Latvians and one Chinese married to a Russian woman. Many had lived for a time in America.

Most of the so-called Americans were not American-born at all, although many of them had at one time or another taken American citizenship. They had nearly all come originally from middle Europe, but they had lived and worked, or been out of work, for years in the States, and talked the worst and most debased form of "N'Yoick" English.

After the Secretary had shown me over the farm, he begged me to go anywhere I liked and do anything I pleased. "Be like home!" was his benevolent parting injunction. I was not like home, far from it, but I was grateful for his kindness, and indeed all the time I was there I met with kindness and friendliness from everybody.

A Great Vision

I found Delafield's descriptions of the residences and farm buildings were similar to the images on Dick's snapshots. She described her first dinner, the big mid-day meal, customary in farm life.

At about a quarter-past eleven, a bell rang and went on ringing for some while. I saw the workers making their way towards the canteen and I went up to an elderly man wearing horn-rimmed spectacles, which made me think he must have lived in America-and asked whether he could speak English. He could. He was a Finn, and had been in California for several years. We went in to dinner together, and I sat next to him, and although he hardly spoke at all he was very kind, and when I asked whether it was possible to have a drink of water he went and fetched one for me....For dinner, a large tin bowl of cabbage soup stood in the middle of each table with an iron dipper beside it. Everybody helped themselves and ate from smaller tin bowls. There was a tin spoon and fork at each place, but no knife. A Comrade presently took away each soup-basin and put in its place a basin of stew. The soup had been good, but the stew meat was tough and quite tasteless. The Finn took a claspknife from his pocket to deal with it, but my other neighbours speared their meat on their forks and tore it apart with their teeth. I had a very small penknife in my pocket, and brought it out, to everybody's great amusement. Several of the women held out their hands for the knife, and looked at it, and laughed a great deal, and I laughed too.... The remainder of the meal consisted of black bread. It was very good.... Milkless tea was in a huge jug. Dinner, and in fact all the meals, were usually very silent, and the workers hardly ever lingered at their tables. They had an hour off at dinner-time and seemed to spend most of it either in sitting or walking about, doing nothing. To finish here with the subject of the meals: the midday one always took place between eleven and half-past, and the next, and last one, at six....Supper was much the same as dinner: always soup, usually made with cabbage, but sometimes with beans or fragments of meat, and always unlimited quantities of bread. The second supper dish was sometimes macaroni, sometimes cheese made with sour milk, and sometimes fried eggs. Except for the meat, nothing was badly cooked, and the tea, or barley-coffee, was always served hot.

Richard March

Delafield complained that the communards lacked table graces; that a few of them ate with their fingers, and many slurped their macaroni. But she maintained that the monotonous diet seemed to sustain her well during her stay and she remained healthy. After that first dinner she prevailed upon her Finnish-American companion to show her where to bathe. She encountered some hot water, and also met Eva, the woman who became her best friend during the sojourn and whom Delafield considered "the most intelligent woman in the settlement and who spoke English, German and Russian fluently."

[The Finn] took me to one of the small houses that were dotted about. Behind a wire-netting door was a tiny dispensary, and at a table sat a very tall woman of about forty, with straight, short yellow hair and a strong, rather handsome face. This was Eva, whose husband was the Chairman of the Executive Board. They were both forceful and intelligent personalities, and I got to know Eva better than anyone else. She was oddly hard and cynical on the surface, and fundamentally very kind.

The Finn, ushering me in, said, "I brought you English Comrade. She can visit with you awhile," and departed.

Eva spoke English fluently, and I found that she had lived in America a long while, and had a sister there, married to an American. The sister often sent her books and papers, but she said that hardly any of them ever reached her. She thought that they were confiscated at the post office.

Then we entered upon the question of washing. "Oh yes," said Eva, there was a wash-house, and she would take me to it at once. "It is nothing to be proud about," she added grimly. (Eva was the only Communist I ever met in Russia who was sometimes willing to admit that perfection had not, as yet, been achieved in every single direction under the new regime.)

Eva showed her a small brick building, both the women's wash house and laundry containing a large vat of steaming water. In the laundry, "most of the women were half undressed, partly because of the heat and partly, I suppose, because they had no change of garment....The actual bath-house could be compared

125

to nothing, except perhaps one's idea of the Black Hole of Cal-
cutta."

When women went in to bathe they left their clothes in the
laundry, and there was always a Comrade to watch them.

Eva warned me never to leave any of my belongings unwatched,
never to take money or my watch to the wash-house, and to lock the
door of my room every time I left it. The Comrades were as communal
in the bath-house as they were everywhere else. I never went in there
without finding several women, all stark naked, swilling themselves
with water or standing about and talking.

Accustomed to more privacy, Delafield used a bucket and a
basin that Eva lent her to carry hot water to her bedroom to wash.
Once during a heavy rain, on Eva's suggestion, she washed her
hair outside in the downpour.

Eva, who had training as a nurse, was the sole health care professional. She treated routine illnesses and injuries. There was
a hospital many kilometers distant. As a last resort, seriously ill
communards were taken there in a farm lorry jolting and bump-
ing over the steppe. Delafield admired Eva's competence, but
she was appalled that the nurse did not wash her hands between
treating patients.

Malaria, the most common illness, Eva treated with imported
quinine, but in recent years the government had rendered it unaffordable by imposing a high tariff. So from her limited pharmaco-
peia, Eva invented a curative serum that seemed quite an effective
cure-all. She regularly injected it into as many communards as
possible to treat such illnesses as measles and influenza and also
as a preventative inoculation.

Delafield inquired about access to a doctor:

Eva, I think, was a little bit offended at my suggestion of a doctor.
She told me rather curtly that when he did come he was principally
occupied in dentistry. She herself had not strong enough wrists.

Despite improvised health care, Delafield noted that nearly
all the children looked healthy and strong. They lived in fresh

air and got plenty of exercise. Regular school was not in session during the summer, but there was a day school for the small children while their mothers were at work.

Eva took me to see the school. It was one of the best of the buildings, although the amount of floor space seemed terribly inadequate for something like fifty or sixty children, all under seven years of age. Most of them set up a most frightful howling at the sight of Eva, and she explained to me that they were afraid of her injections.

Family life and sexual mores in the commune were based on a conception of morality Delafield, an upper-crust Englishwoman, characterized as "widely removed from our own." The early Bolshevik revolutionaries advocated a total transformation of society to eventually eliminate bourgeois marriage and patriarchy. In the Soviet cities, sexuality was debated and became a significant polemic concerning the future of society, but at Seattle Commune, the actual practice of revolutionary sexual and familial arrangements was implemented substantially. No marriage regulations existed, and no registration of them took place. A man and a woman wishing to marry applied for married quarters and received them. Delafield reported:

Did they, I asked Eva, usually remain together?
Sometimes they did, and sometimes they didn't. Those who had been already married before they arrived at the Commune were generally faithful to one another, especially where there were children. The young people were often very promiscuous. They changed partners frequently.
What happened if a girl was left expecting a child by a man who had gone to live with another woman? Eva answered it was right that a father should contribute towards the maintenance of his child....The girl could appeal to the Comradely Court, and the onus of proving he was not the father lay on the man.
Did this frequent re-shuffling of partners lead to quarrels and jealousies?
Apparently not. There had only been one fight in twelve years, said the Esthonian, when a woman had thrown a bucket at another

woman's head. She seemed to think that everybody worked too hard and was too worn-out by the end of the day to have any energy left for emotional violence.

Eva told me the tall Armenian I met on the night of my arrival–he was young, and very good-looking in a swarthy way–had been one of the worst offenders in the matter of promiscuity.

"He took nearly all of the girls behind the pighouse," said Eva. "Not even a very nice place," she added thoughtfully.

It is likely that the communards practiced birth control, since Delafield reported that most couples had only one child and none had more than three.

Delafield praised how much building had been achieved in the commune's dozen years.

The original hut in which the pioneers had lived in 1922 still stood, but most of the houses built since then were of brick or lath-and-plaster. One or two were concrete. Each contained from four to six rooms, and one family lived in each room….Whatever the size of the family, that one room had to serve them as a dwelling place. Unmarried girls over fourteen went to sleep, all together, in a Women's Dormitory, and the boys had a Men's Dormitory. They slept about twelve or fourteen in a room.

There were nearly always some rather pathetic little attempts at decoration and home-making. One woman had put up a frail little pair of muslin curtains that she washed and ironed two or three times a week. She had brought them, three years earlier, from New York. None of them had any possessions worth speaking of. A clock was a very rare object, and there were no pictures, excepting occasional photographs of friends or relations, and the usual coloured newspaper supplements featuring leaders of the Revolution. Except in Eva's home, I never saw any books or newspapers.

Delafield noted that there was a small library, little used while she was there, that she suspected was more popular in the winter. The scarcity of books and apparent lack intellectual discussions must have dismayed Uncle Dick, the studious mariner.

Delafield found it difficult to persuade the communards to

assign her work duties, so at last she decided to just show up and begin helping somewhere. She chose the bakery, which produced the black bread she had praised.

The head baker was a very tall blue-eyed Pole. He always wore a chef's cap and a more-or-less white smock. He also had been in America. He baked his bread in a huge brick oven, and it was always very good. Two of his assistants were women, one Polish and the other Russian, and they kneaded the dough with their knuckles in a huge crock for hours and hours. It seemed to me that even the most inexperienced person could hardly go wrong in so uncomplicated a rite, and I kneaded with them.

One of the women, called Anna, who was about fifty and had a nice, broad, smiling, freckled face, had achieved the distinction of having been married for eighteen years to an American and being still unable to speak or to understand one single word of English. She talked to me in a Russian dialect, and when I failed to understand her, as I generally did, the other woman—Julia—translated. Julia was about forty years old. She was a Pole, and so was her husband. They had been for years in America where Julia had worked in a silk-stocking factory, and the husband—she told me—had been out of work nearly all the time. This was afterwards amplified by Eva, who explained that, in America, Julia's husband had been continually in and out of prison for promoting strikes and general Communistic propaganda. On coming to the Commune, he settled down into a most excellent worker, and never gave any trouble at all. I got to know him quite well--he was in charge of the cow-houses--and he was one of the nicest men in the settlement.

Both Anna and Julia were very kind to me. They had a conviction, which nothing could shake, that I was very frail and delicate and ought not to be allowed to work. I think this was mostly founded on the fact that I weighed so much less than they did. All the women, almost without exception, were fat and heavy. Some of them asked me, via Julia, what they could do so as to become slim, and I suggested a few exercises, which made them laugh a great deal.

Her co-workers marveled at Delafield's possessions in her purse: a powder puff compact with a mirror, reading glasses, and wrist watch. It made Delafield realize what a simple life they lived and how few possessions they had. She discussed the simple commune life with Julia, who could compare her life in the USA to the commune.

I used to visit Julia in her own home-that is to say, the one room in which she and her husband lived. They had no children. She showed me what was evidently her greatest treasure—a photograph album. It was filled with snapshots of American friends...[and] weddings. Her own wedding-group was there. Julia and her husband had been married in a church, and Julia had had her hair waved, and had worn a very frilly white frock and a wreath of flowers. I asked her if she regretted America, and she said: Often. During her first three years at the Commune she had hated being there, and had wanted all the time to go back. Now, she said, she was getting used to it. There were no worries. In America, she had continually been worried, about how to pay the rent, how to live, how to keep a job when she had one and how to get one when she hadn't. She admitted freely that she missed the shops and the amusements and social life, of her American days.

No doubt the Grbac brothers shared Julia's feelings, especially Dick, and had never "gotten used to it." The idea of building a communal utopia in the workers' republic on an isolated swath of virgin steppe would appeal to an idealistic communist, until one encountered the grimy and monotonous reality of it. For someone worried about starvation, this modest way of life could represent welcome security, but not for an adventurer like Dick, who had traveled widely and lived in Chicago and New York City, two vibrant metropolises. It's amazing that he stayed there for as long as three years.

The remote American island in a sea of steppe could not remain fully isolated. The first spring after the arrival of the Grbac brothers, a horrendous famine, the "Holodomor," broke out in a vast area a few hundred miles northwest of Seattle Commune. Many Ukrainians contend that this was their Holocaust. Estimates of the death toll vary considerably, but by the most reliable estimate, between three and four million people starved to death, mostly peasants.

It is controversial whether the famine was intentionally caused by the government in order to break the back of Ukrainian nationalism and the "kulak" (rich peasant) village social system that rejected collective farming, or whether it was caused by a combination of natural causes and disastrously mistaken agricultural policies. The Soviets confiscated the peasants' grain, tried to hide the famine from the outside world and refused offers of food aid from abroad.

Delafield noted in 1936 a large portion of the communards were Ukrainian peasants, some of them possibly escapees from the famine zone. A number of them performed their folk songs and dances at her farewell party. As more Ukranians entered the commune, the American influence was diluted. They changed the commune's name to Seyatel, meaning "sower" in Russian, which sounds a lot like Seattle.

In 1934 Dick married a Ukrainian woman, Aleksandra Vasilievna Groshenko, who had come to the commune for agricultural training. They departed for Moscow where Dick found employment in the Stalin Auto Works, while Aleksandra worked in the central office of Komsomol, the Communist Youth League. In 1935 their son was born. Committed internationalists, they named him Ernst after Ernst Thälmann, the leader of the German Communist Party who had been arrested by the Gestapo in 1933.

Tony, Ana and son John left for Leningrad, where he found factory work as a boilermaker. They had a second son Edik, but Ana died of complications from childbirth. Tony married again, and with his second wife had a daughter Eleanora, named after Eleanor Roosevelt. Dan was receiving treatment in the mental hospital in Rostov.

The Grbac's rural experiment in Seattle Commune had come to an end, but the community continued. Around 1940 they finally yielded to government pressure to reorganize as a collective farm without communal consumption. A 1967 article in a Puget Sound community newspaper noted that more than 40 years after its founding by idealists from the Pacific Northwest, the Seyatel collective farm was going strong with five of its original members still living there.

Herb and Jane in Chicago

In April, 1933, Herb and Jane March, two 20-year-old kids, retraced their hitch-hiking journey from Kansas City back to Chicago and took up residence at the 59th Street Grbac home. They had decided to have a baby. Pa couldn't continue to work as an unpaid organizer, he needed a paying job. Job prospects had improved. Franklin Roosevelt became President the previous month and plans were afoot to implement the National Industrial Recovery Act, commonly called the NRA. As a first step, to spread the work around, the length of the standard work day was to be reduced to eight hours from the ten hours then typical in industry. In anticipation, industries were doing some hiring.

Mom kept her promise to her mother to have her baby in Chicago, plus she would have Nona's assistance caring for the infant. Nona had quite a lot of experience in that area.

For Pa, Chicago was fertile grounds for his revolutionary activities, now as a union organizer working in a packinghouse. Additionally, there were big YCL and CP groups in Chicago he and Jane could connect with. During the previous three years, Chicago Communists had organized a significant movement for unemployed relief, which Jane had already participated in and was emerging as a youthful leader. Unlike Kansas City, Chicago was her familiar home turf where she could engage in community organizing as an authentic insider.

Moreover, Chicago had been a wellspring of American radical movements, notably, the 1886 Haymarket tragedy, a central event in the fight for the eight hour day, the 1894 Pullman strike and boycott, the founding place of the IWW in 1905, and of the American Communist Party in 1919. Chicago boasted a diversity of radicals and radical thought, as well as a strong tradition of unionism. Although generally limited to craft unions of skilled workers, the Chicago Federation of Labor (CFL) had long been one of the most militant sections of the American Federation of Labor (AFL), having attempted industrial organizing of the stockyards in the World War 1 period.

Chicago's location made it a natural center for industry. It had a Great Lakes shipping port, hundreds of railroad lines converged there, and it was connected by canal to the Mississippi River. It had access to agricultural products and natural resources of the West and to population centers and markets of the East. For decades Chicago was the fastest-growing city in the world.

Industries connected to farming and food products were among the first to develop. In the 1860s and 1870s, Philip Armour and Gustavus Swift established meat-packing concerns, profiting handsomely from increased demand during and following the Civil War. Manufacture of farm equipment arose even earlier. In 1847 Cyrus McCormick began to produce reapers. Chicago's steel industry originated in the 1850s, eventually becoming part of the largest steel producing region in the country.

In the 19th Century, northern and central European immigrants and their sons and daughters constituted the bulk of Chicago's industrial labor force: Germans, Scandinavians, Irish and near the century's end, Czechs. As mechanization and expansion of industry diminished the need for skilled workers, it created an insatiable demand for unskilled laborers. Southern and Eastern European immigrants from impoverished villages in Italy, Poland and other Slavic countries poured into Chicago.

They crowded into hastily constructed neighborhoods adjoining the factories, isolated from the rest of the city by railroad yards, polluted waterways and the factories themselves. Stockyards and packinghouse workers resided in an area about two miles square known as the Back-of-the-Yards, or Packingtown, its 55th Street southern boundary just four blocks from the Grbac home. The area was subdivided into ethnic enclaves occupied by Poles, Lithuanians, or Slovaks and later, Mexicans. When African-Americans joined the packinghouse workforce early in the 20th Century, in segregated Chicago, they lived in the so-called Black Belt, a couple miles to the east.

Since attempts to organize unions had failed, Chicago industrial workers were powerless and impoverished. The meat packing companies were especially resistant to unions, systematically exploiting divisions between skilled and unskilled workers as well as ethnic and racial differences. The few highly skilled butchers and tradesmen, mostly German- and Irish-Americans, were organized in craft unions that acted narrowly in their own interests, seeking to retain their relative privilege. Often they opposed gains for semi- and un-skilled workers, mostly new immigrants and blacks. Many of these unions had explicit anti-immigrant and racist precepts. The constitution of one union limited membership to "white free-born citizens of some civilized country."

During meat packing strikes in 1894 and 1904, the packers imported trainloads of strikebreakers directly from Ellis Island and from black communities in the South. The bitterness of white strikers was particularly directed against blacks. In 1904, with effigies labeled "nigger scab" hung from lampposts in Packingtown, there was violence against blacks, whether they were scabs or not. After the defeat of the 1904 strike, the percentage of black packinghouse workers rose from 3 to 25 percent, making them a crucial segment of the workforce.

World War 1 suddenly increased demand for meat products exported to Europe. When the United States entered the war, conscription and enlistment created a labor shortage. Packinghouse workers seized the opportunity to demand higher pay and better working conditions. Assisted by the Chicago Federation of Labor, the various craft unions in the industry formed an alliance, the Stockyards Labor Council (SLC). There were serious tensions within the council. Among its leaders were militant syndicalists William Z. Foster and Jack Johnstone, but also conservatives like Dennis Lane and Patrick Gorman of the Amalgamated Meat Cutters & Butcher Workmen (AMC).

As a strike loomed, to prevent a crippling disruption of meat production in wartime, the federal government ordered binding arbitration. In February, 1918, Judge Samuel Altshuler rendered a decision favorable to the workers—an eight-hour day, across-the-board raises, and equal pay for women—but it did not require company recognition of the union. After the war's end in November, 1918, arbitration remained in effect for more than two years.

The packers were well aware that a majority of the black

workers remained unsupportive of the "white man's union" even though several blacks achieved leadership roles in the SLC. To the packers' consternation, efforts to increase black support were gaining and reached a peak in 1919, when the SLC organized a "checkerboard parade" followed by an integrated picnic. But later that same month, these promising developments were violently reversed.

On July 27, 1919, an Irish gang killed a black youth when he inadvertently swam into an all-white Lake Michigan beach. Irish gangs from the Bridgeport neighborhood followed the killing with a rampage of random attacks on blacks that was conspicuously unopposed by the Chicago police. The next day the gangs moved westward into Packingtown to attack black workers. Packinghouse unionists were convinced that agents of the bosses incited the Irish gangs to come west to attack blacks.

In five days of rioting, 23 blacks and 15 whites were killed. Race relations in Packingtown hit an absolute low in August, when Irish gangs set an arson fire, destroying 49 homes of Lithuanian workers. A rumor circulated that it was an act of revenge by blacks. By the time the arbitration agreements ended in 1921, there was little black-white solidarity left.

In August the packers unilaterally instituted severe pay cuts that provoked the SLC to strike. The AMC, representing the skilled German and Irish butchers, without consultation, broke from the SLC. Black workers were escorted into the struck plants by armed troops. The ineffective strike dragged on until January, 1922. The SLC was totally destroyed, as was any remaining presence of the AMC in the big packing plants.

When Pa moved to Chicago, unions in the giant meat-packing firms had been virtually non-existent for over a decade. He wasted no time seeking work at the biggest and most notoriously anti-union packinghouse, Armour & Company.

I remember the first time I got hired at Armour and Company. The way they used to hire was about the same way they used to buy cattle. We crowded into a great big hiring hall and there were benches that would seat maybe a few dozen people. But hundreds of people were standing, men and women separate. They had a little platform that the employment manager, a guy name of Cecil Gile, would stand on. He looked over all the people, then he would point to one or another person, have them come over and talk to him briefly. If he liked them, he gave them a ticket to get hired. I didn't get pointed at, but after doing this process for a while, Gile and some assistants came down on the floor and circulated. The guy came up and asked me, "Where's your letter?" A lot of people had a letter from some little politician, a precinct captain or ward heeler, or some damn thing, recommending them for a job. I told him, "I don't have a letter. I just came looking for work." The guy looked at me, tapped my chest, felt my arm and said, "You're looking for work, well we'll give you work." And he wasn't fooling! I got some hard work! But I felt as if the guy was buying cattle or a horse. He did everything but count my teeth.

It was the practice then that 20 to 30% of the workforce was hired by the day, having to endure this hiring hall shape-up every morning. Pa was fond of relating that the "princely" wage he received was 32½ cents per hour. Later, when the NRA came into effect, his hours were cut back but he got a dime per hour raise. Working full time, even at the improved rate, he received only $17.00 per week. Not much money, even in 1933.

The heart of the Armour plant was around 43rd and Loomis, and the distance was, what, about two miles or a little more. So when I started working, I used to ride the street car in the morning, for seven cents fare, to get down there, but unless I was real tired, I'd walk home after work to save the seven cents. Seven cents meant something in those days. Sometimes you could find pork chops marked down for a nickel a pound.

He was put to work in various places—the boiled ham department, the salt cellars, on the loading dock—as a common laborer. Early on, he found out the workers managed to get at least a small benefit from working in a food industry.

Well, I was a green worker. The first lunch time came along and somebody said to me, "All you have to bring for lunch here is bread." I said, "What do you mean?" And the guy handed me a slice of ham about a half inch thick and he says, "Here, try this in your sandwich." And after a while the workers got tired of boiled ham, you know, a steady diet of it day in and day out. So somebody would go up to a company cop and give him two hams. One was for him and his buddies, and the other was for trading purposes. He would act as the intermediary. He'd go off someplace and come back by noon with some meat products from other areas, sausages or whatever. And sometimes the guys who were boning meat for sausage would take a nice cut, some beef tenderloin or something like that, and one guy would be designated as cook. He'd have a pot stashed someplace, and they'd run a steam hose into it, cook it. Sometimes guys would lay some meat on sheets of metal up high on top of some steam pipes and grill it. The company knew they had to tolerate a little bit of this. But they wouldn't let you smuggle anything out of the plant.

As soon as Pa told this story, to make sure I didn't get the impression that packinghouse workers had it good, he followed up with this narrative:

Those lunches were some of the sweeter facets. But the working conditions were just horrible. All sorts of terrible accidents occurred. A lot of people would get cut and pretty badly too. The foreman constantly would be pushing us to work faster and guys were working in close quarters with razor-sharp knives. The speed-up led to a lot of horrible accidents. And if you did get cut but you could still manage to struggle along despite of it, you didn't dare file a workman's comp claim. They'd turn around and lay you off.

I remember the Swift gas plant blew up and killed four people—hydrogen gas. They produced hydrogen for refining lard. I remember one time the pork tanks at Armour exploded and a guy was practically scalded through to the bone by steam. He walked out of there and died about two minutes later.

You had people working under refrigeration. What the hell! I'd work in the freezer in the summertime where it was eight below zero and come out and it was 90 outside. Before the union, they'd keep you in there, maybe let you out every couple hours for about five minutes or you'd sneak out. You'd come out, your blood would get thin. You'd get into the summer heat and you were woozy, dizzy, sort of drunk with the heat. Or you'd work in the freezer and they'd bring you out to work on the loading dock a while and it'd be a hundred degrees outside. You'd get sweated up and they'd send you back in the freezer and the sweat would just freeze on you. Guys got pneumonia from it.

There were many, many things wrong. So if a guy chewed on a hunk of meat once in a while, it may have made life slightly bearable but it certainly didn't compensate for the miserable conditions that existed in those packinghouses.

Pa explained that among the "many, many things wrong" was the autocratic power of the foreman in each department. To keep in the good graces of the superintendent, the foreman had to produce his department's required output, if possible, at a reduced production cost. The "drive" system was used to push personnel to work ever harder and faster. Workers were verbally abused and threatened with layoff if they didn't pick up the pace. There was no protection, no seniority. Workers were hired and fired at will. To avoid layoffs, they frequently had to bribe the foreman, bringing him a bottle of liquor or some cigars. Sometimes the foreman induced his employees to "volunteer" to do work painting or repairing the foreman's house. Another common practice was what the workers called "working for the church." The foreman would direct them to punch out on the time clock and then require them to do unpaid work for another fifteen minutes or so. The Armour family's generous contributions to churches were well known, so the workers remarked cynically that it was the value of their unpaid time that generated the money for Armour's donations.

The passage of the NRA not only provided employment opportunities by reducing the work week, but also it contained Section 7A, which according to Pa, "at least in theory, guaranteed the right of workers to organize. And while there were no teeth in it, no real protection, the *illusion* of having rights stimulated people to try to organize."

The first group to stir in 1933 was a new incarnation of the Stockyards Labor Council under its old leader Martin Murphy. It claimed to have signed up 5,000 members mostly from the older skilled butchers who, after the defeated strike in 1921-22, were blacklisted by the big packers, and found employment in smaller, less mechanized plants like Roberts & Oake, C.H. Hammond, and Reliable Packing. Reliable's employees included virtually the entire Polish and Ukrainian leadership cadre of the failed strike. Although the rank-and-file were sincere union members, Martin Murphy was corrupt. He considered the Council his personal possession and prevented any challenge to his leadership with an entourage of paid thugs. Pa characterized them as hoodlums who had never worked anywhere.

Through YCL connections Pa found there was an incipient Communist-led effort to organize a TUUL-affiliated union, the Packinghouse Workers Industrial Union (PHWIU). With his energy and enthusiasm, Pa proved to be the sparkplug of the PHWIU. Although the membership never rose above 500, mostly black workers augmented by some white leftists, the PHWIU was strong with black butchers in the strategically-positioned hog and sheep kills at Armour and among white maintenance mechanics at Wilson. Before getting jobs in packing, many of the PHWIU members had been active and developed militancy in the Communist-led Unemployed Councils.

The third union that now attempted to raise its presence in meat packing was the AFL's Amalgamated Meat Cutters. Unlike the other two unions, it had resources to hire full-time organizers, and they offered to waive initiation fees and dues for new members. Nonetheless they had little success due to their dismal reputation. Workers remembered their treachery that undermined the 1921 strike. "People weren't about to hop in bed with Denny Lane again. Most would have joined up with the Salvation Army before they signed on with the AF of L," commented one veteran worker.

The one area in which the AMC did have success was with the predominantly Irish livestock handlers in the Union Stockyards. Sometimes called "the aristocrats of the Yards," they were clannish, politically conservative but aggressive on job-related issues. Like all workers in the industry, the livestock handlers had endured successive pay cuts from 1930 to 1932. Without seeking the approval of Lane, they went on strike in November, 1933, demanding a restoration of the pre-Depression pay rates. They promptly won a 10% pay increase; the news exhilarated packinghouse workers, enhancing support for unionization, but apparently not for the AMC, revealing its great weakness among the mass of workers.

At this time Pa was working at Armour. He was the Secretary of the PHWIU and an executive board member of the Stockyards Labor Council. With at least three separate organizing efforts ongoing, plus pressure from the employers to join ersatz company unions, it was confusing to workers where to place their loyalties. A series of reversals, firings of several union activists, led Pa and a couple of leaders in the SLC to decide that the Communists' dual-union (and in this case triple-union) strategy was not effective. They decided to combine efforts. The pragmatic way was to merge with the AMC, to take advantage of their financial resources and the no initiation fee offer. Without seeking Party approval, Pa led the merger negotiations; AMC promised to launch a drive to organize unskilled workers "soon," and the incoming SLC and PHWIU leaders assumed leadership positions in the AMC. Pa became the delegate to the Chicago Federation of Labor which was headed by a progressive veteran unionist, John Fitzpatrick. The militant unionists opted to give another try to the "boring from within" tactic, working within the framework of the conservative AFL.

As in Kansas City, the union had to operate clandestinely to avoid firings. Through their spies, Armour management discovered Pa's union activism. Cognizant of his abilities, Armour did not simply fire him but undertook a patient, months-long effort to "hook" him, as Pa called it—to manipulate him into working for them as a stool pigeon (spy) or perhaps a leader of a company union.

When they began to suspect me, they assigned me and a guy by the name of Walter Nelson, a black man, to work together, just the two of us, to clean up an old smokehouse. And what Nelson did was try to smoke me out. He acted very friendly and talked as radical as possible. He mentioned the Unemployed Council and the Scottsboro case and so on. I was kind of young and naïve and went along with him, became friendly, but he did most of the talking. After working with him three or four days, they figured they had enough on me, so they laid both of us off. Actually he wasn't laid off, but I didn't see him anymore for a while.

After that the company evidently decided to see if they could hook me. They patiently took six or eight months to work it through. They let me work along and then, on the very day my oldest son Bobby was born, I went to the hospital in the wee hours of the morning. I called in that I was at the hospital, my wife was giving birth, and I would come in as soon as I could. And I did, I came to work about 12 noon, grabbed a bit of lunch, and worked the rest of the day. As soon as the end of the day came along, I noticed the boss coming up to me with a pink slip, I was laid off.

Then they let me cook for a while by not hiring me back, and of course I was very desperate for cash. I needed work and I kept coming to the employment office every day, the old slave market, but with no results.

Finally I was called in by the employment manager, Cecil Gile, [pronounced like "guile"] who was running the hooking operation. He says, "Your name isn't Marich. It's March, isn't it?" I had been using Marich with an "i" in it in the plant. "We found out about you." He said he knew I had been active in the Young Communist League in Kansas City, that I was a radical and had a past record. But as far as he was concerned, I was young then, he wasn't going to hold it against me. He thought I was a good fellow. But he said there were people higher up in the company who said to get rid of me. Then he said, "Well, if you're really so interested in representing these employees, we could see to it that you played a role in the company's Employee Representation Plan. I'll put you back to work and you just think about it a while.

This was a cunningly timed offer to sell out. The Employee Representation Plan was the company union, a safety valve against real unionism. By then it was thoroughly discredited. Supposedly they could handle grievances. Pa maintained the only time anyone went to them was after having been fired and you had nothing left to lose.

The widely disdained leaders of the company union were C.H. Talley, a black man and James Holmes, a white. They held ostensible jobs in the Armour plant but were free to wander around in their never-bloody white coats, supposedly seeing to the needs of the employees. Mostly they were shaking down workers for ten cent weekly dues and running other rackets. They made $5

loans which were repaid on pay day at $6, a usurious rate. Tall-
ey received a kick-back from a men's clothing store in the Black
Belt neighborhood. Workers were pushed to buy clothes there on
credit, and as long as they were making payments on the over-
priced clothes, Talley saw to it they wouldn't be laid off.

So Gile offered me a place in that company union apparatus. I told
him I wasn't interested. Finally he said, "Well, I'll see what I can do to
keep you covered. I know that you're hard up." And he gave me a job in
the beef curing department—a sort of out-of-the-way place.

Pa mentioned that the job was "no picnic." He had to wade in
ankle-deep brine much of the time.

I worked in that department for about four months when I got
called in again by Gile. He asked me how I was getting along, and he
says, "Herb, I've been taking care of you, doing a favor for you. I wonder if you could do a favor for me?" I said nothing. He said, "There is
a certain person," and he said her name, "who we suspect is active in
the women's local of the Amalgamated. She's currently on lay off, and
as long as we suspect her, she'll stay laid off. But I don't want to do her
an injustice. Could you do me the favor of finding out whether or not
she's active in the Amalgamated? If she's not you'll be doing both her
and me a great big service." Well of course the ploy was just obvious
to me. All I had to do was say OK and come back a week later, say, "No,
I've checked and she's not active." He figured the temptation would
be for me to do that and he'd have somebody listening or record it in
some fashion. If they could prove that I had performed an informant
service for them, they could use that to blackmail me and turn me into
a stool pigeon.

And so I looked at Gile with a big grin and said, "I'm sorry, Mr. Gile,
I'm just not built that way. I'm not interested in helping you get any information of any sort." He said, "OK Herb, no offense." They found out
they couldn't hook me and of course I knew what the consequences
were. Two days later I got bounced, laid off. Boom.

From that time Pa was blacklisted at Armour. I asked if they
ever tried to "hook" him again. "No, they figured I was incorrigi-

ble," he replied.

Pa liked to relate the outcome to the hooking story that took place three years later. Pa thought about it and figured out that management's information on him must have come from Nelson. One day he noticed Nelson had a job along the Armour & Company visitors' route as a janitor.

He had a nice white coat and he would dust off displays in the little office the visitors came through. It was a job doing practically nothing. So I figured Nelson was a stool pigeon, for sure.

Pa had a fantastic memory, especially for names and faces. The packers underestimated his recall powers when they sent Nelson to carry out another stool pigeon assignment.

Well, in 1937 we started our CIO organizing drive at Armour. I hadn't seen Nelson for three years. One of the first groups we organized was the sheep kill. So the workers set up a meeting at a Masonic lodge hall on the South Side. It was our first attempt at an open big meeting and we were going to elect stewards and give them badges. In those days there was still a certain amount of fear, despite the Wagner Act. You were sticking your neck out and might get fired, so it was the bolder ones who came to the meeting, about 50 or 60 of the 120 sheep kill workers, I'd say.

As the meeting began, I was to open it, I noticed a gentleman come sliding into the hall and sit down in the audience and lo and behold it was this stool pigeon Nelson. So as a preliminary, before getting our meeting underway, I made a little speech about how the company is trying to break up our union and trying to use stool pigeons to spy on us, and there may be stool pigeons in the audience. I said, "Now let me give you an illustration. There is this particular gentleman..." and I told them the story of how Nelson had stooled on me. I noticed Mr. Nelson was beginning to squirm. Then I pointed directly at him and said, "The man who performed this stool pigeon work on me is at our meeting, his name is Walter Nelson, and there he sits." The tension in the air was so thick you could cut it. There was a good chance that somebody might clobber him. But I said, "Now don't anybody do anything, but I want to know if Mr. Nelson still wants to sit in on our meeting?" And he got out of the hall so fast it would make your head spin.

Pa was concerned that exposing the stool pigeon in their midst might intimidate the workers, but it actually had the opposite effect. They enjoyed the incident so much that it didn't scare anybody. Their feeling was, to hell with him. They had been pushed around way too long and they were ready to push back.

Despite being blacklisted, Pa made had some success in 1934 to get back in at Armour, but was eventually frozen out from the hiring hall. Like his fellow industrial workers, Pa desperately needed a job, so he sought work at other companies. For a while he worked the graveyard shift (midnight to 8:00 AM) at the Campbell Soup plant running potato peeling machines. He had to pour sacks of potatoes into front-loading peeling machines that looked more or less like clothes dryers. The potatoes tumbled around in a drum that had abrasive walls until the peels were scraped off. He had a long line of these machines to fill. By the time he loaded the last one, it was time to empty the first one. One night he got interrupted and left the spuds in too long. They were scraped down to about the size of ping pong balls. What to do? He'd probably get fired if he sent the mini-potatoes onward. There were few other workers on the graveyard shift, no one around, so he decided to just keep them in the peeling machines until the potatoes were ground down to nothing, totally gone. No one knew the difference.

He managed to get work in a WPA street paving project, tearing up and removing old pavement. Figuring he was a "troublemaker," trying to talk union the supervisor put him with the black workers, the only white among them, to limit his influence. It made no difference. Pa said it was just fine to have a chance to talk to black workers.

I learned about this job in a strange way. In high school I was an enthusiastic folk musician. I bought an LP of blues musician Jesse Fuller and played it on the Hi-Fi in the living room. When the record came to Jesse singing "Linin' Track," a railroad worksong, I was astounded to hear Pa start singing along. I knew his taste accentuated classical music and light opera. "How do you know that song?!" I blurted. Pa said he learned it, and a bunch more work songs on that black road crew. They sang to coordinate the swinging of their picks. To demonstrate, he launched into another work song, swinging an imaginary pick:

"Ham and eggs (whop, whop)
Pork and beans (whop, whop),
I would eat more (whop, whop)
But the plate wasn't clean" (whop).

When Jane and Herb returned to Chicago, Ivan had died, three brothers were in Russia, brothers John and Krešo had their own residences. There were only Nona, Aunt Agnes, Uncle Joe, and his daughter Gloria who was less than two years old. Her mother, Kate Knaus, Joe's first wife had died of uremic fever.

While Pa labored in the packinghouse, Mom found work as a waitress at the "Century of Progress" World's Fair. Celebrating Chicago's centennial, the fair attracted millions of visitors to its grounds along the lakefront. From late May to early fall, Mom waited on patrons in the "Streets of Paris" section. Mom had become pregnant in May. She commented that, as the summer turned to fall, she found it increasingly difficult to hide her pregnancy in the tight-fitting French waitress uniform she had to wear. She let out the seams and did her best not to be noticed. In those days it was considered improper for a pregnant woman to be visible in public. Ultimately, she couldn't hide her condition any longer and they fired her.

Mom's sister Agnes, because of tuberculosis of the spine had to have an operation, fusing vertebrae in her lower back. She was sent out of polluted Chicago to a farm in Michigan to gain strength. The farm, about 130 miles away, belonged to friends, the Kruzich family, Croatian immigrants who had worked in the Iowa coalfields long enough to earn the money to buy a farm near Mattawan in southwestern Michigan. Agnes had the company of the three Kruzich daughters and one son, but after a couple months, farm life became dull to the vivacious 23-year-old city girl. She and 17-year-old Victoria Kruzich decided to run away to Chicago. They hitchhiked to the Lake Michigan port of Benton Harbor where they boarded a ferry. Vicky attributed her decision to run off to the deprivations of the Depression. There would be one fewer mouth to feed on the impoverished farm, but also the allure of the exciting city drew her to Chicago. Prior to departure, she must have been eating well. Vicky claims she was a hefty 157 pound, rosy-cheeked farm girl when she arrived, although I only remember her years later, as a very slim woman.

Vicky took up residence at the Grbac home. She became Mom's closest life-long friend. They adopted each other. Over the years, in their correspondence, they addressed each other as "Dear sister." In an early 1970s interview with historians Alice and Staughton Lynd, Vicky described the scene in 1933 at the Grbac house:

I lived with them at 59th and Ashland. Jane and Herb lived on the second floor and on the third floor they had bedrooms and an attic room. Anyone who didn't have some place to live could always find room there. It was near the streetcar intersection and when there were meetings, blacks could slip into the back door of the house unnoticed. (This was a real problem at the time.) The Marches would have meetings of the YCL in the attic and they'd ask me to sit in. The terminology was like a foreign language. I thought that I better join this outfit so that I would know what they were talking about.

Mom was an active YCL organizer, and Vicky described the discussions through which Mom and Pa educated young working people about unions and socialism.

They pointed out things to me that, in my very unsophisticated and farm-like way, I saw. There was so much food being dumped—the government bought it up—and people were hungry and didn't have enough to eat...the government was set up to keep it this way. They thought that instead of just thinking about ourselves we should be thinking about other people and try to get them together in a union and organize and then maybe we would have socialism where there would not be hunger, war, etc. They initiated me into a lot of political ideas and gave me material to read. We had classes and we would discuss industrial unionism, the craft unions and the history of the labor movement in this country. We talked about Debs, we talked about the eight hour day, many things...

.

Nona willingly allowed her Chicago house to be a center of radical activity—providing lodgings and meeting space. It was a familiar role for her home. Decades earlier in Nerezine, her house was the center for Croatian political efforts.

The YCL had a strategy of "colonization," placing members in jobs in key industries where they hoped to organize. Pa already was working at Armour so it seemed advantageous to have Vicky get into another big packing plant:

> Herb suggested that I get a job [at Swift]. He bought me a steel, with which one sharpens a knife, and I took it with me. He took me down to the stockyards and (he likes to tell this story) I said, "Those beautiful cows! They can't kill those beautiful cows!" At home we just had cows for milking. But here were all these cows and they were going to be killed and they were crying, mooing...But one had to get a job!

Vicky went to the employment office, told the women's hiring director that she had experience butchering hogs on the farm, and was hired on.

She and Mom worked together on organizing efforts. They both were involved in the publication and distribution of pro-union shop papers, one directed at women packinghouse workers called "Stockyards Stella" and another called "The Yards Worker." Because Mom wasn't a packinghouse employee she and other YCL-ers passed them out at the plant gates, although the packers' security cops often chased them away. Vicky smuggled the papers right into the plants in her underwear. Vicky joked that in the morning she'd come into the plant "all busty" with papers stuffed in her bra, then left them in the washroom for other workers to find.

Like Pa, Vicky also described the unsanitary and atrocious working conditions in the packinghouse. Working in the cook room where "drought cattle" were being processed into canned hash to be distributed for relief, she recounted:

> The meat would be cut into big chunks and steamed. Then it would come on a rail and be dumped out on the table. The women

would be all around the table and we would cut the meat up, remove the gristle and bad parts, and make hash out of it. The government inspector would come around to see that bad meat wasn't being thrown into the hash. But as soon as his back would be turned, the foreman would push this stuff right down the chute to go into the cans—all this stuff we had put aside to be thrown away he would push right down in, including gloves, cockroaches, anything. The company didn't give a damn.

The meat would be so hot and steamy your fingers almost blistered but you stayed on. In 1933-34 we worked six hour shifts at 37½ cents an hour. We would have to work at a high rate of speed. It was summer. It would be so hot that women used to pass out. The ladies room was on the floor below and I would help carry these women down the almost vertical stairs into the washroom.

An accident occurred in the hot dog department on the floor below. A woman lost her fingers in a meat chopping machine lacking safety guards. Vicky and two other YCL members decided to take action:

Three of us "colonizers" had a meeting during our break and decided this was the time to have a stoppage and we did. All six floors went on strike. We said, "Sit, stop." And we had a sit-down. We just stopped working right inside the building, protesting the speed and unsafe conditions. We thought people's fingers shouldn't go into the machine, that it was an outrage. The women got interested in the union. We got the company to put in safety devices.

Jane March speaking at Skyline Athletic Club, 1943

After this action, management investigated to identify the

ringleaders. Vicky and the others were fired and blacklisted. She cut and dyed her hair, put on make-up, used a fake name, Helen Ellis, and managed to get hired back into the very same department. After a few days, the forelady who was also Croatian, addressed Vicky in that language, "OK Helen, I know you are Vicky. I won't say anything, but just keep quiet."

Work was unstable. After a few weeks work, there would be a layoff and often weeks passed before being called back. During layoffs, Vicky worked with Mom on organizing activities. They became active in community groups. The Communists developed the International Workers Order (IWO), a fraternal insurance society that had separate ethnic chapters for the Polish, Lithuanian, Croatian and other groups. Vicky and Mom signed up members. They helped to organize events involving ethnic foods, music and dancing to promote fellowship and to provide an opportunity to discuss politics, unions and economic issues. As former Catholics, Mom and Vicky retained ties to people in the neighborhood parishes. Vicky, a single teenager, joined the sodality, a young women's club, at Assumption Church, playing on their basketball team.

As the fall of 1933 wore on, Mom had to face the fact that a big distraction from her activism was inexorably on its way; her pregnancy was advancing, she was going to become a mother. Mom's perspective on these times was expressed in a remarkable letter. Before she passed away in 2009 Vicky gave me a sheaf of letters from my mother that she had saved. In a December, 1990 letter, Mom wrote about what Vicky's arrival in Chicago meant to her:

Vicky, Vicky, I wasn't able to sleep and I am writing this at 5 AM. My mind kept going to when you came to live at our house in Chicago. Me, with my Bobby making me bigger and bigger, I was not sure of what I could do with a baby in that big old, cold, barn-like house with dozens of adults in and out, sleeping on mattresses in the attic. Aggie was about to go to the hospital for a back operation, Mama [Nona] was trying somehow to at least have bread baked for everyone.

Then you came, such a fresh breeze from heaven. The strong-muscled girl with a red-cheeked face, you came and laughed. That laugh has stood me well in many of my darkest, moodiest, saddest hours. I never forget the feeling of hope you brought to me. Could I be happy—I, a poor kid who grew up in war, a starveling? How could I be strong like this absolutely cheery, open-faced girl coming with the reputation of being the champion grape-picker in Welch's grape juice country of Michigan? Well, I couldn't start over. But I did do whatever had to be done to make myself stronger, and (if it had to be) make *my baby* strong, really strong.

It made me resolve to finally go to a pre-natal clinic. I went to Dr. [Joseph] DeLee's, Lying-in Hospital at the University of Chicago, the best damn place going for pre-natal care. A pale-faced intern asked me the usual questions. I must have been scared stiff, for I was 5 months or so pregnant and had not done anything about proper food, care, etc. I was organizing and picketing at a Stetson China factory. We had pulled the women out as they had been working for weeks with only *promises* of pay. The men got a pittance of pay to keep them coming in and not joining the women on strike.

At the doctor's I was wearing a black satin dress Aggie had discarded. It was big on me and hid the tummy. What a sight I was, all of 120 pounds on my scrawny 5'7" frame with boney arms and legs. This very nice doctor measured, weighed, examined me, and then shook his head. "You have to eat." I just stared. Again he said, "Why aren't you eating? It won't go away. You must have an orange a day, milk, fruit, vegetables." I burst out, "An orange costs a nickel, and there are thousands like me out there in the same condition with no nickel for an orange." I was fighting mad. I had had enough of what the Depression had done to us by that fall of 1933, and here was this smug rich kid, studying to be a doctor, telling me what I had to do.

Well, he was a human being. He fell apart. He almost started to cry. So I started to comfort him. "It must be hard for you to have girls come in here and see them in this condition. Well, tell me what should I do? I know good truck farmers who help the unemployed. They are Socialists from Holland. I can go get food from them if as you say, I'll be sick and my baby will be sick if I don't." (Anyway, we had sort of ended the strike as Stetson finally gave the women a little money. They couldn't keep the factory going without the women's china painting.)

He asked if I could get cabbage, peppers and tomatoes. Well, of course I said, that's the main crop in August and September on the truck farms. He said, "Cabbage, tomatoes and even peppers have lots of vitamin C, same as an orange." We talked and smiled and he was happy that with this advice he might help others who may have access to the bountiful produce grown around Chicago. "Eat all of those vegetables raw until the end of your pregnancy." Well, the tomatoes and peppers we made into chili sauce for winter, but by October, the raw ones were few. But cabbage was another thing. We saved the hardest heads for storing, the rest for sauerkraut. I ate cabbage either way until Bobby was born at the end of February.

Luckily Herb and you, Vicky, were working in the stockyards after NRA came in and I had car fare to go with two bushel baskets to the end of the 59th Street streetcar line, walk a half mile and then bring back two bushels once every few days. Did I ever begin to feel good! I ate lots and lots of Nona's homemade bread, with every kind of grain and flour that the relief had started giving to our neighbors and they, not knowing what to do with it, gave it to Ma. Bread we had and luckily, Joe being a plumber, knew how to by-pass the gas meter connected to our furnace, as the gas was expensive. Everyone did it. Joe was smart. He left a few lines run to the meter so no one got wise;...we didn't get caught and had gas for heat and cooking, also we had a little money. We loved and laughed and organized, had room for homeless comrades and bread and tea at every meeting.

My baby grew. Bobby came out skinny for a 23½" baby, but he had the biggest cabbage head you ever saw! It has served him well, as you know of his achievements in nuclear science and astro-physics and so much more.

I love you. I have never before had it hit me so strongly as to what you did for *me*. Now, over 50 years later, after so many struggles I can look back at the people who gave me inspiration. You were my first. I'll never forget.

Have a good Christmas with your family. And oh yes, Happy Birthday! I do remember sometimes that you're almost a Christmas baby like my Buddy.

Love, Jane.

P.S. I weighed 170 lbs when I went into labor. I came out 129 lbs. Cabbage weighs a lot! (Biggest placenta they'd ever seen, the doctor told me.)

Mom's early morning musings reveal the importance she placed on working as an organizer and the value of her friendship network to build the movement. What's more, going to Lying-in for maternity care began our family's long association with the University of Chicago, where both of my brothers were educated, ultimately earning doctorates there. Also obvious is the intense personal conflict Mom felt about having a baby. After becoming a mother, would she be able to continue the activism she was so passionate about?

In her positive message concerning the inspiration Vicky brought, Mom avoided mentioning the two tragic events that occurred on February 28, 1934, the day my brother Bob was born. First, Pa was laid off. But worse, Mom's beloved eldest brother John was killed that morning in an industrial accident.

John became a father figure for Mom when he returned to her household in Nerezine in 1919. After her father Ivan died in 1930, John, the senior male in the family, again assumed a paternal role, taking an active interest in the day-to-day affairs of his mother and younger siblings. He and his wife Kata were infertile, having no children in 15 years of marriage, and John was excited about his little sister's impending baby.

John's trade as a cooper provided reliable employment even during the Depression. Before the era of steel drums, wooden barrels were widely used in industry. In 1934 the factory where John worked used open elevators, little more than large wooden platforms lifted between the floors by cables. There was nothing automatic about the device. Two levers inside the elevator controlled an electric motor that raised or lowered the platform. By today's standards it was obviously unsafe, but in 1934, long before the Occupational Safety and Health Administration (OSHA), employers had little incentive to provide safe working conditions.

While workers injured on the job or their heirs could sue employers for damages, taking legal action was expensive and winning proved difficult. If employers could demonstrate that the employee had understood the risk, that the injury was caused by a fellow employee, or the worker himself was partly at fault, the courts usually denied liability. Studies showed that in court cases fewer than half of the workers fatally injured recovered anything and when they did, the average compensation amounted to less than six months' pay. For employers, accidents were cheap. American industries developed with little concern for workers' safety.

John had given his wife instructions to call him at work as soon as Jacinta gave birth. He wanted to rush to the hospital to see the baby. Bob was born that morning, and before leaving for the packinghouse, Pa called Kata from the hospital. Kata took the call about 10 AM. John was scheduled to work only until noon that day and would be home soon. To her eternal regret, Kata decided not to call the factory.

A little later that morning, John and a co-worker needed to load a batch of barrels into the elevator. As he approached the device, he noticed that the floor of the elevator was a few inches higher than the factory floor. This was not unusual, there were no automatic settings for where the elevator was to stop. Standing beside the barrels, John leaned into the elevator and reached for the levers to adjust it downward a bit. What happened then, we will never know. Did John hit the wrong lever? Did he slip? Did the elevator malfunction? Suddenly the elevator flew upwards. It carried him up and crushed him between the elevator floor and the factory ceiling, killing him instantly.

At Lying-in, Mom couldn't understand why her brother John didn't come to see her. The other family members, still in shock, decided it best not to tell Jacinta about John while she still was in the hospital, in fragile condition.

When she came home, her few days of joy were tempered by grief over John's death, and by worry because of Herb's layoff. Like Mom, little Bobby was born into a turbulent and uncertain world.

The Grbacs faced yet another blow when the priest at Assumption Church refused to conduct John's funeral Mass because of his family's communist associations. Finally he relented. John had never foresworn his religion and Nona emphatically reminded the priest of his late father's importance to the congregation as vestryman.

Tragedies and Triumphs

The premature death of her son John was another shock and grief to Nona, but sadly, also a portent of things to come. Death visited the Grbac house with alarming frequency. Since the beginning of the 1930s, Nona had lost her husband. Her son Joe had lost his wife. Within a decade Nona would have to endure the sorrow of outliving four of her six sons. "The 20th Century was difficult for working class men," Mom mused one time. The wars and dangerous industrial jobs took a big toll, especially on men. While they were in grief over the loss of life, Nona and Mom had a duty to nurture a new life, Bobby, the baby with the big cabbage head.

Nona served as Bobby's chief care-giver; his first words as an infant were in Nerezine dialect. Mom, a caring mother, nonetheless resumed her activism in the YCL as soon as possible. She had the freedom to do so because Nona was at home, a reliable care-giver. They had only one argument about childrearing. Mom was given a modern baby care manual at Lying-in. It prescribed precise amounts and times for feeding a baby. One day Mom came home to discover that Nona had fed Bobby earlier and had given him more than the book prescribed. "That's not what the book says," Mom insisted. "He didn't read the book, you did," Nona countered categorically. "He was hungry and I fed him and that's it!"

Mom did have frequent spats with older brother Joe—a pattern that lasted all their lives. Though it was a loving relationship, Joe criticized his little sister's behavior, even if she never heeded him. "What kind of a wife and mother are you? You're always running off to your meetings. You should be home to take care of the house and your child." Mom did throw herself into efforts to improve home life and care of children, but like Clara Lemlich Shavelson in Brooklyn a generation earlier, not just for herself, but

157

for her community.

Mom had discovered the University of Chicago Settlement House. The Settlement house was in a stark-looking structure on a narrow street in the heart of the Back-of-the-Yards neighborhood. Across the street was a row of taverns known as Whiskey Point frequented by packinghouse workers. The settlement house had been founded in 1894 by Mary McDowell, a close associate of Jane Addams. Supported by funds and volunteers from the University of Chicago's Settlement League, an all-female organization, they aimed to improve local conditions with education and assistance for immigrants. Moreover, documented settlement house efforts were a laboratory for the departments of sociology, social work and economics at the university.

Settlements were a reformist movement in England and the US that began in the 1880s and peaked in the 1920s. They were founded in poor urban areas, where middle-class volunteer "settlement workers" would reside, eager to share their knowledge and culture with their neighbors, providing education, training in handicraft skills, child care, nutrition and health care. By 1914 there were over 400 settlements in 32 states. The leaders of many settlements became convinced that the poor were oppressed by economic factors that could not be addressed merely by the settlement's educational efforts and became supportive of unions to improve conditions for impoverished workers.

Mary McDowell, who called herself "an immigrant from Evanston," the prosperous suburb north of Chicago, became known in the neighborhood as "the angel of the stockyards." She served as "head resident" at the U of C Settlement for 34 years, moving into the neighborhood just weeks after the 1894 strike, and assisted workers and their families in the strikes of 1904 and 1921. Upton Sinclair resided at the settlement house while he conducted research for his influential 1906 book *The Jungle*.

The settlement house was fiercely opposed by the Polish Catholic priests of the neighborhood. They resented the educated, upper-middle-class settlement workers, their English and Scotch-Irish backgrounds and especially their Protestantism. McDowell attended a Methodist church in the area with a largely Slovak congregation, and the priests viewed the settlement workers as nothing more than intruding Protestant missionaries. To compete with McDowell's efforts, in 1915 Father Grudzinski, the pastor of St. John of God, the most prestigious of the Polish parishes in the neighborhood, bought a lot and built a facility nearly next door to the settlement house, the Guardian Angel Day Nursery and Home for Working Girls.

McDowell had retired as head resident a few years before Mom arrived but remained involved with the settlement until her death in 1936. Mom appreciated the Settlement House pro-labor, educational and social improvement traditions, while they welcomed her Spanish-speaking ability. Because there was no Catholic church in the neighborhood hospitable to them, the many Mexican immigrants who arrived in the 1920s used the Settlement House as their community center. She and Vicky became regular frequenters, joined by other leftist women, their friends, Mary Szewczyk (Siporin), Hermione Orear and Estelle Zabritski.

These young women convinced the YWCA to open a branch in the neighborhood, on Ashland Avenue, just a stone's throw from the settlement house. The two organizations collaborated closely. Mom's cohort formed a club called "Modern Mrs." which sponsored children's activities and the general enlightenment of women on consumer, homemaking and health issues, including information about birth control.

The accomplishments of Mom's cohort were warmly praised in an April 7, 1940 article in the virulently anti-labor Chicago Tribune, which usually relished every opportunity to smear Pa. The article lists the "girls" who were officers and committee members, including Mom, her sister Agnes, and close friends Estelle and Hermione.

This group of dedicated community organizers, many of them communists, learned how to bridge the neighborhood barriers of ethnic and religious rivalries. Through years of work they laid the essential groundwork and provided the model and the muscle to establish the Back-of-the-Yards Neighborhood Council (BYNC), the organization upon which the famous community organizer Saul Alinsky made his reputation. While the crucial contributions of Mom and her cohort are given only passing mention in the historical writings about the origins of "Alinskyism," the work of the

Back-of-the-Yards Council led the movement, thanks to Mom's community and Pa's union organizing.

After playing a key role in the merger of the stockyards unions, Pa and his cohorts continued without success to push the Amalgamated Meat Cutters to launch an organizing drive in the Armour, Swift and Wilson plants. They remained reluctant to organize despite the enactment of the Wagner Act in July, 1935 which offered legal protections for union activity and established the National Labor Relations Board (NLRB). The AMC leaders were content to represent the skilled butchers in retail stores and in a handful of small packing plants. An influx of new unskilled workers of differing racial and ethnic backgrounds might threaten their personal positions of power in the union.

In the summer of 1935 Pa seized an opportunity to put additional pressure on the AMC. For several years the Chicago Federation of Labor hosted a Labor Day gathering at Soldier Field, Chicago's big football stadium, attended by thousands of union workers. Use of the facility was regulated by the city parks commission. In 1934 former Armour & Co. Vice President Robert J. Dunham became the parks commissioner. Dunham vetoed allowing the CFL to hold their event in Soldier Field, calling it too controversial. When the decision was announced at the CFL board meeting, Pa, the AMC's representative on the board, made a bold suggestion: "Why not hit Mr. Dunham where it hurts? If we can't use Soldier Field, why don't we hold a Labor Day Parade right through the stockyards area?" The idea was enthusiastically accepted by the other CFL delegates. When they found out, the AMC leaders Dennis Lane and Patrick Gorman were far from enthusiastic.

Since the Chicago Federation of Labor was honoring the proposal to march through the stockyards on Labor Day, the AMC couldn't decline. But they were unhappy about my having raised it. And so to guarantee the purity of the Labor Day parade, they called upon what was known as the Red Squad, the Industrial Detail, to closely supervise the parade. If any radicals attempted to march, to see to it that they were arrested or gotten rid of.

I remember the parade well. I had never ridden a horse before and I was called upon to ride a horse in front of a group of packinghouse workers leading the parade. I had a general idea of how to steer a horse but we had some fancy trained parade horses that the CFL had rented. The marching band started playing, and this horse was trained to dance and prance when he heard music. He started kicking up his heels and I was hanging on for dear life. I must've been quite a sight.

Pa expressed dissatisfaction with the turnout. Because they "were used to sitting on their butts," it was not as big as the Soldier Field gatherings. Nonetheless thousands of Chicago union workers attended the parade, which started at the AMC headquarters and ended with a rally at Sherman Park in the heart of the Back-of-the-Yards, the same place big union rallies were held in 1919.

The Chicago Police Industrial Detail, the Red Squad, was headed by "Make" Mills, a Russian who reputedly once had been with the Tsarist secret police. His cops were out in force to harass and arrest known labor radicals. Pa went on:

Of course there were a few nasty incidents. Just to get them out of the parade, a number of people who were left wingers in various unions were arrested, taken down to the stockyards station, held for a while and then released.

You know a funny thing, they arrested my wife and my son Bobby. He was about two years old. He was pinched too. I understand when the police picked him up he assaulted a policeman by kicking him in the shins. He was real militant but no charges were filed.

The police were looking for me, too, but they couldn't find me. They saw me on the horse but they had me confused with my brother-in-law, Krešo Grbac. When they questioned Jane at the police station, they kept insisting the guy on the horse was her brother Krešo and kept asking what the hell was he, a pharmacist, doing in the parade with packinghouse workers? How they could have mixed us up I'll never know. We don't look much alike. Besides, Krešo had a moustache and I was clean-shaven.

The thousands of workers who turned out for the procession

thwarted Dunham's attempt to squelch the CFL's Labor Day observance while calling attention to the meat packing industry as a target for unionization.

Flushed from the success of the Labor Day Parade, Pa and rank-and-file activists from the militant unions in the AMC called for a special order of business at the next CFL meeting. The Amalgamated was feeling pressure from above and below. The CFL was considering direct support for the militant insurgents. The Amalgamated was invited to send a representative to present their program. They sent "Big Bill" Tate, one of the AMC's few black organizers and a former sparring partner of Jack Dempsey. Unfortunately the "program" he proposed was worthless. Pa expressed utter disgust that Tate proclaimed, "When you go into a butcher shop, how many of you look around to see if there is a union-shop card? It would help us a lot if you would refuse to patronize a store that does not display the card...it would give us all the assistance we ask of you." Since the retail butchers were about 90% organized, this would do nothing to organize the packinghouses. That was the last straw. The militant stockyards unionists gave up on the AMC's self-interested leaders.

Because packinghouse workers were pressing for a union drive, the CFL agreed to set up an organizing committee over the objections of the AMC. The chairman Art Kampfert and vice-chairman Frank McCarty were veterans of the 1920s SLC. Pa, the young upstart, was made the secretary. But Pa complained they were given no finances, "We couldn't get money, not even money for leaflets."

But new possibilities were emerging. At the stormy October, 1935 AFL convention in Atlantic City, industrial organizers complained that AFL craft unions were deliberately hindering organizing efforts. United Mine Workers of America (UMWA) president John L. Lewis, who had been a typical conservative AFL leader, decided the time was ripe to advocate industrial unionism. After an exchange of insults, Lewis vaulted a row of chairs and slugged the 300-lb Carpenters Union leader William "Big Bill" Hutcheson, a craft union stalwart. Pa reflected on the emerging dispute:

About that time at the AF of L Convention, John Lewis and several others, including reps of the Amalgamated Clothing Workers and the Typographical Union, pressed for a campaign to organize the unorganized. The discussion reflected a concern of a section of the labor movement about Hitler's coming to power in Germany. They argued we must bring democracy to industry to stop the rise of fascism here in the United States.

In November, 1935 they established the Committee for Industrial Organization (CIO) within the AFL, predecessor to the independent Congress of Industrial Organizations formed by unions that broke from the AFL the next year.

Meat packing wasn't an early CIO organizing target. Lewis pressed AMC leaders Lane and Gorman to join the CIO, but they dithered. The first large CIO organizing drives took place in 1936 and 1937 in the steel, rubber and automobile industries. Pa had close friends who played leading roles in those drives, including the militant sit-down strike in Flint, Michigan against General Motors that won union recognition in 1937.

With the Depression easing, demand for steel was increasing. After seeing successful union drives by rubber workers and auto workers, US Steel, the largest corporation in the nation, opted to negotiate with the CIO's Steel Workers Organizing Committee (SWOC) rather than risk sit-down strikes. They reached agreement in March, 1937. The so-called "Little Steel" corporations like Inland Steel and Jones & Laughlin (which were big, powerful corporations, only "little" in comparison to US Steel) held out against the SWOC.

The hardest nut to crack was Republic Steel, whose virulently anti-union chairman Tom Girdler assembled an arsenal of military-style weapons inside its Chicago mill. Chicago's CIO unionists called for a Memorial Day picnic and parade to support the strikers at Republic Steel. Of course my family went to the event, which became known as the Memorial Day Massacre. I heard accounts of what happened that day from Mom, Pa and brother Bob, for whom it was one of his earliest memories. Pa recalled:

I was working in the stockyards at the time, the packinghouse. My brother-in-law Nick Daniels [Agnes' husband] was working at Carnegie Illinois then and I knew a lot of other steel workers too....My brother-in-law said, "Memorial Day we're going to have a big union rally out at the union headquarters." They had rented an old building, I'd say about a quarter of a mile from the mill gate of Republic Steel. Some national CIO leaders were coming to speak.

A couple of days before, on the picket line there had been some arrests and beatings by Chicago Police. So the SWOC officials decided to put on a mass picket after the rally, as a protest and to strengthen the morale of the strikers. We came out to the meeting, Jane, Bobby and I, and some friends of mine who worked at Inland Steel saw I was there with the wife and kid, so they told me, "Look, the police have been rough the last couple of days." They said, "You better keep your wife out of this picket line, because if rough stuff starts, she and the baby might get hurt." So I told Jane, "You stay out of the picket line please. I don't want Bobby getting messed up; if they start shooting tear gas around, the kid'll get sick." He was about three years old then.

So that afternoon after the speeches they requested people to join the picket line. A number of us wet our handkerchiefs and put them in our pocket in case we got tear-gassed, a little protection. We started out marching across this wide open field at which point we could see a line of police stretched out, facing us. And there were some box cars on which were mounted machine guns. They were never used, fortunately. The only thing that seemed peculiar was that the police were brandishing bright yellow clubs which were about twice as long as the regular police clubs.

I was in the forward section of the group. The police had said they wouldn't permit any mass picketing, but this was a holiday. There was nobody coming or going from the plant. This was a purely symbolic thing. When the beginning of the picket line arrived, the police blocked their further progress. So we stopped. Some of the SWOC officials were trying to talk to somebody. The crowd kept advancing so you ended up with a mob of police and a mob of picketers facing one another.

All of a sudden the police started shoving, clubbing. When they did, the people fought back. And tear gas started to fly, and then some workers back of the line started throwing rocks. But what amazed me was, just after the tear gas went off, the shooting started. I was right up front, the tear gas came at me, I turned my head away, and a club hit me, right between the shoulders, knocked me down. I was very fortunate that I was knocked down because that was when they opened fire with their pistols. All I could see around me was clubs flying and pistols going off. I was in a pile of people right up front.

The police went through there clubbing and shooting. I saw them shoot people who were prone. I saw people get clubbed even after they were shot. The police were just in a frenzy. They acted like they were drunk, and I believe some of them were drunk.

I spent the rest of my time with several other people picking up the wounded and carrying them back to the union headquarters. It was quite a haul. I wound up with my shirt just soaked in blood.

Ten of the demonstrators were killed by gunfire and more than 100 were injured. All the gunshot wounds were to the backs or sides of the fleeing victims. Under a headline "Police Repulse Mob Attack on S. Chicago Mill," the rabidly anti-union Chicago Tribune peddled the Police Captain's story that, stirred up by radical CIO agitators, frenzied Red unionists attempted to storm and seize the Republic Steel plant and the police only acted in self-defense. Footage shot by a Paramount Newsreel cameraman, filming from behind the police line, clearly revealed the lie. Paramount declined to screen the newsreel in theaters, stating that it might inflame audiences. A subsequent US Senate investigation determined that the police attacked a peaceful demonstration with "inappropriate force."

Mom recalled that when the shooting started, bullets whizzed past her and Bobby. She hit the ground and lay still until the gunfire stopped. Bob says he can't remember the shooting but remembers the aftermath. The union headquarters was a building that had formerly been a neighborhood bank. Bob recalled that Pa made a moving speech holding a blood-stained flag one of the marchers had carried. He also remembered that a black man had become locked in the otherwise empty bank vault. That part of the story seemed strange, but seventy years after the event, I learned that three-year-old Bobby's memory was correct.

On Memorial Day, 2007, my wife Nikki and I took 91-year-old Vicky Starr to the Steelworkers Union hall located at that very site to attend a 70th Anniversary commemoration for the victims of the Republic Steel Massacre. After the speeches, songs, and dramatic presentations, we mixed and chatted with other participants. Vicky introduced me to everyone as "Herb March's son." I'll never forget the reverent reaction of Eddie Sadlowski, a progressive Steelworkers Union leader, at the mention of Pa's name. 52 years after he had left, Pa's reputation among Chicago unionists was still venerated.

Driving back to Vicky's apartment, she reminisced about that fateful Memorial Day. She was inside the union headquarters with Henry "Hank" Johnson, then an organizer for the SWOC helping him with some business in the office, and despite her suggestions that they join the group outside, Hank kept delaying. When they heard the shooting, he panicked. Fearing the police might enter the hall, he took shelter in the bank vault and closed the door, inadvertently locking himself inside. Vicky informed the returning marchers who were setting up a triage center in the union hall that Johnson was trapped in the vault. Someone knew how to contact the former bank manager, who arrived presently to open it. "Hank wasn't all he should have been," Vicky mused. Perhaps he was haunted by the lynchings of black men and women at that time.

The Memorial Day Massacre was the final incident in the United States in a string of mass killings of strikers from the 1886 Haymarket Tragedy to 1937. Coming nearly two years after the passage of the National Labor Relations Act, it was a bloody anachronism and ultimately had consequences. Although the Little Steel strike was lost, in five years the War Labor Board required the steel makers to use NLRB procedures and recognize the SWOC. A more immediate consequence was that Chicago Mayor Edward Kelly, harshly criticized for the actions of the Chicago Police, and needing labor's support for his reelection, moved decisively to mend fences with the labor movement and proved a reliable ally in subsequent years.

Organizing the Packinghouses

Packinghouse union activists despaired of working through the Amalgamated Meat Cutters (AMC). Seeing the dramatic gains of the CIO, they longed to lure the nascent labor federation into meat packing. Core groups met in secret, laying groundwork for a union drive in packing.

Early in 1937 a "Committee of 18" was formed with reps from each of the developing "locals." Pa and a delegation from the committee met with the CIO's Midwest rep Van Bittner, a former coal miner and an associate of John L. Lewis. The committee hoped to convince him to put some resources into organizing meat packing. Pa recalled that Bittner said,

"Quit kidding yourselves. You're not going to get anything from the Amalgamated leadership." And he said, "If you can show us that you really have sentiment for organization among your people, then we'll give you funds to support a drive."

So we got a card printed that said, "I want to organize a union that will be part of the CIO." In a couple weeks we brought down over two thousand signed cards.

In the spring of 1937, they launched a drive with CIO support. CIO gains were national news. Association with the CIO stirred workers, particularly at Armour, the largest plant and lynchpin of the industry. The union began to hold regular meetings at Sikora's Hall in Packingtown, where the Polish owner didn't object to inter-racial union meetings. In October, 1937, the CIO officially established the Packinghouse Workers Organizing Committee (PWOC), provided funds for a secretary and for Sikora's to become the union hall. They hired Frank McCarty as an organizer and brought Henry "Hank" Johnson over from the Steel Workers Organizing Committee.

Johnson was a gifted orator, who as assistant national director of the PWOC demonstrated to black workers that blacks would

167

be well represented in the top leadership. The son of Texas share-croppers, Hank's father had been an IWW member in the timber industry. Hank worked as a plasterer and a longshoreman before attending the City College of New York in the early '30s. There he became a member of the Communist Party, and in 1934 he was assigned to organize Negro sections for the International Workers Order in Chicago. Hank's oratory, delivered in clear college-educated diction, influenced black and white workers alike.

Pa organized in the stockyards for four years. He achieved a few solid beachheads of unionism, but most packinghouse workers remained unorganized until Pa led a successful union drive in 1937. Midwest industrial workers were flocking to the CIO. During seven years of organizing in Kansas City and Chicago, Pa had acquired the tools and the credibility to become a critical leader with powerful oratorical skills. He was an astute strategist with courage and a track record of laboring in the packinghouses that earned the workers' trust.

With scant support from the established "labor movement" or the CP, Pa welcomed the CIO support. But factionalism emerged, a perpetual bane of American labor. The national CIO leaders assumed they should exert top-down authority over the PWOC through their lieutenant Van Bittner. Rank-and-file packinghouse workers had little regard for Bittner, a brusque authoritarian type whom they derided as a "coal miner" who knew nothing about meat packing. They supported home-grown leaders who came out of their recent struggles, Herb March foremost among them. The local leaders wanted openness, equality, and democratic control.

Ultimately, the CIO couldn't exert top-down authority in packing. They initially put only McCarty and Johnson on the PWOC drive, adding Pa and a young Polish unionist Sigmund Wlodarczyk a few months later. But packinghouse unionists were accustomed to self-reliance. Their power stemmed from a growing ability to hold up production at the shop floor level. The companies found, like it or not, they would have to deal with them.

Support for the union snowballed. Even before he was officially hired by the PWOC, blacklisted and unemployed, Pa delivered rousing speeches every day at noon outside the packinghouses at the location known as "CIO Corner." To well-attended rallies, Pa advocated industrial unionism. Department by department, whenever a grievance came up over a firing , an unjust lay-off, a speed up, a dangerous work process, the issue became fodder for Pa's speeches and stimulus to join the union. When they had enough strength in a department, on an agreed-upon day, the workers all put on union buttons.

The stewards had big oval buttons Pa characterized as "big as a locomotive's headlight." Only months earlier, wearing them would have been grounds for firing. Indeed Armour did fire a couple of the early activists for refusing to remove union buttons. Bittner submitted the cases to the NLRB only to encounter long bureaucratic delay. So without seeking Bittner's blessing, the nascent union took matters in their own hands, applying pressure at the point of production. Pa related a couple examples. The first concerned the Armour Soap Works.

One of the first groups that came around to the union office was from mechanical maintenance at Armour Soap Works. This was an important group because these men circulated all over the plant. We proceeded rather quietly for some time and built up a nucleus. Then we began to pass out leaflets, and of course, management reacted to it. One of the secrets of successful organizing is to anticipate that management is going to react, and to be prepared to meet their response with your own counterpunch.

Well, management picked out two key guys in the mechanical maintenance department and disciplined them—a suspension or a discharge, I don't remember which. We asked management to hold a grievance meeting with us the very next morning at eight. The plant opened at seven and we wanted to settle this thing. At least management always agreed to meet, just to talk, you know. That was the limit of their so-called compliance with the Wagner Act...We said we were bringing our grievance committee and they said all right. So we set up a committee of three or four people from each department in the plant who were key operators and without whom work could not go on. So at eight we went to the meeting with about 50 to 75 people. The manager's office was just packed. Within minutes, he started getting calls from this department and that department. Without these key operators, production stopped everywhere. "Hey, is this a strike or what?" "No, we're just here for a grievance meeting." And so they settled the thing by immediately returning the two fellows to work. Well, that just broke the union through. That victory resulted in people in the plant signing up left and right. In a couple months Armour Soap Works was 100% union.

The union's protection of workers' jobs was a powerful inducement to join. Heretofore they had been completely at the mercy of the bosses whims. The union's defense of Walter Stabrawa, a Polish-American worker in the pork cut department, was a key incident leading to a breakthrough in the main Armour packing plant. Born in one of the toughest sections of Packingtown, Stabrawa became an officer of the nascent Armour local. Benjamin Appel, a regional writer, caught up with Wally in 1939:

"I'm Walter Stabbers." Stabrawa smiles with full red lips. A man of twenty-five, he has a butcher's meaty complexion "It's a nickname, it's been in the family. I was born and raised right here Back of the Yards... When I was a kid, I'd go with a gang. The old man wouldn't give you no money, so we grabbed apples...sniffed around for what we could get. The cops chased us. We'd sell junk to the ragman, copper, brass. There was fifty of us. Now about six are dead, killed by cops. Ten or fifteen are in the penitentiary.... I went to work because the cops got too rough."

His low-paying, grueling work as a scaler ignited Stabrawa's passion for the union. He described his backbreaking job. The freshly slaughtered hogs went first to the cooler, and then came to the pork cutting floor where the basic processing was done:

"I started working when I was sixteen. I scale [weigh] and pack pork loins. It felt like a prison when I started, the boss yodeling at us. I got two bits an hour and I worked as high as eighty-five hours a week. I scale and I pack and I throw the box on a conveyor. Those boxes weigh from fifty to one hundred and forty pounds. All the time I have to keep up with the speed of the table. The butchers cut over nine hundred hogs an hour. There was eight of us on the loin gang. Four packers, two nailers, two scalers. Always it was thirty-five degrees in that room. All day, the pork loins kept coming through. You could work up an appetite after that. I carried a lunch that looked like a laundry bag. I averaged ten sandwiches a day.

Scale and pack and holler at each other when we want to talk! It's noisy in there. Talk about baseball, about women, how drunk you got last week and how drunk you were going to get. But in them days, when you got through, you were too tired to get drunk. I'd go to work around six o'clock when it was dark. And get home when it was dark. At eight, nine or ten o'clock. Only saw the light on Sundays."

When union efforts revived in 1933, Wally signed up. When the PWOC began, he was already a union veteran. Pa recalled that the pork cut department had "a large group of active union guys, one of whom, Stabrawa, was treasurer of the council. The company decided they would get him, fire him." The company tolerated workers eating a certain amount of meat. Wally's informal assignment in his work gang was to cook some meat on the steam pipes for their lunch. Without warning, he was fired because of it. Pa said:

We decided we wouldn't accept this discharge. Of course we were a little worried. We didn't know what would happen if we struck. So we got a committee of workers who were stewards from several departments and met with them. I told them to go to the meeting with the employment manager and the plant superintendent, and I told the boys, "Go in and say, 'Are you going to put Wally back to work or not?' That's all. If they attempt to discuss it with you, don't discuss anything. Say, 'All I want to know is are you going to put him back to work?'" So that's what they did. Of course the plant manager attempted to discuss that you can't have employees steal the product. The fellows kept on shaking their heads just saying, "Are you going to put Wally back to work?" After they asked it the fourth time and started to walk out the door, the plant super called them back and said, "All right you bastards, we'll put him back to work."

The superintendent offered to refer the matter to the NLRB. "You're looking at the Labor Board in this plant right now," the workers replied. Seeing stewards from several departments, the bosses knew they couldn't sustain this firing without a major disruption in production. The union members learned not to rely on governmental procedure but upon themselves. It took 11 months for the NLRB finally to rule concerning the two firings Bittner submitted. The NLRB was slow, but the workers learned they had another option: solidarity on the shop floor gained prompt results.

The union developed varied tactics. A steward would signal the start of a routine known as "rizz-a-ma-tizz" by walking through a department with arms folded and his cap cocked to one side. Everyone would feign work at a fast clip, but actually slowed real production, minimizing output. It was only at the end of a shift that a shocked foreman would figure out they had not hit the production quota. Another tactic, which required considerable coordination between departments, was known as a "stop-and-go strike." Workers would halt production in their department over a grievance. After the foreman summoned the superintendent to the idled sector, they resumed working. At that moment a work stoppage would occur in a completely different department in a distant part of the plant, and so on until the issue was resolved. These actions involved hundreds of workers. The militant workers were winning *de facto* recognition. As Pa stated, "It gave them the experience of being organized before we'd won the [NLRB] election, much less had a contract."

Armour management tried a give-and-take strategy to head off growing militant sentiment among its workers. When they settled grievances favorably or raised pay, they gave credit to their puppet company union. Most workers saw through this ploy. When the company failed to act on grievances, building up a backlog of unresolved cases, the workers responded with militancy. At an afternoon grievance meeting a mass of workers descended on the room. At 4:30 when the superintendent tried to adjourn, they blocked the exit and refused to let him leave. No violence was used, but the bosses understood the threat and stayed until 9:00 PM until the backlog of cases was eliminated.

From its inception the union forged racial solidarity. The symbol of the PWOC was a black and white hand clasped in handshake. The proportion of black workers in the packinghouse workforce had been increasing for years. With African-Americans constituting more than 30% of the personnel, racial solidarity was imperative. Lowell Washington, an early recruit to the movement, a ham-boner (whose own hog butcher father had spurned the "white man's union" in the 1920s), referred to Pa and his radical cohort, "Here were these white fellows who were helping us out, really meaning it. I'd never seen anything like it." Blacks were well represented in union leadership. A majority of the shop stewards were African-Americans. Many immigrant Eastern European workers with a limited command of English appreciated the articulate, quick-witted African-Americans on the shop floor to argue their case.

Race relations among packinghouse workers were advanced by a surprising happenstance. To accommodate Polish-American workers, some union meetings were conducted in Polish. A popular speaker at these meetings was John Hackett, an African-American hog butcher who spoke fluent Polish. He learned the language during World War I, as a prisoner of war. The American Army was segregated. The captured white American officers objected to Hackett's presence among them, so the Germans sent him to a camp with Polish prisoners. It was language immersion and Hackett learned well. Pa recalled:

Hackett came back from Europe with a good command of Polish that he polished in the packinghouse. The Poles would get a big charge out of him speaking. They'd say, "We want John to speak!" and he'd get up there and sound off in Polish and they thought that was great, they loved it.

Armour used to place a black star on the corner of time cards of African-Americans, marking them as priority for lay-offs. When a veteran black worker Charles Perry was laid off despite his seniority, the union initiated job actions until the company agreed to put him back to work and to remove the black stars from all time cards. The union also pushed for no discrimination in hiring and for integration of all-white departments.

The union was concerned with racial discrimination outside of the plant. A race relations incident involved Walter Stabrawa, who was engaged to his sweetheart working in the Campbell's Soup cannery. Their combined income was too low for a nice wedding. But things improved due to union pressure, with Wally's pay increasing from 25¢ to 65¢ per hour.

Wally learned that St. Rose of Lima church, formerly an all-Irish parish whose congregation had steeply declined, was offering a $15 deal on a wedding ceremony. But through his union activity, Wally had become fast friends with many blacks. Pa recalled:

A number of black guys from Wally's department came to his wedding, and with the tacit knowledge of the pastor, the ushers asked them to leave. This was an issue in the union and we protested. A committee went to the church to raise hell with the pastor. "You embarrassed Wally and excluded his friends! This is not acceptable!" The heat was on that church from then on, and eventually they had to come around. St. Rose's became part of the Back-of-the-Yards Council and opened its doors to Mexicans who had a colony right close by.

The PWOC sponsored inter-racial social and recreational activities, a weekly bowling tournament, baseball and basketball games, family picnics and dances, utilizing the facilities of the union hall, the YWCA and the U of C Settlement House.

In 1937 the union complained to the NLRB about the illegal company union and requested a union representation election at Armour. The request finally was approved in September, 1938. Armour management was livid, stonewalled, delayed, and refused to cooperate with the NLRB. Nonetheless, the election finally was set for February, 1939.

Armour unleashed a furious wave of violence. Because the NLRB ruled their company union illegal, Armour got the Amalgamated Meatcutters to grant it a charter, creating AMC Local 661. The AMC was only too happy to play company union for the bosses. The renamed company union was staffed by notorious Capone Gang veterans Tom Devereaux, John Saltis and George Dashill. This arrangement gave Armour a degree of deniability from the violence. They claimed it was altercations between two rival unions.

Four days after the NLRB ruling, the PWOC headquarters in

Sikora Hall was bombed. There were several drive-by shootings into the building over the ensuing weeks. With a new militant spirit in the neighborhood, youth gangs voluntarily took on the duty of defending Sikora Hall.

The PWOC leadership assumed a major strike might be necessary to win recognition. Widespread community support for the strikers would be crucial from churches, local businesses and ethnic organizations. The union hoped to stop the packers from enlisting conservative Catholic priests and black ministers to preach against the union.

The union's early championing of racial equality both in the plant and beyond garnered support in the black community. African-American union leaders like Hank Johnson frequently spoke in black churches. There were more than twenty black ministers of small congregations who worked in the packinghouses and many were stewards. This wasn't the AFL's "white man's union" of the past, the *Chicago Defender*, a major black newspaper editorialized. Noting that before the union, it was common knowledge that "no Negro had better show his face west of Ashland Avenue after dark...Today because the PWOC planted the seed of unity in the stony soil of Packingtown, Negroes walk freely and in safety."

Most white workers were Eastern European ethnics who lived in the Back of the Yards neighborhood. They were not unified, harboring Old World intolerances for other ethnic groups. Poles opposed Lithuanians, Czechs disdained Slovaks, and vice versa. The elderly pastors of their parishes were conservative, but younger assistant pastors, mostly American-born, tended to be liberal and pro-union. A priest at St. Michael's, the Slovak church, Fr. Ambrose Ondrak, had worked as a scaler in Morris & Company, a small packinghouse and was a strong union supporter.

The community work that Mom, Vicky and their cohort had been doing helped to gain wider support for the union. The women were energetic and young in their mid-twenties. Mary Szewczyk Siporin, a Gorale Pole, proved to be a key organizer in her ethnic group. Gorale are the "hillbilly" Poles from the Tatras Mountains in southern Poland. Estelle Zabritski was Lithuanian and effective among that nationality, and Hermione Orear was poised and educated, good at approaching local politicians, clergy and officials.

Their organizing efforts had deep roots in the community, reaching back to the early 1930s with Mom's work in the Unemployed Council. With the PWOC's backing, the women conceived a plan to seek funds from the National Youth Administration (NYA), a New Deal agency, to hire unemployed neighborhood youth in a project to turn some nearby unused railroad property into a playground and recreation center.

Around this time, Saul Alinsky, a University of Chicago-educated criminologist working for the Institute for Juvenile Research (IJR) was assigned to research the causes of juvenile delinquency in the Back of the Yards. Sympathetic with the CIO and the PWOC drive, Saul sought out Pa. The two of them hit it off, forming a long-lasting friendship. They shared an urban non-observant Jewish upbringing, Pa in Brooklyn, Saul in Chicago. Intelligent and educated, both used blunt, unpretentious working-class mannerisms and language. Pa was more radical, but he appreciated the pragmatism of Saul's unaffiliated, progressive political stance. When our family later moved to the Hyde Park neighborhood near Saul, Pa, Saul and the union's lawyer and future president Ralph Helstein socialized, taking in White Sox baseball games and playing cards.

In Sanford Horwitt's biography of Alinsky he contended it was the women's efforts that laid the groundwork for the Back-of-the-Yards Neighborhood Council (BYNC) on which Alinsky made his reputation:

> About the time when March and Alinsky began to talk, a small group of women who, like Herb March's wife Jane, were staunch union members or supporters were moving ahead with their own youth program and would soon organize the Packingtown Youth Committee.... To drum up support, the young women made the rounds of the sodalities, clubs and sports teams and talked to as many of the priests as would see them. At each meeting, the young women would explain that there might be a way to bring jobs into the neighborhood. Would you please come to a conference in a few weeks, they would ask, where we can all talk about how we might be able to do it?

The women were more successful than Saul Alinsky might

have guessed. As the time for the conference drew near, Mom's friend Vicky, one of the organizers, heard about Alinsky's work with delinquents and thought he would be interested in their efforts. They arranged to meet at the Jucus restaurant in the Back of the Yards. She planned to ask him to speak at the conference. They talked about delinquency in Chicago and he recounted his work with gangs. Vicky was impressed. "I figured this man could really talk and would make a real contribution to the conference. He could talk about crime and how kids needed places to play. I asked him to be a speaker, and he turned us down."

Vicky was angry, having expected Alinsky to accept. Why had he refused? Alinsky was vague. "He didn't feel like it," she remembers him implying. Maybe he thought the conference wouldn't amount to much, or he didn't want to be identified with the young communists in the women's group. Vicky said, there were people who saw her and her friends as "a bunch of Reds," and felt the PWOC was "a radical Red organization." Still, the conference was a success. Twenty-six ethnic groups and parishes were represented at the Packingtown Youth Conference. There was such a sense of purpose and accomplishment that word quickly spread about the successful meeting. An eyewitness to it, standing at the back of the room, watching and listening but never speaking, was Saul Alinsky.

Saul saw a big opportunity. The Packingtown Youth Committee had united a critical mass of neighborhood organizations and interest groups around their project. With the approval of Mom and her cohort, Saul and Joe Meegan, the recreation director at nearby Davis Square Park, became the public faces of the emergent neighborhood organization. To avoid Red-baiting, the Communist women avoided the limelight. Moreover, as women they were used to accepting the sexist idea that the official leaders should be men. Alinsky proved to be a prodigious self-promoter and cultivated his reputation as a formidable organizer, though Thomas Gaudette, a community organizer, claimed that his mentor was less an activist than an investigator who preferred to remain in the background as "the thinker."

My parents had a copy of Alinsky's 1946 book *Reveille for Radicals* in which Saul inscribed, "To Herb and Jane, who lived it," a

tacit acknowledgement that they lived the life of organizers and
he only wrote about it.

Taking on the Stockyards

As the union drive accelerated in Packingtown, the Stock Handlers local, which had gone on strike 1933, left the AFL for the CIO in 1937. They demanded recognition and a contract but made little headway. The Union Stock Yards and Transit Company proclaimed that in 70 years of operation they had never signed a contract and never would. In a wave of anti-union violence, thugs invaded the home of Ben Brown, president of the stock handlers and brutally beat him with baseball bats, breaking both arms. With the company receiving a union charter with the sell-out Amalgamated Meat Cutters, they called in the Chicago police to forcibly remove the stock handlers' bargaining committee from their premises and staged a lockout of the 600 CIO unionists.

The infuriated stock handlers immediately turned the lockout into an effective strike. Pa relished the story:

Livestock Handlers were primarily Irish, mostly second generation, but some were Old Country Irish who had been in the IRA and had a militant tradition. They were excellent, excellent union men. They were enraged when there was the beating of Brown, then shortly thereafter the lockout, and the handlers struck! They were ready for a fight!

Now the year before all of this, the Memorial Day massacre had occurred in South Chicago and Mayor Kelly came out with none too savory a reputation with the industrial workers of Chicago. His police committed this brutal massacre and many blamed him for it. Kelly was up for re-election in a few months and was beginning to realize how deep and intense was the sentiment against him among union workers. So Kelly sent out word to us he was interested in seeing what he could do to resolve this stockyards situation peacefully. We said, "Well good, we appreciate your help, but in the meanwhile, don't interfere with our right to picket and carry on a lawful strike. Let's see whether the police can behave much better than what occurred down in South

Chicago."

The strike was around the annual Livestock Exposition time, so there was extra livestock in the yards. The company hadn't really picked the best time to lock out the union workers. The guys decided they would make sure no scabs stayed working in the yards. They stopped all work but remained on the inside. The stockyards stretch for over a half mile along Halstead Street, and these guys kept running around to all the locations, seeing to it that nobody was working, nobody. The police were brought in to get the union boys out. The company said, "These men have told us that they're striking, but they're trespassing. We want them out." It took at least 36 hours before they got the last of them out of there. There was a whole network of barns and pens and the cops couldn't find them. They kept moving around, there was real confusion about who was who in there. The result was to really clean out the yards. At the end of 36 hours, there was nobody left in there. They struck at midnight the night before and by six o'clock the next day, they were a little hungry and tired but they had totally shut down the stock yards.

The company concocted a strategy to break the strike. Tom Devereaux, the gangster leader of the AMC local, announced a back-to-work movement to take place in three days. The AFL-chartered local abandoned any pretense of unionism and undertook an undisguised role to serve as strike-breakers.

The night before Devereaux's announcement, another crime was directed against the union. Wally Stabrawa, the local's treasurer, received a substantial amount of dues at the evening union meeting at Sikora Hall which he planned to deposit when the bank opened the following morning. According to the Chicago Times, Wally "was robbed of $700 union dues and his car by a young man who entered his auto when he stopped at a light...." Wally felt this was no ordinary armed robbery and carjacking, attributing it to Devereaux's gang.

Undaunted by Brown's beating, the robbery, and a plan to introduce scabs into the yards, the livestock handlers pressed on. Pa continued:

With everybody out, the company brought around this scabby ele-

ment that was in the company union. They...announced they were going to have a big back-to-work movement about three days later. Well,
the packinghouse workers said they wouldn't handle any scab-provid-
ed livestock, so it appeared that the strike might spread. While the
union didn't have everybody organized yet, one place where the union
was very strong was on the killing floors, the first place the livestock
would hit.

Anyway there was a big mobilization of packinghouse workers
on the morning of the back-to-work movement. They came over to
Halstead, east of their usual territory, to help the livestock handlers
picket. This back-to-work deal was announced for 6:30 or 7:00 AM,
and their assembly point was at the Amalgamated Meat Cutters Hall.
Well we had so many pickets there, we didn't know what to do with
them, literally a couple thousand guys, maybe more. So we formed a
sort of parade and marched them up Halstead. We were approaching
the entrance of the Amalgamated Meat Cutters Hall just at the time
when the back-to-work group was supposed to come out. There was
every bit of thirty or forty of them. Then they saw this mob of a couple
thousand packinghouse workers and livestock handlers coming up the
street. There was a narrow door that ran up a flight of stairs, and did
those scabs ever step on one another trying to scramble back up the
stairs! I never saw a more horrified scramble! And the police, instead
of bothering us, were peaceful and quiet. Nobody struck a blow. The
scabs were intimidated, and well they might have been. Those Irish-
men are tough. They weren't fooling. They wouldn't have permitted
these fellows to walk into the stock yards. They would have beaten the
hell out of them. The stock yards had been there seventy years and
everybody knew if so-and-so's father or grandfather had ever scabbed
back in the early days. At any rate, that ended the back-to-work movement.

The battle was won on the streets and in the yards, but the
victory had to be sealed in the corridors of local political power.

Then the question of getting a contract came up, and these gentlemen [the company] indicated, "No contract under any circumstances." We met with [Mayor] Kelly and Kelly said, "Well, you just leave it
to me. These gentlemen get their water from the City of Chicago at a

very, very good price." If they didn't have a cooperative attitude, they might have their water cut off. So we did leave it to him and by God they came through with the first contract in the history of that company. They capitulated!

Though the livestock handlers got their contract, anti-union violence continued in Packingtown. A few days before the settlement, Pa narrowly escaped an attempt on his life, the first of the assassination attempts made on him.

The PWOC repaid the political debt to Kelly by getting out the vote for him and actively backing Earl Dickerson, a pro-union African-American aldermanic candidate. With Dickerson on the city council, Kelly often was reminded to retain union support. Ed Kelly remained in office until 1947 and he and the Packinghouse Workers union maintained a mutually-supportive relationship.

Herb March, Paul Robeson, Chicago Mayor Ed Kelly

A short time after the stock handlers won their strike, the NLRB election was scheduled in the big Armour plant. As the election loomed, Armour management refused to allow polling places on their premises. The NLRB had to rent a storefront across the street from the main plant entrance, not an ideal solution, because many employees worked far from there. To make matters worse, on the day of the election, Armour locked the main entrance, forcing workers to use doors far from the polling place. Foremen warned workers not to participate in the election and management posted supervisors on the street outside the polling place as intimidation. Nonetheless, about half of the Armour workers overcame the obstacles and voted overwhelmingly for the PWOC. Armour refused to recognize the results. Contending that a majority of the total workers had not voted for the PWOC, they filed frivolous lawsuits that the courts soon set aside.

The union pressed for the legally required contract negotiations. It seemed a strike was looming. It became essential for the union demonstrate its strength and its strong community support. The Back of the Yards Neighborhood Council made its grand debut with a large community congress scheduled for Friday, July 14, 1939, just two days before a rally featuring CIO president John L. Lewis in the Chicago Coliseum, a large downtown auditorium.

Bishop Bernard J. Sheil, the second-ranking prelate of the Chicago Archdiocese, was a nationally-known, pro-union liberal concerned about the well-being of his flock. Bishop Sheil was known to quote from Pope Leo XIII's 1891 encyclical *Rerum Novarum*, which provided a Catholic rationale for a worker's right to organize for a wage sufficient "to maintain himself, his wife and children in reasonable comfort."

Through the liberal assistant pastors and park recreation director Joe Meegan, Mom, Vicky and their cohort interested the Bishop in the Packingtown Youth Committee. Saul Alinsky was especially interested in cultivating a powerful connection to the liberal wing of the Catholic Church and worked hard to deepen Bishop Sheil's involvement in the young Back of the Yards Neighborhood Council. Bishop Sheil consented to be the featured speaker at the founding congress.

On the day before the Congress, a story in the Chicago Daily News stated that "Something new in community organizing" was about to occur in Back of the Yards. Using his burgeoning PR prowess, Saul Alinsky was the source for the story which stated, "The council is the conception and individual project of Saul D. Alinsky." The article noted Bishop Sheil's endorsement and stressed the Council's support for the CIO drive in the meat packing industry. It noted also that John L. Lewis' arrival in Chicago to boost the PWOC drive was coming hard on the heels of the Council's founding congress.

When the evening of the BYNC Congress arrived, Pa picked up Vicky at her place and they headed to the event together. Mom did not attend, having given birth to my brother Bill two months earlier.

The founding Congress was a rousing success. Bishop Sheil's appearance helped attract a big turnout. Community residents representing dozens of neighborhood groups crowded the activities center of Davis Square Park. The resolutions passed that evening were to pursue the Packingtown Youth Committee's recreation facility project, to develop child nutrition and health programs and to urge Armour to forestall the impending strike by negotiating a fair agreement with the PWOC. Pa was delighted. This represented a big setback for Armour, but they had one more trick up their sleeves. The company had hired gun thugs, who were on their way to visit Pa with murder on their minds.

Assassins At the Door

When I was a curious little boy in the early 1950s exploring my parents' bedroom closet, I discovered a dark leather shoulder holster hanging next to Pa's ties. When I asked Mom, about it, she said, "Oh your father used to have to carry a gun, but he doesn't anymore. You shouldn't worry about it, dear." "But where's the gun?" I asked. "It's put away in a safe place. Don't ask, honey."

Later I asked Pa and learned that indeed he had a .45 caliber automatic pistol, and that no, he had never shot anybody. In fact, he had only fired it on a couple occasions: once on a friend's farm to learn how to shoot, and once again in the backyard of the old house on 59th and Ashland one 4th of July, when he shot holes in an empty oil drum to ventilate it so it would burn trash better.

Pa often repeated the story of why he carried the gun, the most gripping, most oft repeated of his family stories. The first assassination attempt occurred during the stockyards strike in December, 1938. Pa described it as follows:

"In the midst of the livestock handlers strike I decided one day that I'd go home for lunch. I lived then around 59th and Ashland, and the hall was at 47th, not too far. I had an old '32 Dodge so it didn't take much time to get home. I was on my way back and I started to approach the corner of 51st and Ashland. In those days two street car lines intersected there, it was a very busy area. It was about one o'clock in the afternoon in broad daylight, in December. I heard the screech of tires as a car pulled up alongside of mine and started attempting to curb me, and I looked down the barrels of two .45 automatics, one guy driving and two guys with guns pointed at me. Well needless to say I was not happy. I was scared but at least I had enough presence of mind to hit my brake and gas successively so that my car was jerking, and they started firing. As a matter of fact, as I slowed down, they got

185

out on the running board and kept on shooting. They had a V8 Ford, I remember, and were banging away. I jammed the brake until the car was going slow enough so I could get out the passenger door. I let the car run and it ran into a parked car and then I headed for the sidewalk and I dove, face down with my feet toward these gentlemen who had almost come to a stop. I hugged the ground and they fired about nine more shots at me. I busted my nose but didn't even notice it at the time. That pavement was sweet.

Pa's stoic tone matched his real-life actions. He dismissed his broken nose for which, to Mom's dismay, he never sought any medical attention. In fact, Pa thought it was amusing that after dealing with the Chicago police, who had taken him off in a squad car after the shooting, he had to hurry back to the union hall, a little late for an appointment to speak to a group of young women from the Chicago Teachers College. With face bloodied and swollen, he spoke and took questions about unionism and violence in the Back of the Yards area.

Later that same afternoon Pa had a verbal duel with the superintendent of the Armour plant about being late to a grievance committee meeting:

The superintendent said to me, "March, (Mister was never used) what kept you so long?" I said, "I don't know, but I think Armour and Company knows a hell of a lot more about why I'm late than perhaps I do." I hadn't given him any reason, but very indignantly he said, "You ought to be very careful...what you say about Armour and Company." I said, "That doesn't scare me in the least, because I don't think Armour and Company can do anything more to me than has been tried right now," and that ended the conversation.

Pa was pleased the attack backfired. He survived the shooting, still made a speech and used the shooting incident to advance the union's cause:

This shooting resulted in terrific indignation among the workers. Word got back into the plant that the shooting had occurred and guys went and got my car. The thing was full of bullet holes. I was just lucky, my guts would have been ripped open except for the fact that one of the bullets hit the rods of the window-lifting mechanism, you know, just dead center....Well there was that car, banged full of bullet holes, and a steady pilgrimage of people came out to look at that thing.

Pa used this tone when speaking of a second assassination attempt which occurred half a year later as he was on his way home from the BYNC founding congress. Pa noted that Bishop Sheil came to the meeting in highly protected circumstances:

Bishop Sheil had been threatened when it was announced he was going to be at this founding meeting of the Back of the Yards Council, and he borrowed from a friend a bullet-proof automobile. I was not threatened at all. I was just shot on the way home from the meeting.

He was appreciative of Bishop Sheil's support of the union, but Pa's quip made it clear he knew he, Herb March, really was the guy in the trenches fighting for it. Pa continued the story: After dropping off Vicky, he drove home.

I was very cautious for some time after that first shooting incident. I lived at 59th and Ashland, so when I came to 58th, I took a left turn and went around the block and parked my car right in front of my house, about three steps and you were right in the door, so that I wouldn't present too comfortable a target. That was the amount of protection I had. And also, at that time, I kept a .45 automatic pistol in the glove compartment of the car. I never wanted to be confronted with a situation like the first time. I couldn't get a license for it, but I decided I shouldn't need a license to stay alive. As I turned left to go down 58th, some lights hit, I heard the screech of tires, and rather instinctively I kind of threw my shoulder up. (My arm was on the open window of the car.) As I threw my shoulder up and glanced back, I heard the loud report of a pistol and bits of glass hit my face, and I felt a sharp blow on my shoulder. I immediately lay down on the seats and pulled the emergency brake on. By that time the car had run up the curb and run into a sapling tree and knocked it over. I didn't do it much good.

Years later, while driving by that spot, Pa would point out that crooked tree and took the blame for messing it up in its infancy.

I reached into the glove compartment, came out of my Plymouth with that .45 in my hand, and all I could see was tail lights half a block away. I figured what the hell could I do, so I tossed the thing on the back seat of the car, and I was shaking my head when a man came out of the house in shirt sleeves who was an off-duty policeman who lived there. He said to me, "What happened, what happened?" I said I didn't know who the gentlemen were but somebody had pulled up alongside of me and shot at me. He said, "Well, were you hit?" And I said, "I don't know." He looked at me and said, "Yeah, there's blood coming from your shoulder." You know in the excitement I hardly knew. And he said, "Did you have a gun?" And I said, "Yes, it's in the back seat of my car." Well, they called the police and the police placed me under arrest for having a gun. They took me over to the South Town Hospital which was a few blocks away.

Before that happened, a woman who came around, said, "Can I do anything for you?" I told her to go around the corner and see my wife and tell her there'd been a shooting incident, that I was hurt but not bad, and tell her not to worry because I was going to be taken to South Town Hospital. So she came and saw Jane. Jane then had Bill as a babe in arms. She was nursing him when the woman told her, and she got busy and called the doctor, a personal doctor of mine. Well, I was held for a while in the hospital. They just examined me, and apparently made the determination to take me down to the Bridewell [prison] Hospital. They were about to lead me out of the place when Jane and my doctor, Shayle Miller came in. He said, "Wait a minute, that's my patient." The cop said, "He's my prisoner." The doc said, "He's my patient and I want him taken up to emergency for an operation right now." Well, they were very unhappy about it but they assented and he took me up to fill me with local anesthetic. It was funny. I noticed when he took it out, first he took out the bullet, then a piece of my coat, then a piece of my shirt and then a piece of underwear.

Herb was still under arrest so the ordeal continued. They took him to Bridewell for a tetanus shot, then in a Black Maria, in considerable pain after his anesthetic wore off, they bounced him around all night moving him to different jails. Meanwhile,

Bishop Sheil, the union leadership and Mayor Kelly's office had been notified about the incident. As Pa put it, "the wheels within wheels started turning." About 6:00 AM at the police station near 60th and Vincennes, a plainclothesman that Pa recognized as one of the mayor's bodyguards asked him what he'd say about how he got the gun. (Actually he had gotten the .45 US Army Colt from a Chicago police marksmanship instructor.) He told the mayor's bodyguard he had found the gun in the attic at home, that it belonged to his father-in-law, who had been dead for years. "That's a good story, stick to it," the cop said. But Pa never had to use the story.

An attorney showed up who had been hired by the union. I think his name was Al Kamin. And I appeared in Stockyards Station. They had a little municipal court there of the lowest order, I would say. All I remember of the so-called trial was Kamin kept on talking rapidly, and every third word kept mentioning that Bishop Sheil was very concerned about this. And the judge, after hearing Bishop Sheil's name repeated four or five times said, "Case dismissed. Mr. March, would you like to have your pistol back?" And the arresting officer there appeared very apologetic and said, "Your Honor, I'm very sorry but we've just recently received a general order that all weapons stamped 'Property of the US Army' must be retained and returned to the Army." So I thanked the judge and left.

Pa found it absurd. He was the one who was shot, but he was the only one arrested, for ineffectual efforts to defend himself. As soon as his supporters in high places weighed in, the authorities offered apologies. Pa figured Mayor Kelly's support still was fence mending after the Memorial Day massacre. On some level he realized his fearless leadership was a bigger deal than he was willing to make it seem in his story. Pa was content to get his accolades from others.

The second assassination attempt happened as the organizing drive in meatpacking was nearing its peak. On July 16, just two days later, the huge rally at the Chicago Coliseum was attended by an estimated 15,000 packinghouse workers and their supporters. CIO head John L. Lewis and Bishop Sheil were featured speakers. In his book *Down on the Killing Floor*, historian Rick Halpern wrote:

> For most of the workers gathered in the Coliseum, however, the high point was the arrival of Herbert March....[Union activist] Pat Balskus recalled that the sight of March, swathed in bandages and wearing a sling, in the hall caused a murmur that grew into a roar which distracted the speaker. "Lewis was a hero, a big man," she explained, "but Herb was a real life hero because he was one of us. Herb was the union, and to see him there that night gave me a kind of strength that ten John L.'s couldn't have come close to.

Pa was willing to make himself a personification of the union and became a lightning rod for the violence employed against it. In *Out of the Jungle*, Les Orear wrote, "Herb March became the driving spirit of the Packinghouse Workers Organizing Committee (PWOC) set up by the CIO. Workers gathered at 'CIO Corner' from all over the vast Chicago stockyard region to hear March preach a gospel of rebellion against the indignities and injustices of second-class industrial citizenship." His fiery, preacher-like orations were attested to by others also. According to longtime UPWA President Ralph Helstein:

> [Herb] was ready to stand up in the front and get shot at if that's what it meant, but on top of that he was a fine orator in mass meetings. He'd get out in front of three, four, five thousand of these guys out on "CIO Corner" and start making these speeches that really pulled them out of their shoes. He had them roaring and yelling till you weren't sure if they were going to pull down the plants.

Mom's stories of those times had a darker, dramatic tone describing the experience of living in fear. She said that one evening, Pa was at a meeting and Mom, pregnant with their second child, was home with Bobby, who was five years old. They lived in the upper flat of the house. There was a long straight stairway from the outside entry up to the flat. Late in the evening, Mom thought she heard someone open and close the entry door downstairs, but there was no sound of anyone coming upstairs. She became convinced there was an assassin at the bottom of the stairs waiting for Pa to come home. "What could I do, what could I do?" she said. "If I shouted out the window to warn him when he pulled up, it would probably be too late. But if I went out on the stairs, the guy could just shoot me and Herb, too." She sat there paralyzed by terror. Finally, when she heard Pa's car pulling up, she screwed up her courage, said "What will be, will be," and went out the apartment door to the stairs. There was nobody there. She collapsed on the landing, sobbing. Pa came in, dashed up the stairs—"What's the matter, Jane, what's the matter?" "I don't think he ever understood just how scared I was in those days."

Mom told me she could never have survived that period had it not been for the tight support network of her family and their many comrades. "I knew if Herb and I were killed, you kids would be taken care of, no question," she told me. But Herb kept his tone lighter, content to portray himself as an incorrigible trickster, a perpetual thorn in the bosses' sides. You can be serious, but don't take yourself too seriously.

Chistka, Voina i Blokada:
The Purge, the War and the Siege

In the 1930s, widely dispersed families like the Grbac clan kept in touch by putting pen to paper. There existed quicker means of communication, but sending letters across the world's wide oceans was the only affordable way for working people. People were accustomed to a slow pace of communication. It might take weeks for a letter from another continent to be delivered. And it might take months for the recipient to write back. Nonetheless, these family conversations went on, with long pauses between messages.

The geographic distances between the Grbac siblings were immense. Nona, the matriarch and five of the Grbac siblings, four after John was killed, lived in Chicago. The two eldest sisters were in Portland, Oregon, and Maritza was in Nerezine. The three brothers in Russia, by 1935, had scattered a considerable distance from one another, Dick in Moscow, Tony in Leningrad and Dan in Rostov. All through the 1930s into the 1940s, as the world plunged into turmoil, Grbac family letters managed to get through, during times of war, occupation, purges and repression. When letters from a family member ceased, it was a bad sign.

Most of the family letters have been lost, but fortunately Mom squirreled away several precious trans-continental letters from her brothers in Russia. Over 70 years after they were mailed they are a window into a time and place long past. A lot of the content is pro forma courtesies: "Dear Family, We are all fine. We are living well. It's good to hear that you are fine, etc."

For example, a 1937 letter to Nona from Dick, in literary Croatian with a tinge of Nerezine dialect and also of Russian, was written on a sheet of onion-skin paper folded in half to form a little four page booklet:

A Great Vision

Dear Mother,

It makes us very happy to read your letter which informs us of your good health, and in it you tell us a little about everybody. It is very dear to me to hear that [brother] Joseph's little daughter [Gloria] is healthy and fine. So for you, in your old age, it seems you have another child to bring up. You still look good in the photo, so does our Katarina [brother John's widow], and how beautiful and green it is in her yard, so you can pass time in such a beautiful place.

Recently I received a letter from Dinko [brother Dan]. He sent me 100 rubles for me to buy something and send it to [sister]Maritza and her children. Today I bought a warm cap for [brother-in-law] Celestin because it seemed to me that he will need it when he goes out fishing. I received a letter from them recently. They write that they all are fine. They also write that they received that bacon that I sent to them and that the kids love it. In the next few days I'll look for something else to buy to send them because, as you know, the fascists there are doing everything to kill off the people, but believe you me, mother, they and their politics won't last long. The time will come when the wide masses of the Italian people will see that Mussolini and fascism are leading to disaster, and they will throw him and his gang of head-choppers out where they belong.

We, mother, are living well. I wrote a lot about it to Jacinta [to Mom, in English] and I hope that she will read it and tell you about it. And how is it going for you with English? Probably you can already understand everything? Otherwise there isn't any way for you and Katy [Joe's Irish 2nd wife] to understand each other. It would be interesting to hear you talk. Oh, how I desire to see you again and to converse with you from the soul.

It is dear to me that you heard from Miki [An aunt in Nerezine] that they are all fine. I hadn't heard anything from them for a long time. I recently got a letter from [brother] Anton. He writes that he and the family are fine. Receive our numberless greetings, kisses from all of us, Aleksandra, Ernest and your unforgetting son, Rade.

Many greetings to Katarina, Krešo, Josip, Agata, to all, Good bye.

Then on the back panel, following his journalistic impulse, he wrote an English message to Mom about possibly publishing the letter in the Croatian-American press.

One can infer that Nona had written earlier to Dick with news from other relatives in Nerezine, that his little brother Joe had gotten married again, this time to Kate McGowan, an immigrant from County Mayo, Ireland, who of course spoke no Croatian. Dick was clearly amused that after fifteen years in Chicago, Nona finally had a strong motivation to learn English.

It may seem surprising that Dick and Tony said they were living well materially in 1930s Soviet cities, that Dick even sent care packages to his sister's household in Italian-occupied Nerezine, and Dan had 100 rubles to spare for presents for Nerezine relatives. They mention scant details about their lives in Russia, making claims of prosperity suspect, yet it seems Maritza and Celestin, the poor village relations, indeed received bacon, a cap and other presents. Dick even sent a Soviet flag as a present to the family in Chicago. With Dick and Aleksandra both working at decent jobs, they had some discretionary income.

Dick's globetrotting habits diminished after his move to the Soviet Union. In his early years there, travel was difficult from Seattle Commune, but Dick didn't just stay down on the farm. He made it to Kharkov in 1933, where he had his portrait taken on the occasion of the 15th anniversary of the October Revolution and also made the excursion to the spa in Zhelesnovodsk. In 1935, shortly after he and Aleksandra settled in Moscow and their son Ernest was born, the Soviet Union closed its borders. Dick probably wasn't planning a trip then anyway.

The sealing of the borders was a harbinger of the terror Stalin was about to bring to Soviet society. The Soviet 1917 revolution was followed by civil war lasting into the early 1920s, justifying Lenin's strict rule under war powers and mercilessly rooting out perceived enemies of the revolution. With forced collectivization in the 1930s, uncooperative peasants were persecuted, and millions died. In the later 1930s, the Chistka, meaning purge in Russian, was carried out by the NKVD, the feared secret police, engulfing Soviet society in a web of denunciations, disappearances and executions.

Historians have attributed the Chistka variously to Stalin's desire to eliminate possible rivals to power, his desire to strengthen the Soviet Union in anticipation of an attack from Nazi Germany, and his need to terrify the population into accepting totalitarian rule.

During the height of the Chistka there were show trials in 1936, 1937 and 1938; many of the prominent old Bolsheviks who participated in the revolution were tortured into offering implausible confessions of espionage and counter-revolutionary plots. A majority of the generals and admirals of the Red Army and Navy were accused and tried in secrecy. The big fish were promptly executed while lesser figures were sentenced to long prison terms in Siberia and the far North. Exact numbers may never be determined, but some historians believe that about 500,000 were executed and over 3 million were sent to labor camps.

The wave of arrests snowballed. Prisoners were forced to implicate others who had supposedly "recruited" them. As a way to quickly settle scores, opportunistic accusers could dispatch adversaries with allegations of "counter-revolutionary activity." It is not surprising that the outspoken Richard Grbac acquired enemies and fell into this sort of trap.

Meanwhile, in Chicago, although Mom was cheered by her successful organizing efforts, she was concerned about a long period without letters from her brothers in Russia, especially Dick, who always wrote often. Mom's life was busy; she didn't have time to dwell on it. Then shortly before Bill's May, 1939 birth, Nona received a shocking letter from Dick dated April 12, 1939. He began with an indirect apology for not writing sooner:

Dear Mother and Brothers,
Quite some time has passed already since I received your last letter. I am in good health and I am working as much as I can to help build socialism. We are spending some time in isolation because I didn't have the true proletarian spirit to fight and work for the interests of the working people. I know for this the Soviet Government is not at fault. I got tangled up and it is hard to get it all untangled…. Dear mother and brothers, don't worry about me. In time everything will be all right. Your unforgetting son and brother, Rade

The letter was written 13 months after Dick had disappeared. The family now learned he was in a prison camp.

We have only ambiguous information as to the reason he was sent there, from vague, veiled statements by Dan and Tony. We think Dick became involved in a dispute with some managers at the Stalin Auto Works. As an experienced auto worker in two Ford plants in the United States, he likely was dismayed at practices in the Moscow factory. He may have been concerned, too, about corruption on the part of the managers. Not one to hold his peace, Dick was a particularly vulnerable Soviet worker then, a foreigner, an American. With Stalin's growing xenophobia, foreigners became prime targets for accusations of espionage. Moreover, Dick had become a candidate for membership in the Communist Party, which ironically made him even more of a target.

Late on the night of March 8, 1938, there was pounding on the door of the Moscow apartment Dick shared with Aleksandra and two-year-old Ernst. NKVD agents rushed in. They tore the apartment apart in a thorough search, seized whatever papers they found and ordered Dick to go with them immediately. He tried his best to calm his young wife. The agents took him away. Aleksandra never saw him again.

Aleksandra made persistent inquiries at Lyubyanka Prison, an imposing edifice in the center of Moscow. Instead of answers, she herself was arrested and imprisoned behind Lyubyanka's walls. Ernst was taken away to an orphanage in the town of Tambov. After months of harsh interrogation, without explanation, Aleksandra was released on October 27, 1938. When she learned the location of her son, in a feat of daring, she kidnapped him from the orphanage and fled to the south of Russia, to the Stavropol region, not far from Seattle Commune. She dropped her married name, reverting to her maiden name Groshenko for herself and son Ernst.

Dick spent months in Lyubyanka where, doubtless like other prisoners, he was brutally interrogated until he either "confessed" or was "convicted" of the crimes of "counter-revolutionary espionage and anti-Soviet agitation." He was sentenced to five years imprisonment in Kargopol Lag concentration camp, a much shorter sentence than average. In her memoirs, another prison camp internee sentenced to five years recalled that a fellow prisoner exclaimed, "Only five years! Then you must be completely innocent!"

From Moscow's Yaroslavl Station, Dick was shipped in a cattle car hundreds of miles north to the Arkangelsk region. In his book *The GULAG Archipelago*, Aleksander Solzhenitsyn wrote that while being transported along that same railroad line, he worried that his destination might be Kargopol Lag, a particularly notorious prison camp.

Kargopol, a town on the banks of the Onega River, was a trading center for salt, furs and amber. At its peak in the 18th Century it had 3,000 inhabitants. In 1936, with the onset of the Chistka, Kargopol's 16th Century monastery was converted into a prison camp. On its grounds twelve wooden barracks were constructed. Each housed 150 to 200 prisoners. The corrupt guards granted privileges to ordinary criminal prisoners, using them to spy on, bully and steal from the political prisoners. Ill housed, ill fed and ill clothed, the political prisoners endured hard labor, digging a canal and cutting timber in the snowy forests in extreme weather. What happened to Dick we can only speculate. In such a camp, his five-year sentence likely turned out to be a death sentence. He was never heard from again.

When he was in the Rostov mental hospital, Dan wrote a letter on a scrap of a paperboard box, scribbled in Croatian to his mother with a blunt pencil. The first time I held the missive in my hands it gave me a chill. It reeked of the paranoia of that time and place.

Dear Mother,
Here I want to let you know that I am fine. I am in a hospital now, but it isn't so bad. I'm being treated with electricity because I suffer from nervousness. I am getting a little better.

There follows a confusing sentence in which Dinko castigates "those who testified falsely, and will soon be cast into their own pit of evil death and deceit."

Is he referring to the men who condemned Dick? He continues:

I still am not completely free but I expect I soon will be. This is

a great school in the struggle for our salvation from the damned remainder of the enemies of the working class. Don't worry about me in
the least. Everything will end well for us and for all the workers of the
world. Receive my many greetings to everybody.

I remain, your son Dominic

Then he drew a line straight across the page and below it in
Russian wrote a message to his brother Tony, asking him to forward this note to their mother and requesting paper and enve-
lopes. He promised to write to everybody. He says it is good to hear
that "we are fine and that Rade is fine too and that he should soon
be coming back." Dan's undated note must have been written in
1939, because by 1940, Tony wrote Nona that he hadn't heard from
Dan in a long time.

Is Dan's note the ravings of a madman? Tony sent it on to
Chicago so maybe he didn't think so. Tony seemed prone to write
overly reassuring messages. I have two postcards and a letter Tony
sent to Nona in 1940 and 1941. Tony wrote in beautiful, neat hand-
writing in a Croatian that had by then been significantly influenced by Russian. He even occasionally erred using a Cyrillic letter in a word otherwise in Latin script.

Leningrad, January 30, 1940
Dear Mother,

I am letting you know that I and the family, wife, children are in
complete health. I am working, the same as before. We live well and
happily. I had a letter from Rade. He writes that all is well. I haven't
heard from Dinko in a long time. He wrote before and I don't know
why he doesn't write now. It was very cold here but now it has become
a little nicer. We are living and by us there is no danger that could harm
our children or us. Materially we are living well. Don't worry about us
because we are fine.

Anton, your son

I think his letter was a bit too cheery to be true. I'm sure Nona
thought so, too. The only ominous note is that Dan had stopped
writing. The next postcard Tony sent is dated November 5, 1940.

A Great Vision

Dear Mother, brothers and sisters,

I want to let you know that I received your letter for which I thank you very much. I am working. Everything is fine, brother Rade is fine. I don't know anything about Dinko. The children are growing and Jan goes to school. He is learning well. The wife is working in a factory on a machine. They make film projectors. Her work is not bad. I wish you all the best. Forgive me that I didn't write sooner. Your son and brother Anton

The final letter that got through was sent after the June, 1941 start of Hitler's Operation Barbarossa, the German invasion of the Soviet Union.

Leningrad, August 26, 1941
Dear Mother, sisters, brothers and all our comrades,

To all of you I wish all the best from my heart, my children and my wife and all of our comrades. I am alive and well. I work in a factory. The children are in the country on a collective farm. They live very well. They have cows, potatoes, all sorts of greens and berries. So don't you fear for me. We are living out of any danger. The sons live in the Leningrad provinces, 70 kilometers from the city of Ashtashkov.

There followed a passage in which Tony seemed to be responding to an offer from the family in Chicago to have Krešo take one of his two boys, John or Edik and Agata would take the other.

They [John and Edik] will be fine there on the farm, I think, until this war ends. As to brothers Dick and Dinko, I haven't heard anything for a while. They are fine. I am eating well, I work hard and at present everything is all right by us. I don't doubt our war effort. We have very good discipline. So don't cry for me. As long as I am alive I will write to you often. I think that soon there will be a different time when the Germans will be running from us and conditions will be better here.

Help us however you can in morale or materially. I love you all, Mother, brothers, sisters and all our comrades.

Your son, brother and comrade, Anton

The heartbreaking letters sought to reassure the family that they were safe and well, but the effect would have been just the opposite. The writing and sending of such letters was less an act of communicating information than an act of love. The words are formulaic; each sender had no desire to worry distant loved ones with the actuality of his dire plight. Each wanted to comfort and reassure that he was all right or at least that in the end everything would be all right.

Even if the Kargopol prison authorities had allowed Dick to write letters, he wouldn't have chosen to devastate his loved ones by telling the truth. He would not have written that his had been an error due to youthful idealism to move to the Soviet Union along with his two brothers, where a people's revolution has been betrayed, where a brutal dictator and his minions ruled with the same cruelty and injustice as the tsars had. Though he died an unknown death in Kargopol Lag, no, Dick did not wish to subject his beloved family to that bitter, bitter truth.

Tony was never a deep thinker like Dick. Mom described him as a "good time Charley" during his years in Chicago. Nonetheless, he would have felt the same impulse not to frighten his family in Chicago and Nerezine. In 1941 he also parroted reassurances that his nine- and seven-year old boys were fine—on something like a holiday in the country, surrounded by abundance on a collective farm that boasted all the resources to succor and shelter a sudden influx of evacuated city children. Such words must have been unconvincing to Nona, who during World War I had already experienced the evacuation of four of her boys, including all of the three sons then in Russia.

It was probably similarly unconvincing that he and his wife were quite safe in Leningrad where they were working hard and eating well, and that the evacuation of the children did not portend an imminent threat to the city's population. It would have been difficult to give credence to Tony's words that the mighty Red Army was already poised to throw back the wretched German invaders.

Less than two weeks after he dated his last letter, the Germans sealed off the only remaining land routes to Leningrad. He could not have known that on Hitler's orders, the German Army Group North would begin a bitter siege, the Blokada that would last nearly 900 days, explicitly intended to starve to death the civilian population of the city.

Hitler planned to wipe Leningrad from the map, a city of three million. The German High Command ordered, "St. Petersburg must be erased from the face of the Earth." The Command rejected occupying the city "because it would make us responsible for food supply." Their decision was to keep the city under siege and bombardment, starving its population.

The Nazi genocidal plan resulted in one of the longest and most lethal sieges in history, causing the deaths of one million Leningrad civilians, an incredible horror. Thousands died daily. It would be nearly impossible for the city authorities to dispose of the mounting heaps of corpses, especially during the long winter months when the earth was frozen solid.

While the weaker Leningraders died, a trickle of food and other supplies managed to be brought in from November through March on the so-called *Doroga Zhizni*, the Road of Life, an ice road across thirty kilometers of Lake Ladoga. Convoys of trucks managed to evacuate 1.3 million of the three million city residents, and on the return trip they carried into the besieged city, 360,000 tons of goods, mostly foodstuffs, during the duration of the Blokada. The Road of Life became bordered by walls of snow more than two meters high, limiting visibility to attacking German aircraft which harassed and bombed the convoys. Tony became one of the truck drivers. In the middle of the winter, the ice was more than four feet thick, relatively impervious to German bombs, but as Spring approached, the ice thinned. It was in late March, when Tony's convoy was bombed, the ice breached. Tony and his truck vanished into the icy waters of Ladoga. His death did not go unmarked; he was posthumously awarded the Order of Lenin for his sacrifice.

Dinko, the remaining Grbac brother in Russia, like Dick, suffered an unknown death. There are two family stories about his demise, presumably learned from Tony's descendants with whom we were in contact after 1958: Mom heard that Dinko died in a "mountaineering accident." Mom thought he committed suicide by jumping off a cliff. Uncle Joe contended he heard that the Rostov mental hospital where Dinko was a patient was bombed by

German planes and he perished in the bombing.

The idealistic quest of the three Grbac brothers to the workers' paradise tragically took them all to untimely deaths.

Victory at Armour and Inter-Union Strife

Happy he had been shot but not killed, Pa now found himself in the strange circumstance of being befriended by two of Chicago's prominent public figures, Bishop Sheil and Mayor Kelly. As chair of the union's Anti-Discrimination Committee, Pa asked Bishop Sheil to author a pamphlet opposing on religious grounds any form of racial discrimination. The Bishop complied and the CIO printed the pamphlet and distributed hundreds of thousands of copies.

When Pa's request for a permit to carry a handgun was denied, Mayor Kelly ordered Chicago Police bodyguards to protect him. Pa knew the Chicago hoodlums were well aware of the consequences of harming a cop, they were the toughest gang in town and could exact their revenge with impunity.

Two older officers nearing retirement were assigned to this light duty and became quite friendly. Pa tried to make their duty easy as possible. In the evenings when Mom and Pa wanted to go to a movie, they encouraged whichever cop was on assignment to bring his wife. It became sort of a double date.

Fortunately the bodyguards never had to fend off another assassination attempt. Pa related:

> I told the two cops that I was going to get a gun, and I wanted to know if they had any objections. They said to me, "No, three guns are better than two." The fellows were pretty nervous at first. There had been threats. There would be phone calls to the union hall saying, "This guy March is going to get it next week."

The year of accompanying him on his rounds was quite educational for the two officers and it contributed to their positive relationship.

I had to go into packing plants where there was a stoppage; they went right with me through all these things. They saw the conditions; they saw all these events taking place.... So they got to like me pretty well, strange to say. One of them, an old Irishman, told me he loved me like a son. He said, "I only got one thing against you, Herb. I never see you with a rosary." Other than that I was okay.

Brother Bob had an amusing childhood memory involving the police bodyguards. On Flag Day, six-year-old Bob was getting out a flag to display just as the bodyguards arrived. Bob decided that of the two flags available, he preferred the pretty red flag that Uncle Dick had sent from the Soviet Union. It would be different from other flags in the neighborhood. The cops convinced him to fly the American flag.

The time around Pa's shooting was a turbulent era in American labor. After its stunning initial successes, the CIO's unionization drive lost momentum. The Little Steel strike was lost; a major effort to unionize textile workers in the South stalled.

The rapidly created CIO unions developed factional splits. Lewis became locked in a leadership struggle with Sidney Hillman, of the Amalgamated Clothing Workers. Hillman was supportive of President Roosevelt's policies, serving as labor's representative on the President's War Preparedness Board. With the 1939 outbreak of World War II, Lewis became increasingly unhappy with Roosevelt as he inched toward involvement in the European war. Lewis feared a repeat of the anti-labor repression that followed World War 1 and remained a staunch anti-interventionist.

A purge also began of the most dedicated CIO organizers, the Communists. Although he was staunchly anti-communist, John L. Lewis was glad to use Communist organizers, feeling they were effective and presented no real threat to his power. Lewis is supposed to have said, "When you go hunting, who gets the rabbit, you or the hunting dog?" But other CIO leaders like Hillman, Walter Reuther and Philip Murray were swayed by red-baiting and worried that the "Reds" might become rivals for union leadership.

Pa's Communist affiliations became a serious issue in his union activity. From his initiation of organizing efforts in meat packing, Pa was known as a Red. He didn't deny it, generally deflecting inquiries about his personal political beliefs and preferring to concentrate on union-specific issues.

Anti-communist CIO officials were not the only problem. Pa expressed annoyance also at the "grandstand quarterbacks" of the Communist Party who "didn't know a packinghouse from a pickle" but wanted to dictate his organizing strategy. In 1939 when the PWOC was locked in a deadly struggle with the packers' gangster surrogates, the Party declared the CIO had become "a decadent organization," and ordered Pa to abandon the PWOC and work with the AFL—the guys who were shooting at him! Disenchanted with the Party leaders and busy with union work, he ignored them.

Armour persisted in their refusal to recognize the February NLRB election, falsely contending they already were in compliance with the law by working with their AFL-chartered company union. With a major strike looming, Secretary of Labor Frances Perkins initiated conciliation efforts.

Armour's general manager and his attorneys, summoned to Washington in September, refused to meet in the same room as PWOC representatives; Secretary Perkins served as go-between. AMC president Patrick Gorman inserted himself into the dialog, claiming that a majority of Armour workers actually favored the AFL—a ludicrous claim. Nonetheless, it caused enough uncertainty among the Labor Department mediators that the PWOC consented to repeat the NLRB election in November with the AMC on the ballot.

Armour figured they had a winning strategy to swing the election and install their phony company union. Gorman stepped up his rhetoric that the PWOC was a Red conspiracy, and at the suggestion of the meat packers, Texas Congressman Martin Dies brought to Chicago his traveling show, the House Un-American Activities Committee (HUAC), subpoenaing the leaders of the PWOC, Pa, Hank Johnson and Wally Stabrawa. The hearings were in a downtown hotel just three days before the NLRB election. Pa recalled the day:

> It was a Saturday at one in the afternoon, something like that. I got down there just in time to pick up the Chicago Tribune Sunday edition

with big boxcar headlines, "Red Czars of CIO Meat Packing Hailed Before Dies." And there was a full story of what had already occurred at the hearing that I was about to go into. My attorney was Art Goldberg, who subsequently became a Supreme Court Justice. At that time Art was a left-winger, active in the National Lawyers Guild.

I got in there and I'm confronted by Dies. Was I a member of the YCL in Kansas City? I said, "Yeah, I was young then."

Pa glossed over a part of his testimony that more than twenty years later would prove to be a problem for him. The hearing transcript:

DIES: Are you a member of the Communist Party?
MARCH: I am certainly not.

Actually this statement was a half-truth at the moment, because he had ceased to be active in the CP months earlier.

DIES: Have you ever been a member of the Communist Party?
MARCH: I have not.

This was a lie, no doubt told with legal advice from the future Supreme Court Justice. Pa felt the HUAC hearing was an abuse of legislative powers, intended to swing the union election. Recalling the hearing, Pa emphasized the zingers he delivered to Congressman Dies:

I said, "Martin, if you are concerned about un-American influences, I know of some. Can I tell you about them?"
He said, "You do? Go ahead."
I said, "There is a criminal conspiracy to deprive people of their civil rights and their rights to organize, through force and violence by the meat packing industry."
I detailed the fact that I had been shot at two times and shot the second time, and that I had evidence that gangsters Thomas Devereaux and Jake Saltis were among those responsible for it. I had a paper all prepared and delivered it to him.
He said, "I'll show you that I'm impartial. I forthwith subpoena, ah,

what's his name?" Of course nothing ever came of that.

Hank Johnson also lectured Dies that the Congressman should investigate the un-American activity of lynchings in their mutual home state Texas.

Confident they would get a favorable outcome, Armour allowed the NLRB polling places on their premises. Despite the highly publicized red-baiting, the PWOC won by a bigger margin than the first election, receiving over 4000 votes to about 1000 for AMC. Pa heard workers comment, "Well, we're all Reds now."

Armour finally had to negotiate but refused to use the word "contract." They negotiated a "memorandum of agreement." When it was signed in the spring of 1940 it was really an anti-climax. Armour workers received a modest pay increase, and the hard-won gains in working conditions, already won through shop floor actions, were codified. Still, it meant a lot to packinghouse workers. Gertie Kramarczyk, a veteran Armour employee, typified the attitude: "I felt like a human being with real rights, a real whole person for the first time in my life."

The key battle in meat packing was won. There were still the other packers to bring to the negotiating table, but *de facto* they had to offer comparable pay and conditions to Armour.

With recognition, the CIO national leadership moved to impose more centralized control on the PWOC and get rid of leftists. Van Bittner, the autocratic CIO-appointed union leader discharged Pa, the most influential local leader.

"They laid me off, thanked me for my service," Pa commented with undisguised irony. "But actually I was still around. I was drawing unemployment, still speaking to workers, giving advice when they asked for it." Bittner did not find this amusing. He needed Herb March out of town. At Bittner's instigation, Philip Murray offered Pa a job as organizer for the SWOC, at the Sparrow's Point Bethlehem Steel Plant in Baltimore. Needing work, Pa took the job—"stupidly" he said later.

Mom and Pa and the two boys moved to Maryland. Initially they found lodgings at a boarding house near the harbor. Bob recalls that old salts who roomed there were happy to have an interested young boy to regale with tales from their voyages. Later the family moved to a house in an outlying area—an exotic experience for a Chicago Southside boy to attend school with rural children.

While Pa worked in the successful effort to organize Bethlehem Steel, politics in the CIO hit a breaking point. 1940 was a presidential election year. John L. Lewis' opposition to Roosevelt had grown intense. He tried to build labor support for Montana Governor Burton Wheeler, a Western populist who shared Lewis' isolationist views. With Wheeler failing to inspire an enthusiastic following, Democratic sentiment was strong for a third Roosevelt term.

The Republicans passed over the front-runners Robert Taft and Thomas Dewey for Wendell Wilkie, a liberal lawyer and former Democrat. Lewis found Wilkie unsatisfactory, too, because he shared Roosevelt's interventionist ideas. Nonetheless, in an October radio address, Lewis endorsed Wilkie.

In the CIO, Phil Murray and Sidney Hillman fiercely opposed Lewis' position. Lewis pledged to resign as CIO head should the membership fail to follow him. When Roosevelt was re-elected, Lewis stepped down, supporting the accession Philip Murray.

A dispute between Lewis and Murray prompted John L. to pull the UMWA out of the CIO. He then tried to create a rival federation using District 50 of the UMWA, a catch-all district comprised of non-mining workers. Lewis hired organizers to raid existing CIO locals, asking them to jump from the CIO to District 50. Unionists were confronted with a tough choice—to stick with the CIO or with John L. Lewis. Chafing under Van Bittner, Hank Johnson and other members of the PWOC leadership opted to go with Lewis.

Meanwhile, still in Baltimore, Pa heard from his Chicago colleagues about serious problems. Hank Johnson, working for the UMWA District 50, was pushing to raid PWOC locals. Also a mysterious figure named Scotty McKenzie had shown up in Chicago a year earlier. He was hired at Armour in the early days of the union contract and was one of seven workers suspended, a major grievance. The union threatened to strike, mostly a bluff, but McKenzie and the others were reinstated with a peculiar agreement. Pa related:

Armour and Company regarded me as an object of particular enmity. I was the incarnation of the devil. So Armour made a deal with the top leaders of the PWOC that these guys would be reinstated, at the price that I would not speak for the union any longer at meetings with plant management. They figured that would destroy my prestige with the workers. So they put the guys back to work, including McKenzie, and he started taking on increased responsibility in grievances and eventually became Grievance Chairman. The old role Armour had played with the company union they began to play with McKenzie. They would settle grievances for him that they would not settle for anybody else.

Armour was trying to build up McKenzie as a union leader.

While I was out in Baltimore, McKenzie made an alliance with the Lewis forces, and got elected to the union's council. About that time I heard from people in Chicago and I got concerned. My attitude wasn't based on the fact that McKenzie was with the Lewis forces. His whole career began to smell funny.

McKenzie claimed to have been a militant unionist with oil workers on the West Coast. Pa asked West Coast friends to check up on McKenzie's story. They reported he had been the leader of a company union in an oil refinery in California. Pa said: "It was evident that he was an operator, a professional labor spy."

Pa decided to get back to Chicago as soon as possible. "Packing people were saying to me, 'Jesus Christ, Herb, you belong back here. You're letting the whole thing go to hell.'" Pa quit the SWOC and, unemployed, he needed a job. John L. Lewis figured that Pa was embittered toward Van Bittner, so he offered him a job as a District 50 organizer in Chicago. Pa took it and returned to Chicago in February, 1941. He arrived in the nick of time. At Hank Johnson's urging, the Armour Soap Works was about to vote to leave the CIO for District 50.

There was a move underfoot to swing the Armour Soap Workers Local 100 out of the Packinghouse Workers into the United Mine Workers. And I was on the United Mine Workers' payroll. It was a plant

I had organized from scratch. I intimately knew some of the people there who had been convinced of the need to make the switch. I met with them and changed their minds. Then I appeared at the membership meeting and spoke on the importance of all workers of Armour and Company remaining in one union to the degree possible. The membership overwhelmingly voted down the switch of affiliation.

Ever the maverick, instead of doing as directed, Pa did what he felt was right and foiled the plans of his current employer.

Following on the heels of the soap works vote, the big Armour PWOC local 347 was facing a similar issue. Scotty McKenzie was pushing to take control of the local. Pa arrived while the meeting was underway and a lot of bickering was going on. A split in the local seemed to be brewing, with a segment poised to break off with the Lewis forces.

All I did was walk into the hall and the meeting was interrupted for five minutes by applause and people coming up to shake my hand. I had come back to Chicago. A lot of people felt very badly about my going away and I guess I did too, by then.

When the meeting resumed, Pa asked to be recognized and detailed the information he had about McKenzie. He asked that the members re-examine how McKenzie had come to prominence in the union, that he must have had the cooperation of the company for what he accomplished. Pa offered a motion that passed overwhelmingly: to suspend McKenzie from the union pending an investigation. Pa said, "I think McKenzie left there with about four supporters and there must have been over four hundred people at the meeting."

Confirming Pa's allegations, McKenzie suddenly was hired by Armour as a supervisor, remaining with management until he and a group of fellow supervisors were discharged for theft of meat products.

Despite his disagreements with the national CIO leaders, Pa had no intention of allowing the packinghouse unions to be split up by District 50 raids.

The UMWA decided it was a mistake to have me with them because I was frustrating their aims in the packing industry. They wanted to fire me, but they wanted to do it with a little grace. So after about a month I got a letter from Martin Wagner, the secretary of District 50, stating that it had been called to his attention that I referred to Miss Kathryn Lewis, John L. Lewis' daughter and the nominal head of District 50, as a 'big fat slob.' What did I have to say for myself? This was more than a little ridiculous. Well, I sent him a letter. My tongue in cheek couldn't be seen, but it was pretty obvious. My answer was: "Dear Brother Wagner, Please be advised that I am not in the habit of calling young ladies big, fat slobs, particularly those to whom I have not been formally introduced." Needless to say, my discharge was shortly forthcoming.

Pa's credibility with the packinghouse workers was so strong that the CIO leaders realized they wouldn't be able to withstand the UMWA's raids without him, so they hired him back. His sparring with the Lewis forces had not yet ceased. Hank Johnson still was working to engineer a faction of Local 347 to bolt to District 50. Johnson was aided by two key African-American union activists, Arthel Shelton and Frank Alsup.

Lewis sent goons to Chicago to press District 50's cause. Two big thugs stalked into the union office, wearing coats tight enough to reveal the bulges of their guns in shoulder holsters. Speaking in thick Kentucky accents they threatened Pa. He got rid of them and called District 50's Martin Wagner. "Now Martin, these goons may be pretty tough guys down there in the coal camps, but you know, this is Chicago. Do you have any idea how many unemployed gangsters there are around here? Since Prohibition came off, they lost their jobs protecting liquor shipments. Do you know how cheap it is to have a guy knocked off in Chicago? For their own protection, I think you had better get those two hillbillies out of town." He never saw them again.

Threats and violence were a constant issue. Shortly after his return to Chicago, Pa and his friend Bob Travis, a leader of the Flint, Michigan sit-down strike, now with the militant Farm Equipment workers' union, saw that the CIO's Chicago Council had become conservative, excluding leftist unions, so he formed a rival Cook

County Industrial Union Council.

With threats coming from a leader of the CIO Chicago Council, Bob and Pa decided to have the fellow's leg broken. Bob spoke to a thug who was in the business. Pa remarked that the hoodlum had a regular menu: one leg broken, $50, a leg and an arm, $75 or two legs for $100. They ordered one broken leg and paid a $25 deposit on the job. Pa had serious misgivings about going through with it and persuaded Bob to call the thug and cancel the job. He offered to return their $25 deposit:

"No, you just keep it," Bob replied.

"Well, OK, you've done a favor for me so I'll do one for you," he said and gave Bob a tip on a horse in a race. Bob told Pa about it, who wanted none of it. But Bob was curious; he called a bookie and bet $2. Sure enough the horse won the race. The thug called Bob back.

"Well, did you put some money on that horse?"

"I just put $2 on him."

"Two bucks! No, no, I'm going to give you another horse for tomorrow and put some serious money on him, like fifty bucks."

Pa still wasn't having any of it. He never asked Bob if he went ahead and bet on the second horse. Pa learned that the mob made payrolls by fixing a horserace somewhere in the county every day and providing the information to whomever they were paying. I asked Pa why he wouldn't place a bet. "I didn't want to be in the position of having accepted a favor from the mob," he said.

The packinghouse workers remained within the CIO fold despite the efforts of Johnson, Shelton and Alsup. Their story had an unhappy ending three years later in 1944. Art Shelton had been working to organize a local of utilities workers in northern Indiana. He became disturbed when Hank Johnson stepped in, took over forming the local, denying Shelton credit or payment for his work. In an internal District 50 procedure, Shelton filed a complaint against Johnson and Ed Heckelbeck, the Chicago District 50 head. Two UMWA officials were sent from Pennsylvania for the hearing.

When it became apparent things were not going his way, Shelton pulled a .45 caliber pistol from his brief case and fired, wounding the fleeing Heckelbeck and Alsup, and emptied the pistol into Johnson. Shelton then walked to a police station and surrendered. He was convicted of murder and served nine years before being paroled. Shelton never played any further role in the union movement. Hank Johnson died a day after the shooting, a sad ending to the life of a talented man who, had he made different decisions, might have been a significant African-American labor leader.

US entry into World War II came a year after the family's return to Chicago, bringing big changes. Pa reached the height of his career. Since the CIO unions were important players in strategic wartime industries, Pa became an influential labor leader, respected by workers and viewed by the government as a key person to keep labor peace, not only in meat packing but in all of Chicago's CIO unions. Mom's life changed, too. After years out of paid employment, like many other women she joined the wartime industrial workforce at Studebaker, an automobile factory that had retooled to produce fighter plane engines.

With the Soviet Union and the United States allied against the Axis, harsh anti-communist rhetoric was temporarily muted, bringing an unprecedented period of seeming tolerance of communist viewpoints. Hollywood films extolled Soviet resistance to the Nazis. There was even a pro-Soviet popular song, "Stalin Wasn't Stallin'" by the Golden Gate Quartet, celebrating Soviet advances on the Eastern Front.

In wartime, Pa's importance as a labor leader was more important than anti-communism. The War Labor Board sought harmony, mediated disputes and needed cooperation from union leaders like Pa, who supported a wartime no-strike pledge.

The Communist Party supported the no-strike pledge. Party Chairman Earl Browder avidly advocated close cooperation between the US and Soviet Union, optimistically predicting continued cooperation in the postwar years. Browder went so far as to predict "eons of class harmony" from the Soviet-American alliance. Envisioning American Communists as a pressure group within a broad US governing coalition, in 1944 he directed conversion of the CPUSA from a political party into a "Communist Political Association."

During the war Pa became more active in the Party. He was

back in Chicago on the PWOC payroll. The packinghouse CP club, which he had substantially recruited and organized in the 1930s, became crucial for developing union leadership. Pa needed to be in that group, especially to counter the influence of Hank Johnson and his raiders. The emerging African-American union leaders were CP members—Leon Beverly became president and Sam Curry an officer of Armour local 347, Sam Parks and Charles Hayes were the top officers in Wilson local 25. To these African-Americans, the CP represented the most militant organization fighting for black rights. They had come to view the NAACP and the Urban League as "silk stocking" groups dominated by the African-American upper middle class where packinghouse workers couldn't advance to leadership roles.

As war clouds gathered, the Roosevelt administration favored binding labor contracts to ensure stability in industries indispensable in wartime. Pressure from the federal National Defense Mediation Board on both management and labor began even prior to Pearl Harbor. Pa was quickly exposed to its powers. In fall of 1941, they imposed a settlement with a small wage increase on the reluctant Armour management when the first contract reopener came due.

In 1941 war spread with alarming speed. In April, the Axis invaded and dismembered Yugoslavia; Mom's Croatian homeland became engulfed in war. In June, Hitler invaded the Soviet Union. The CP's prior anti-war stance ended abruptly and "defend the Soviet Union" became its rallying cry. Mom had to live with anxiety over the fates of her brothers and their families in Russia.

After Japan's attack on Pearl Harbor in December, all the country's major labor unions agreed to a no-strike pledge that often put Pa in an awkward situation. Seeing potential for vast profits in wartime production, the big packers, especially Armour, sought to speed up work processes in violation of the contracts. The companies stonewalled on grievances concerning the speedup, so shop floor actions were the union's only effective counter-measure—slowdowns or short term work stoppages, like "riz-a-ma-tiz" and "stop and go" strikes that had proved effective in the organizing era. It was crucial to prevent these disputes from turning into large-scale wildcat strikes, which was precisely what Armour was hoping to provoke. Management regularly complained to the War Labor Board that the union was violating the no-strike pledge and demanded to have the union decertified.

Working with the active cadre of stewards, Pa frequently had to play a cat-and-mouse game between aggrieved workers, foremen, plant superintendents, and the War Labor Board. Moreover, the game included internal union politics. The CIO national leadership, which supported the no-strike pledge, used unauthorized job actions as a pretext for seizing control of independent-minded locals and removing leftist unionists. Within the packinghouse union there were divisions. The Trotskyist faction, strong in Minnesota locals, did not support the pledge at all, making it an issue to challenge the union's leadership.

Management was pleased that wages had been frozen, but they resented having to recognize the union and collect union dues through a check-off. Unable to get a pay raise because of the freeze, the union fought for and gained other advances: changing into work clothes and knife sharpening were put on work time instead of prior to clocking in. With meat demand high, most workers benefitted from overtime pay, despite the pay freeze. To counter the company speed-up, the union needed to tolerate a level of job actions, but had to maintain deniability. Sometimes a steward surreptitiously informed trusted co-workers, "I'm going to tell you to get back to work, but don't you dare listen to me."

To resolve the backlog of grievances and disputes in meat-packing, the War Labor Board empaneled a sub-committee headed by Clark Kerr, a young economics professor and labor relations specialist. At a hearing, Pa charged the company with utilizing the "Armour formula" union-busting strategy. Pa related:

The company response was a peculiar one. They attempted to prove that this union was not deserving of union security because, while the company was accused of having a formula, the union in reality was following a thing they described as the "March pattern." They were asked to describe what they meant. "Well, it's a campaign of using sarcasm and scurrilous propaganda to undermine the status of the supervisors." Their poor supervisors were being held up to ridicule, attempting to destroy their image in the eyes of the workers and they couldn't tolerate that. For example, in the Armour plant in Chicago the workers had given this supervisor by the name of Renfrow a nickname. They called him "Tee Hee" Renfrow, because when they would take up a grievance with him, he wouldn't settle anything, and when they kept pressing him, he would giggle in a silly way. This they claimed was part of the "March pattern."

They squawked that I was the Red influence in the union and I was trying to undermine capitalism, and the way I had chosen to do it was to make all bosses look contemptible. The funniest thing was, to prove the March pattern had spread, they introduced as an exhibit a handbill distributed at the Armour plant in St. Joseph, Missouri. It irked them that there was drawn on the leaflet a rather skillful picture of a dog, and in place of the dog's head was a very remarkable likeness of the plant superintendent. The hearing officers couldn't help but laugh. It almost broke up the session, much to the displeasure of the Armour side.

Pa had no idea sarcasm was such a revolutionary activity.

A major accomplishment of the packinghouse workers during the war was to establish the United Packinghouse Workers of America (UPWA), their own independent democratically run union. At the beginning of the war they were still the PWOC, an organizing committee whose leaders and officers were appointed by the national CIO without worker input. The unpopularity of the appointed PWOC head Van Bittner and two subsequent appointees made the PWOC vulnerable to raiding by UMWA District 50, compelling CIO head Phil Murray to promise to allow packinghouse workers to form an independent union. A Murray loyalist, rubber worker Sam Sponseller was the latest appointed PWOC head. Murray figured he would become his hand-picked president.

When the founding convention was called in October, 1943, the packinghouse workers defied the attempt by the national CIO to ram through their selected leadership. Leaders of locals from around the US and Canada hammered out a compromise slate of officers. The most able and dedicated unionists were considered too radical for some of the new union's factions and were passed over for less capable national officers. Pa, who assumed no national post and settled for Director of District 1, might have been president had he pushed for it. His esteem was described by David "Speedy" Cantor, who in 1943 was a young journalist working on the union newspaper:

> Herb March...was absolutely revered, strong square-jawed...a brilliant orator. At Armour Square, smack in the middle of the stockyards, we used to have these mass meetings at noontime where all the workers would come out and...they would have this big raised platform on which Herb March would stand. Herb was great because he appealed with the street type of language that the workers could understand. His rhetorical devices were great. His articulation was great. The man had a bellowing voice. He was full of humor.
>
> Herb was a hero in the eyes of the membership. He could do no wrong...This man wasn't a tin god. He was a real god...a brilliant organizer. He got more people into the union. He had an open door to his office. There were guys that would troop up straight up from the kill, with dirty uniforms, tracking mud and everything like that, walked into Herb's office.
>
> The union brought him in as head of the negotiating team. Armour refused to recognize him 'cause they knew he was a tough son of a bitch. They knew that he could...just sit there and look at them, and stare at them.

Since Pa was popular and respected, I asked why he never tried to become UPWA president. "I never cared what kind of a title I had," he replied. "I could be there regardless; I could influence the direction of the union. I didn't care if they called me the janitor." He explained that conservative locals in Iowa and Nebraska, where there were few black workers, considered him too radical on political and civil rights issues. "I didn't want to be a divisive factor," he said. "In Chicago I had something like 70% support. And the Chicago District was the core of the union. From there we set the pattern nationally."

Neither trappings of office nor the prospect of a high salary motivated him. The UPWA endeavored to keep staff salaries at about the amount a mid-level to better-paid worker would make in a packing plant. As long as he could pay the family bills, Pa didn't care about making money. In the 1960s he turned down an offer to become a partner in a prominent liberal law firm in Los Angeles. Instead he took a lower-paying job as staff lawyer for a local of the public employees union AFSCME.

We lived in unpretentious homes, drove functional used cars, enjoyed dinners out at low-priced Chinese restaurants. Pa always ordered Egg Foo-Yung. Pa didn't want any personal luxuries. He dressed respectably but not fashionably, used a cheap wristwatch. He didn't drink in bars. He didn't want expensive whiskey; the cheapest beer was fine with him. He didn't crave travel except to visit friends and relatives. Tours or fancy resorts held no attraction for him. He liked being respected, even revered, but felt the respect carried an obligation to live up to a high ethical standard. Working for human rights and equality was his true pleasure. He remembered and relished every victory, little and big. And since he didn't want much for himself, he was incorruptible and hard to intimidate.

During the war Pa helped solidify the place of the CIO in American industry. But since he was a thorn in the side of the packers, in 1943 they used their influence to have the Draft Board take him out of the picture. They nearly succeeded. Pa received notice from the Selective Service to report for induction into the Army. A huge send-off party was arranged in the ballroom of the prestigious Skyline Athletic Club, addressed by Mayor Kelly, and attended by a bevy of politicians and scores of unionists.

My brother Bob, then nine years old, recalls that Pa spent time with him before school on the morning of his expected departure. But word of Pa's conscription reached key people in Washington, where his role as a union leader was deemed essential. The draft board's order was quashed. Upon returning home from school Bob was amazed to see his father back home.

Jane Who Made the Planes

When the family returned from Maryland to Chicago, Nona had sold the Grbac house, so Mom found an apartment in the Murray Park area, a few miles southwest of the old neighborhood. They didn't stay long. Mom characterized it as a "lace curtain Irish"

community with high-toned airs where our family wasn't accepted. Seven-year-old Bob's memories of attending the local Clara
Barton School are anything but fond. "They had a dress code.
The boys had to wear a dress shirt and a tie—in a public school!"
Neither did Bob get along with the other kids. He felt ostracized
both as an outsider and as a "brainy" kid who, like Pa, had already
learned to read before entering first grade.

Mom's earlier connections to the University of Chicago, two
births at Lying-in Hospital and her U of C Settlement House
work, led her to seek a residence in the Hyde Park area near the
University. She knew people there and the schools and university
community atmosphere would be better for Bobby. As was common for men of his era, Pa left the domestic decisions up to Mom.
She found an apartment in the Woodlawn neighborhood, at 61st
and Ingleside, the southwestern fringe of the University area.

No longer in an extended family household, Mom was more
occupied at home, caring for her boys, especially toddler son Billy.
But entry of the US into World War II prompted her to wider civic
engagement. On lots near Lake Michigan she helped plant community "Victory Gardens." Late in 1942, she joined the wartime
industrial workforce, taking a job at Chicago's Studebaker auto
plant.

During the war, the number of working women increased from
12 to 18 million. Women have always been in the paid workforce,
especially the poor and women of color. Working white married
women, especially during the job shortages of the Depression,
had been disparaged as "greedy," unjustly taking jobs from male
"breadwinners." Ironically, even Secretary of Labor Frances Perkins, the first female Cabinet Secretary and a married woman,
stated that wives who worked were "a menace to society." But with
the massive mobilization of men for the military and a shortage of
labor in war industries, working wives no longer seemed so menacing.

By late 1942 continuing labor shortages prompted the government to launch a propaganda campaign to recruit more women
workers. Middle-class housewives and their husbands needed to
be convinced it was acceptable and patriotic for women to take
paying jobs. The government public relations campaigns featured

the famous "Rosie the Riveter" and the lesser-known "Wanda the Welder" images. Popular songs like "What Job is Mine in the Victory Line?" and "The Janes Who Make the Planes" played on the radio. About 6 million women took jobs for the first time, including about 25% of married women. The idealized role of at-home mother and homemaker was reluctantly deemphasized in patriarchal American society, though at war's end, it quickly became apparent that toleration of women working "men's jobs" was temporary.

The first hired were young unmarried women who already had an accepted place in the labor market. Citing concerns about ill effects on family life, many employers wouldn't hire women with children under 14. In 1944 due to ongoing labor shortages, the hiring restriction generally dropped to women with children under six.

With a history of activism since her teens, Mom was anxious to get out of the house and into the thick of things, despite two boys at home. Billy was only 3½ when Mom went to work at Studebaker, so she must have figured a way to avoid any "mother of small children" restriction.

For Mom, Studebaker was her first job as a union member. The plant was organized by the United Auto Workers, UAW-CIO. She became an engaged member, serving on the political action committee and advocating for equal treatment of women workers, despite push-back from both management and the union.

Studebaker had been an auto plant prior to the war, an industry with one of the lowest percentages of women workers, only about 4%. After Pearl Harbor, the number of women actually diminished for several months while all-male crews retooled production from civilian to military products.

When she took the Studebaker job, Mom hired Lucinda Cox, an African-American single mother in her early 40s, to keep house and watch the two boys. Lucinda lived about twenty blocks north at 39th Street and Cottage Grove Avenue in the recently constructed Ida B. Welles housing project. Although the place became notorious decades later as a hell hole of crime and grime and has since been demolished, at that time it was a desirable address for Chicago African-Americans. The two-story brick townhouses were surrounded by greenspace including a park. A New Deal project built from 1939-1941, these new housing units were a significant improvement over the dilapidated Chicago tenements most African-Americans occupied. The federal programs of that era retained neighborhood segregation by explicitly designating the project as housing for African-Americans only.

Despite the hierarchical racial relationship inherent in a white hiring a black domestic worker, Mom did her best to counter that tendency in her rapport with Lucinda. She countenanced no "ma'am" or "sir" and made efforts to have the two families socialize outside the work context. Bob fondly remembers visits to the Cox household. At age ten, he had his first pre-pubescent crush on Lucinda's teen-aged daughter Brenda. "I thought she was absolutely beautiful," Bob reminisced.

At Studebaker Mom was a quality-control inspector. With a micrometer she carefully checked the dimensions of steel rods that were to become crucial parts of radial aircraft engines. Air-cooled radial engines have cylinders which point outward in a star pattern from a central crankshaft. They were more suitable for warplanes because they are lighter and less susceptible to damage than liquid-cooled, in-line cylinder engines like the automobile engines that Studebaker long had.

Unfortunately, the Studebaker workforce had trouble acquiring the new, more precise skills required to produce radial engines. Mom consistently had to reject the rods she inspected as outside the allowable tolerance. As quality issues failed to improve and Studebaker fell short of fulfilling government contracts, tensions in the plant mounted. Mom was in a difficult position as a female who repeatedly rejected the production of mostly male machinists. Moreover, it was well known that she was the wife of Herb March, the notorious Communist union leader. Walter and Victor Reuther, leaders of the UAW, already were moving to eliminate communist influence in the autoworkers union. Mom was a Red and as an inspector, a female authority figure who found the men's output unsatisfactory. A confrontation was inevitable.

Her opponents used Mom's work on the CIO political action committee as a pretext to criticize her. With the presidential election between FDR and Republican Thomas Dewey looming, Mom was assigned to distribute pro-Roosevelt materials on her break time. The election outcome wasn't really in doubt, so she didn't devote a lot of time or effort to the election. Still popular, FDR handily won the 1944 election.

Two weeks before the election there was a sitdown strike by 300 workers. Their demand: get rid of Jane March! After a two hour work stoppage, Mom was moved to another department. It made the Chicago Tribune. The strikers alleged that Mom was away from her job "for hours every day, collecting CIO political slush funds...and teaching communism." In typical red-baiting style, the Trib pointed out, "She is the wife of Herb March, nee Marich...who is said to have communist affiliations." Three days later, after daily work stoppages, there was a hearing of management, union representatives and spokesmen for the complaining workers. As the Tribune put it, "Officials of the CIO Automobile Workers union, including Carl Swanson, a left-winger, backed Mrs. March. A showdown was forced at a meeting." In the end, Jane agreed to a transfer.

With scores of fellow workers against her, Mom felt rather than endure it, she would leave. Mom's departure was an early instance of what women encountered at war's end, when they were pushed out to make jobs available for returning male veterans.

After all the stress at Studebaker, Mom needed a break and took an opportunity to vacation in Florida. Mom accepted a left-wing Chicago physician's offer to stay in a house a short distance from Atlantic coast beaches. Pa was busy with union business, so Mom enlisted Vicky to come along, and with the two boys they took a train to Florida.

Herb and Jane had a good and loving marriage which lasted nearly seventy years, but it wasn't a perfect union. I learned from both of them that there was some infidelity on both their parts. Mom confided that she had a flirtation with a man named Johnny during the 1944 sojourn in Florida. "Because I was lonely, I necked with this guy a little bit. So what?" Pa must have found out somehow. Late in life, when he was beginning to suffer dementia, he dwelled on the distant past. He scribbled notes concerning his feelings about Mom's "affair" 57 years earlier. "1944, the best year of my career," he scribbled, "and the worst year of my marriage." He challenged Mom's contention that she never loved Johnny. "How could a man propose marriage to a woman that would involve two divorces and four kids if the woman never said she loved him?" I don't think the issue was ever resolved during the few months Pa had to live.

Mom also confided that Pa had had an affair with a woman who worked in the UPWA's Milwaukee office. He wasn't very discreet. "He wanted to get caught," Mom contended. She put an end to the affair. Much later my brothers and I learned there is a woman in Milwaukee who might be our half-sister. Nonetheless their marriage withstood these stresses.

After the Florida vacation, the travelers returned to Chicago where early in 1945 sister Agnes recruited Mom to become involved with a Yugoslav war relief organization. Aggie and husband Nick Daniels had moved to Detroit in 1942, where they helped organize the All Slav Congress, an ethnic political event that advocated support for Eastern Europeans in the coming post-war world. Through the group, United Committee of South Slavic Americans (UCSSA), Croatian-, Serbian- and Slovenian-Americans, urged US support for Tito's Partisans and raised funds to assist war victims in Yugoslavia.

The garrulous and charming Nikola Grgurović Daniels joined our family in the summer of 1935. Mom's brother Joe met Nick at a Lake Michigan beach. They struck up a conversation and Joe invited Nick to visit the Grbac house. There he met Agnes who had recently recovered from her back operation, and their life-long romance began.

Nick was born in 1907 in Stupin, a rocky poverty-stricken village near the Croatian coast. At age 12 he shipped out as a cabin boy on merchant vessels, serving as a seaman for 15 years. Life at sea was his university. He became conversant in several languages and skilled at maintaining ships' engines, even learning to fabricate engine parts. Nick was popular with children. As a boy I loved hearing the wild and improbable yarns from his seafaring days. At Croatian picnics, he brought a pocketful of dollar bills and handed them out to all the kids. It was a substantial gift. You could get ten bottles of pop for a dollar.

Like many mariners in that era, he was exposed to leftist ideas percolating among seamen and became a convinced communist. Nick jumped ship in New York early in the 1930s, entering the country undocumented. With his machinist's skills, he got work in on-shore factories.

Like Pa had done in New Jersey, Nick stenciled communist slogans with red paint on Chicago streets. He and some comrades cut a hole in the floorboard of his car. While stopped at intersections, they hastily stenciled slogans on the pavement. Nick chuckled that cops directing traffic saw the slogans appear, seemingly out of nowhere.

After Nick and Aggie married Nick worked in an east side steel mill. With the entry of the US into the war, due to fears of sabotage and espionage, tight controls were put on factories. Nick, an undocumented immigrant, couldn't get a job in any industrial plant. Through connections to Vicky's family, they learned of and purchased a vineyard in Michigan where they figured they could spend the war years raising Concord grapes.

Driving from Chicago to the farm, Nick and Aggie stopped in a rural bar for lunch. Nick got into a conversation with a stranger. He complained that despite having machinist skills that could assist the war effort, he couldn't use them because of his immigration status. The stranger, whose name was Brennan, became intrigued. "You tell me you really can do all these things?" he queried. "Yes," Nick assured him. "Wait a minute. I'm going to make a phone call."

In a few minutes Brennan returned. Well connected in Detroit, he said he had just been assured of financial backing if Nick would become his partner in a machine shop. Improbably, it all came to pass. They rented the farm to some locals. The Brennan & Daniels machine shop in Hamtramck, Michigan proved to be lucrative. They fabricated parts for the tanks, jeeps and planes Detroit was producing. Nick and Aggie bought a substantial brick duplex and Nona moved in with them.

Much like Chicago, Detroit had a big community of Croatians and other South Slavs with a strong leftist movement. Aggie became noted in the community as a singer and on-air hostess of the Croatian Radio Hour.

When news of the anti-Axis uprising in Yugoslavia first

reached the United States in 1942, there were only unreliable reports. The Yugoslav government in exile in London shouted the praises of Colonel Draža Mihajlović and his Četniks. By that time however, the Četniks had ceased resisting the occupiers and tacitly allied with the Italian Army. The Partisans, multi-ethnic guerillas under Communist leadership, aggressively attacked the occupying forces and gained effective control in the mountains. Their slogan was "Death to fascism, freedom to the people." The Partisans asserted they would not accept a post-war return of the dictatorial royal government.

A propaganda battle ensued in the US; a royalist Serbi-an-American newspaper was mouthpiece for the Yugoslav ambassador, while leftist South Slav papers touted the Partisans and Tito. Aggie and Nick worked in Detroit to urge financial and political support for the Partisan cause and persuaded Mom to assist the group's efforts in Chicago.

Based on reports from British officers who clandestinely entered Yugoslavia, Churchill declared the Partisans a "far more formidable" force, waging a "wild and furious war" against the Germans. The US State Department still wavered, reluctant to abandon the royal government. UCSSA efforts helped turn the tide in US policy and Allied support swung completely to the Partisans and their vow, "Death to the Fascists!"

The Difficult Decade, 1945-1955

The decade following the end of World War II in 1945 was the hardest of Pa's life. He went from the pinnacle of success to being exiled from his calling at the age of only 42, at loose ends and forced to find a new life in a new city.

At the start of that fateful decade, the last year of the War, 11-year-old Bob knew our father was an important man. He only had to look at our car. It sported A, B, and C gasoline ration stickers, the maximum, entitling Pa to more fuel than needed. To the packinghouse workers he personified their militant union, speaking often to admiring crowds at CIO Corner. He traveled to Washington, DC, where met with high officials like Vice President Henry Wallace, with whom he shared progressive principles.

But a decade later, in the spring of 1955, I saw his life totally changed around. Pa and I sat together in Aggie and Nick's Los Angeles living room watching cartoons on TV. Even as a third-grader I knew it was strange. In Chicago it had been my duty, as Pa was leaving in the morning, to shout down the stairway from the third floor, "Will you be home for supper?" The usual answer was "No!" He was a busy man, his life filled with meetings and people to see. Now he was watching Bugs Bunny. I enjoyed his company, but my father seemed moody. Today I would say depressed.

By 1955 he was expelled from the CP. He had perennial quarrels with them, yet the Party was like a surrogate family. He hoped it might yet come to its senses. He had decided to quit his job as an organizer for his union home, UPWA Local 347, the Chicago Armour local, where he was only treading water. By 1955 he was desperate for a change.

When the Difficult Decade began in 1945, there was built-up worker discontent in American industries. Wages were frozen at 1941 levels, and in spite of supposed price freezes, the Labor Department estimated cost-of-living had risen by 28% from 1941 to

1944. Industries reaped record wartime profits, but now with the war ended, workers lost the overtime hours that augmented their frozen wages, effectively, a pay cut. After four years of adhering to a no-strike pledge, the workers were ready to act.

During the year following World War II there was a wave of strikes, more than in any other twelve-month period in American history: 4,630 work stoppages involving 5 million strikers. The Truman Administration had tilted toward business and had no intention of placating workers, a sign of worse things to come. In fall, 1945, oil workers went on a coast-to-coast strike. Calling the strike a threat to national security, Truman ordered the Navy to seize the refineries. The Oil Workers Union complied with Navy commanders and ordered its members to return to work with only a vague promise of a government inquiry into their grievances.

In November, 1945 the UAW led auto workers out on strike. The government intervened and recommended an inadequate 17½¢ raise. January, 1946 was the height of the strike wave. Autoworkers, electrical workers and steelworkers were on strike, as were packinghouse workers, who walked-out against the Big Four meatpackers (Armour, Swift, Wilson and Cudahy).

Unlike the UAW and the Steelworkers, large bureaucratic CIO unions, the UPWA ensured there would be democratic participation in important strike-related decisions. They formed a broad-based strike strategy committee and a 200-member conference group with all locals represented. The membership voted 20 to 1 to authorize a strike to begin January 16. The leaders of the Amalgamated Meat Cutters reluctantly bowed to their membership's wishes and agreed to have the Big Four workers they represented also go on strike with the UPWA. Broad community support for the union was aroused by Chicago's Back-of-the-Yards Council.

The work stoppage was effective, curtailing meat production. Ten days into the strike, Truman sent the Army to seize the packing plants, ordered the workers to return and as in oil, auto and steel, offered only non-binding government recommendations for a raise. This was worthless. In the auto and steel strikes, GM and US Steel refused to honor the government proposals. The UPWA defied the Army's back-to-work order unless they received assurances that the government recommendations would be binding.

The Army might take over the plants, but "you can't skin a steer with a bayonet," Pa declared. The UPWA's militant stance paid off; they got assurances, but not before the AMC, in its treacherous manner, immediately called off its strike and ordered members back without even consulting the UPWA.

The 16¢ raise the UPWA received was less than the 25¢ goal they set before the strike, but in a low wage industry like meat packing, it was still significant. The well-disciplined strike persuaded the packers to bide their time, agreeing to an additional 10¢ raise at the next contract reopener the following December.

During the strike it became obvious that Louis Clark, the compromise selection for UPWA President at the 1943 founding convention, was incapable of competent leadership. The union's general counsel Ralph Helstein had to step in for the confused president. Clark's performance was so bad that sentiment prevailed to replace him at the next union convention that summer in Montreal. A consensus emerged that despite never having worked in a packinghouse, the union's lawyer Helstein, an honest and progressive man not associated with any internal faction, was the logical person for union president.

As the intention to replace Clark with Helstein became known, the move was vociferously opposed both by national CIO leaders and the Communist Party. CIO and CP leaders descended upon the convention to throw their weight around. Pa responded to their threats by telling them to "Go scratch! We're doing this thing!" Ralph Helstein was elected then and re-elected at every UPWA convention until 1968.

The brewing Cold War and the domestic anti-Communist hysteria commonly called the McCarthy era provided an opportunity for the industrialists to weaken the CIO. In the growing red-scare climate, they claimed the CIO was "Communist-controlled," that disloyal Communist union bosses could manipulate union members and might cripple the country's economy, using strikes to advance the interests of the Soviet Union. Congressional "investigators" of the House Un-American Activities Committee and Joe McCarthy's Senate Internal Security Sub-Committee brought their traveling shows to union towns to smear leftist unionists, the hearings widely trumpeted in the press. In the media's message, militant unionism equaled communism.

The National Association of Manufacturers and large firms like General Electric and Inland Steel loudly advocated for legislation to outlaw the most effective union tactics, eliminate the leftists, the most dedicated unionists and plunge unions into fratricidal red-baiting fights. Republican victories in 1946 brought a conservative Congress to Washington, ready to do their bidding. The Taft-Hartley Act, which curtailed union rights and political liberties, was written by industry lobbyists. It was so extreme that Truman, worried about losing labor support in the next elections, vetoed it. Nonetheless Taft-Hartley passed over Truman's veto in June, 1947.

The law had dozens of provisions to weaken unions. Among its most anti-democratic sections was a clause that required officers of all unions to sign "non-communist affidavits," swearing they were not members of the Communist Party. If a union was deemed out of compliance with Taft-Hartley, it would not be allowed protections of the National Labor Relations Board, opening them up to be "raided" by a rival union. Their name would not be allowed on an NLRB election ballot.

During the 1930s, Communist Party members like Pa and friends such as Bob Travis and Wyndham Mortimer in the Auto Workers, Joe Weber in the Steel Workers, and Ernie DeMaio in United Electrical Workers were among the most dedicated and effective union organizers. They won the respect and trust of non-communist workers by militantly advocating for the workers' interests. They operated in an honest, pragmatic manner and frequently had to ignore misguided dictates of the Communist Party.

Ironically, at the peak of the red scare, the Communist Party had adopted an evolutionary line. In 1944 CP president Earl Browder decided that capitalism and communism could co-exist, dissolved the Party, and asked Communists to work within the system to advance progressive causes. The Hollywood writer Ring Lardner, a Browder supporter, explained: "The change [was]...in line with reality. Our political activities, by then, were virtually identical to those of our liberal friends."

At war's end, Browder's move met with Stalin's disapproval. In

July, 1945, the Party was reconstituted. Browder was replaced by William Z. Foster. The Party's politics, however, remained scarcely revolutionary. In foreign affairs they encouraged US-Soviet friendship and their domestic agenda supported liberal causes. CP officials went so far as to order Pa not to "allow" the packinghouse workers to go on strike lest it threaten national security! But as far as the promoters of the Red Scare were concerned, the CP was a useful bogeyman, dangerous revolutionaries conspiring to overthrow the government by force and violence.

Unions that were supposedly "Communist-controlled," such as the UPWA, the West Coast longshoreman's union (ILWU), United Electrical Workers (UE), and Mine, Mill and Smelter Workers were the most democratic. They had the highest levels of rank-and-file power and fought for racial and women's equality. For years leftist unionists struggled against bureaucratic officials in the AFL and CIO; now Taft-Hartley's non-communist provision handed a mighty weapon to the conservative unionists.

Initially the AFL and CIO condemned Taft-Hartley and vowed to work for its repeal. John L. Lewis denounced the act as "the first, ugly, savage thrust of fascism in America." But united resistance crumbled. Unwilling to do without NLRB protections, the AFL and CIO soon agreed to comply and seized the opportunity to raid locals of leftist-led unions.

When Taft-Hartley passed, Pa was director of District 1, a post that made him an executive board member. Ralph Helstein and a majority of the board opposed signing the affidavits rejecting communism, although a conservative faction, hoping to get rid of Pa, warned that the NLRB protections were essential to UPWA's survival. They demanded that Pa and Meyer Stern, a second Communist on the board, either sign, resign or be kicked off. Pa argued that a union cannot rely upon government benevolence for its strength. They must, in an era of repression, rely upon their own unity and militancy, just as in the pre-Wagner Act days.

Citing their constitutional rights, Pa and Stern refused to sign or resign. The majority on the board understood that the two Communist directors were popular in their districts. If they were booted, they would just be re-elected. Hoping the law might be declared un-Constitutional, the UPWA voted to continue to resist

Taft-Hartley.

At the beginning of 1948 packinghouse contracts came open. Again the main issue was low wages. The UPWA demanded a 29¢ increase while the packers offered only 9¢. In February, 90% of the members voted to authorize a strike. With the legal advantages provided by Taft-Hartley, the packers were keen to take on the union. A bitter 10-week strike began which demonstrated how much Taft-Hartley shifted the playing field in favor of employers.

Again, the union lined up strong community support. Local businesses extended credit, landlords were patient about rent and whole families could get meals in strike kitchens—including a Mexican kitchen that union staffer Refugio Martinez set up.

Pa hoped to avert a strike:

> One of the first things we did was attempt to get the City of Chicago behind us to get a settlement without resorting to a strike. So a delegation of us met with the new mayor Martin Kennelly, a so-called liberal Democrat, a so-called reform mayor who was as phony as a nine dollar bill. He spoke about his pro-labor sentiment....At any rate, we went to see Kennelly, and...we pressed him to use the favors and benefits the City was providing the packers as leverage to get them to settle without a strike.
>
> One comment I made in the meeting was that we should avert a strike because if it comes to one, it wasn't likely to be a Sunday School picnic—we're dealing with people with deep feelings and if there is an effort to break the strike, our membership will fight back. Kennelly used that remark as an excuse to visit upon us as much repression as ever was seen in a strike in Chicago.

After the delay required by the Taft-Hartley Act, giving the packers additional time to prepare, the strike began on March 16, 1948. The difference in the city government's attitude was immediately apparent.

> On the night the strike was called—it was called at midnight— there were so damn many police, they must have had about 8,000 police around the gates of the stockyards. A third to a half of the entire Chicago police force was involved in strike duty. They had so many

cops that night they marched in military formation. When our pickets got out to the gate, it looked like it was raining police.

It wasn't feasible to run the packinghouses with scabs, the product they produced was virtually useless. Nonetheless, to crush strikers' morale, the packers brought in scab labor. Through "scab-herding," they tried to incite confrontations on the picket lines, knowing that a serious incident would enable them to get an injunction from a compliant judge to restrict picketing.

The packers ordered all their supervisors to stay in, to sleep in the plant and used some agencies to dig up scabs from all over. They brought in Pullman cars to house some of the scabs and the elevated was used to bring them into the plants.

The packers had invested big money building a spur line of the Chicago elevated railway that ran directly into the plants. It was possible to take a train to the packinghouses where passengers could exit without ever touching the street. In his story of how the strikers dealt with this challenge, Pa didn't quite approve of their tactics, but his chuckles made it clear that he admired their militancy.

In the '46 strike the street railwaymen's union refused to run the special stockyard El train, but with Taft-Hartley, they were required to do it. In the early part of the strike, a few scabs used the El to come into the yards, especially the Swift plant. We decided that we'd have a little demonstration to discourage anybody from scabbing. We asked the Veterans committee of our union to wear their uniforms, you know with the discharge patch, the thing called the "ruptured duck." About a hundred and fifty vets showed up on a Monday morning about 6 AM and started riding the El. We told them to sing "Solidarity Forever" and speak to people about not going in. If they were office personnel, not to bother them, but if people were attempting to scab, to see what they could do to persuade them not to. Well, they got tired of singing after a few minutes, and on the first trainload with a number of scabs, they made them promise not to get off at the stockyards. They ran into a few who got snotty and were unwilling. So what the boys did, from what was told to me later, they knocked on the little cubicle the engineer was in, asked him to stop the train and he did. Then they grabbed the scab who was the most obnoxious, and two of the guys, one holding each ankle, dangled him out the train window head down. They directed the engineer to slowly start up and they kept dipping this guy saying, "Are you going to scab, you son-of-a-bitch, or are you going to be a decent man?" The guy was screaming, squawking, promising, "I'll do anything you say. Please take me up!" He was 30 or 40 feet above the ground, dangling out of an El train window, and of course everyone around saw this happening. As a result, for at least four weeks afterwards, no scabs attempted to take the train in.

Packinghouse union rally

If this epitomized the militancy of the packinghouse workers, Pa's next account indicated the deadly ends to which the packers would go to break the union. In '46, Teamsters used to respect the picket lines; now this was illegal. The packers sent truckloads of supplies through the picket lines, leading to a fatal confrontation at the Armour soapworks.

The Armour soapworks plant was shut down tight. There were a few supervisory people who were attempting to carry on a pretense of operations. Some truck drivers were delivering materials. There had been arguments at the soapworks plant gate and the Industrial Detail, headed by Police Captain Barnes decided they were going to take over the situation. I subsequently learned from a reporter, before this incident occurred, that Captain Barnes boasted that he was going to see to it that situation was "straightened out...."

The next day a big semi-truck arrived from somewhere in Ohio. It pulled up with a load of material and a small picket line was circling in front of the plant gate. The driver got as far as the picket line and stopped. When he did that, Captain Barnes himself climbed into the cab alongside the driver and he told him to proceed. The driver was hesitant at first, but Barnes insisted that he move. He did and the picket line sort of backed up. They were sort of intimidated; they continued to circle and picket, but backed up slowly as the truck inched forward. Then Barnes told the driver, "Come on, step on it, go right on through." The pickets scattered but some of them were unable to get out of the way fast enough. One of the pickets, Santo Cicardo, a young man in his thirties, a father of two kids, was run over by the truck and killed. Following that there was an immediate injunction slapped on picketing at the plant gate at Armour soapworks.

The Chicago Tribune ran an implausible story that a mob of strikers attacked the truck and, attempting to escape, the driver ran over Cicardo. An inquest was held, without the driver required to attend, which whitewashed the entire incident. Pa firmly believed Captain Barnes deliberately set out to kill or injure a picket. The union held a mass funeral. Six thousand solemn, angry strikers marched down Ashland Avenue. The authorities must have been conscious of the workers' rage, there were no police in sight.

Two other strikers were killed in Iowa; the governors of Iowa and Minnesota called out bayonet-wielding National Guardsmen to escort scabs into the plants. The packers were determined to hold out and do anything necessary to destroy the UPWA. After ten weeks, the members voted to accept the miserable 9¢ raise and end the strike.

When the workers returned, foremen and supervisors attempted to lord it over them. This made it obvious to the workers that they needed their union. Pa had an anecdote about the taming of a scab that exemplified the post-strike militancy.

Immediately after the workers went back, with Armour & Company acting arrogant, a remark made at one of the first meetings after the strike summed up the workers' feelings, "They're treating us like dogs, but every dog has his day." We were determined to rebuild the union and things started happening, you know. For example there were some guys who scabbed in the mechanical department. Well tools started dropping off of scaffolds close to these guys....They made the scabs know how they felt about them. And there are a million and one ways when an overwhelming majority is pro-union. Most of the scabs just left because life was made miserable by the union men.

Then the guys decided in Armour that the best way of letting the company know where they stood was to make it a union shop. We didn't have a union shop agreement so they decided they were going to make it a union shop themselves. They raised the cry, "In the union or out of the plant." And they proceeded to go to work. There was one guy in the beef-boning gang at Armour who came in as a scab in 1921 and he scabbed in 1946 at a time when they couldn't even use him. He just sat in the damn place during the ten day strike. And he had scabbed again in 1948. He was a pretty hard-nosed character who thought himself tough and he wouldn't let anybody push him around. He had never joined the union. So the guys in beef boning decided that they were going to make that son-of-a-bitch join the union. I told them to forget about it. What's one lousy scab? "No sir, no sir," they told me, "You leave it to us. We'll take care of it."

One day the whistle blew at noon and this scab started to leave the boning table for lunch and there were about fifty other beef boners around him, each with his knife pouch on. If you know these boners, you don't have one knife, because you're working piece work and you've got to go like hell and you got to keep a bunch of knives sharp.

The guy said, "Get out of my way." And they said, "No, wait a minute, we want to talk to you." And he says, "I got to go." And they said, "Not until we're through talking to you." This went on and before long there were about four hundred guys gathered around. He didn't want to talk and they said, "Well if you insist that you don't want to talk, all you have to do is just sign the check-off card for your initiation fee and union dues." He wouldn't do it and they said, "All right then, we'll wait," And they did, for some hours. Armour sent over their deputized police force. They had guns and clubs. By that time there were eight hundred or so people crowded into the place, and of course, work wasn't going on. This was payday so I guess a few of the guys had gotten a half pint and were making a celebration out of it. Finally some of the guys started getting angry. They started hollering, "Let me at him!" So the stewards took him into a room for his protection. The men were getting angrier and banging on the door; one of the stewards asked the company policemen, "What are you guys going to do?" They said, "Nothing. We're just looking." And that's all they did, look. See, there was this bitterness among the workers and determination to stick to the union was such a force the company couldn't contend with it. Well this guy signed, and when he did, everybody else that was not in the union signed and the stewards proceeded to go from department to department and mopped up the rest of the scabs.

The packers may have thought they had broken the union when they won the strike. But they soon learned otherwise. The workers revived shop floor militancy to reassert their power in the plants.

After the loss of the strike, the union's board decided that they had no choice but to become compliant with Taft-Hartley. The Amalgamated Meat Cutters, with the connivance of the packers set out to raid UPWA locals. Twenty-four union representation elections were slated. Pa still was adamant that he would not renounce his political affiliations under government duress. Rather than sign an affidavit, he resigned as District Director to enable the UPWA to appear on the NLRB ballots.

He wrote an impassioned statement in the union newspaper asserting that his communist views were well known to the membership, that he had a right to his beliefs, and that union members had a right to elect him to office. Nonetheless he consented to step aside to avoid a split in the UPWA over the issue of Taft-Hartley compliance. It was a time when the union needed unity more than ever.

The UPWA appeared on the NLRB ballots and they swept all 24 elections with an average margin of 4 to 1. Packinghouse workers had no truck with the collaborationist AMC and remained fiercely loyal to the UPWA.

After his resignation as an officer, Helstein hired Pa as Field Representative, a staff position. This arrangement satisfied legal requirements, but there still was political pressure from the CIO brass to get rid of him. In 1949 Philip Murray expelled eleven left-leaning unions from the CIO and raided their ranks. Under the threat of expulsion, Ralph Helstein buckled to CIO pressure and fired Pa.

In a tense meeting with Helstein and union vice president Tony Stephens, Stephens told Pa he was "too heavy for them to carry." Helstein made up a bogus rationale that Pa was hard to work with and unreasonable. Pa responded, "I'm not worried about myself. I'll just go back to work for my local. I'll be around. What I'm worried about is, what does this say about you, Ralph?"

Ralph Helstein paid for firing Pa. Their mutual friend Saul Alinsky was furious with him. It broke their friendship. Years later Pa and Ralph met up in California, talked heart-to-heart into the wee hours and Pa forgave him. Pa contended that Helstein did a good job of preserving the UPWA as a progressive, democratic union. He felt only that "Ralph could have fought a little harder" to resist the anti-leftist wave, to hold out until the implosion of McCarthyism which turned out to be only a few years off.

After his firing from the International's staff in 1949, Pa worked for six years as an organizer for UPWA Local 347. He continued to be the face of the union, accessible to members, a frequent speaker at CIO Corner. I had the good fortune to see this. Mom started to work outside the home again and sometimes Pa took me to his union office. I remember walking with Pa on the dirty, narrow stockyard streets flanked by the stark brick packing plants and down packinghouse hallways painted in shiny institutional green. It seemed to me that every few strides Pa stopped to talk with a burly worker. Their bloody aprons were at my three foot-high eye level.

Decades later I realized Pa was using me, the little boy tugging his arm, as a handy excuse to shorten those conversations. When he couldn't take me with him through the stockyards, I was comfortable being left for a while in the union hall. The workers kidded me gently and kept an eye on me. One time I was playing the pinball machine in the hall when, to my shock, bells started chiming and a stream of nickels came pouring out of the coin return. I started to cry. I was scared stiff that I had broken the thing and would get in trouble. A worker rushed over and doffing his cap, used it to gather up my jackpot for me. He explained that I had "hit a twenty," winning a dollar's worth of nickels.

Pa's recollections of that era are rife with having to contend with the unrelenting hostility of the companies. "Two-bit confrontations" he called them.

I was driving the sound truck; we were announcing a meeting and Armour complained to the police. The police came down, arrested me, had me drive my sound truck over to the Stockyards station and threw me in the cell. I sat down, made myself comfortable, took out my newspaper and relaxed. But I didn't get much of a chance to read the paper before they came and said, "Will you please leave; all charges have been dropped." A number of workers saw the arrest and they went to Armour & Company management and said, "Look, you had Herb and our sound truck arrested. If you don't withdraw the complaint and release him, we're going to walk out."...There was this kind of crap day in and day out.

Another confrontation involved an altercation with Captain Barnes.

On a given date the union stewards would be in all the plant gates and el stations to check whether you carried a card. We called upon everybody to cooperate by carrying their union dues card and showing it when they came in. The office personnel who were ineligible for the union showed their company pass. Well, whenever we conducted these things the packers would get all shook up. They felt there was intimidation of non-members, and I guess it was. The bulk of workers were in the union and non-members were not held in high esteem. You gave them a card to sign. Quite often guys signed up at that time. It was a recruiting thing that was effective with new people.

Well we had a dues card inspection one day and Captain Barnes and his squad were down, Chicago policemen, most of them plain-clothes men. We had a couple of our guys checking in the El station. One was chief steward of the pork cut. He and another steward were there and Barnes came trotting down. Barnes was dressed in plain clothes, so one steward asked him, "Show me your card." And Barnes' response was a little bit of vulgarity, you know. He cussed him and told him to go to hell or something like that. And the steward said, "Now wait a minute, we're just talking to you. Show us your identification." What Barnes could very well have done, and he had two plain clothes men behind him, was to show his police card and that would have been it. But he says, "I don't have to show you a goddamn thing!" He pushed this steward, and of course the chief steward and the other steward pushed back and Barnes went down on his fanny. These fellows were not delicate little wallflowers. Barnes popped up indignantly and he and his two cohorts placed them under arrest, took them right over to the police station.

Well I learned that this had happened and I went up to see Barnes, who had set up a little command post right in the middle of the stockyards. I said, "Look, Captain, I want you to drop charges against these men. What's the idea of arresting men for carrying on dues inspection?" And he said, "Well, they pushed me." And I said, "Well you must have pushed them first." He said, "Don't tell me how to run my business. They're arrested and they're going to stay right there." Well I got perturbed and I said, "Look Barnes, I'm going to tell you something. Those men are the leaders of the pork division." This was early in the morning. "If they don't start work this morning, nobody is going to work there and in a couple hours Armour & Company is going to lose about $25,000. Now if you don't give a damn, I don't give a damn, so suit yourself!" I started to walk away. I got about fifteen feet and he came charging up to me, "Herb, Herb, we'll release the men, we'll release the men, we'll work out a deal."

Spoiled Meat

The adversarial relationship was personal between Pa, the company supervisors and their police stooges. The packers had done their utmost to smash the UPWA and failed. The union was still strong in their plants. The 1948 strike had cost the companies millions of dollars. Moreover, the Big Four were losing market share to a host of smaller meat companies, a trend that was accelerated by the strike when their customers sought new sources of meat during the long shutdown. The last thing they wanted was another strike. During the decade following 1948, they dragged their feet, but were obliged to consent to union demands for wage hikes, working condition improvements and racial equality.

All the while, the packers were making plans to abandon the large unionized packingtowns, Chicago, Kansas City, and Omaha. Owing to automation, the developing interstate highway system and refrigerated semi-trucks, they began to shift production to small plants in small towns nearer the big western herds of cattle where there were no unions.

By the 1950s there was equilibrium and Pa didn't get much satisfaction dealing with two-bit confrontations in the Armour plant. Those could be handled by stewards. He began to focus on issues of racial equality, both in the industry and the wider community.

A dedication to civil rights had been important to him ever since his pioneering efforts on the Great Plains, fighting legal lynchings. In 1936 he was one of the few whites in the core group that organized the National Negro Congress. A prominent slogan of the UPWA was "Negro and White, Unite and Fight," the black and white hands clasped in a handshake on the union logo.

By the 1950s, the proportion of African-American workers in the packinghouses had grown, as white workers moved to higher paying jobs. African-Americans constituted about 70% of Chicago's packinghouse workers. In 1945, under the co-chairmanship of Pa and UPWA Vice-President Phil Weightman, an African-American, the union formed the Anti-Discrimination Committee (the A-D Committee) to fight racism. In the plants, they pushed for integration of lily-white departments like sliced bacon and mechanical maintenance, and they undertook efforts outside the plants to end discrimination in the wider community. Pa led a delegation to meet with Chicago Transit Authority officials to demand that they begin to hire African-Americans as train engineers.

Pa's anti-racist fervor was obvious to his African-American colleagues, and their affection and admiration for him was likewise palpable. The noted civil rights and feminist activist Rev. Addie Wyatt, who in 1941 began work in Armour's canning department, was influenced to become a union activist by Pa's CIO Corner oratory. In 1950 she became a union staff member where she worked with Pa for the next five years. She eventually attained the offices of president of a local and international vice-president of the union, the first woman to do so. When, in her old age, I introduced myself to her as Herb March's son, she fervently gripped my hand and exclaimed, "Herb!"

Chicago was and remains an intensely segregated city. In the 1940s and 50s, the strict boundaries of the Black Belt began to be challenged. Urban segregation had been imposed both by custom and law. Until 1948 there were legally-recognized restrictive covenants that forbade blacks from living in specific areas. Brother Bob recalled that when we lived on 61st and Ingleside, he frequented a radio repair shop on 63rd Street. The business was run by two African-American technicians who had become skilled in radio while serving in the Army. Even though their homes were in a black neighborhood, their landlord received complaints about the presence of a black-run business in a "whites only" zone, forcing the shop to close.

Bob grew up near Cottage Grove Avenue, and used the streetcar along that thoroughfare. The streetcar stops were on pedestrian islands beside the tracks. Bob recalls that blacks, when waiting for a northbound streetcar, which stopped by the island on the east "white" side of the avenue, waited on the west side, crossing only when the streetcar came, so they could board without lingering on the "wrong" side of the street.

Housing issues exploded in Chicago after the war. The federal government funded more projects like the Ida B. Wells Homes, still requiring that the racial composition of neighborhoods should not be altered by new developments. That became harder to enforce after a 1948 Supreme Court decision banned restrictive covenants. It became impossible to contain in the Black Belt an African-American population swelling from a wave of migration from the Deep South. The city's power brokers allowed the ghetto to expand only into nearby older neighborhoods while preserving actual segregation. Integrated neighborhoods were actually "neighborhoods in transition" changing from all white to all black.

Private realty companies and speculators reaped huge profits by "block busting." After "Block busters" sold a property to African-Americans, they provoked panic selling among white residents with rumors that the neighborhood was "changing." They pestered worried whites with offers to buy, gobbled up properties at low prices, and resold them at a profit to African-Americans.

In these neighborhoods, it became common for black home buyers to be "greeted" by white mobs. Chicago was boiling over with race riots that the white police did little to contain. The UPWA publicly decried racist outbursts and organized inter-racial squads of packinghouse workers to guard besieged new arrivals through the worst of the disturbances. The UPWA also picketed City Hall to demand effective police protection in the areas hit by rioting white racists.

Sam Parks, a militant black packinghouse worker, became active with the A-D Committee. He participated in campaigns to pressure banks, department stores and other companies to hire blacks. He and two other packinghouse workers staged a sit-in at the lunch counter of the Goldblatt's Department Store at 47th and Ashland, the store where Mom had worked as a teenager. The lunch counter waitresses often ignored black patrons until they finally left. Parks' sit-in got results. "We kept on there until the head of the Goldblatt chain came out, one of the old Goldblatt brothers, and promised me, 'Mr. Parks, from now on you all will be able to sit in any Goldblatt's store...and eat like dignified ladies and gentlemen.'"

Originally from Memphis, Parks moved to Chicago in 1940. In 1944 he was elected president of UPWA Local 25 at Wilson. In a 1980s interview, Parks declared that he originally did not intend to become a trade unionist. When he came to Chicago, work at Wilson was just his "day job" while he attended evening law school. "I was going to get to be a lawyer quick, and after I got my degree in law, I was going to fuck over, freak up, rob Negroes, make me some money and get rich." His fellow workers at Wilson, however, noted Parks' assertiveness and pressed him to represent them in grievances, and later to run against Dock Williams, the black, non-militant president of the local.

Like several African-American UPWA activists, Parks joined the union's Communist Party cell. He viewed the CP as the most militant organization on racial issues. Although CP members fought Jim Crow and discrimination, the CP adopted a perplexing party line on race relations in the US, influenced by Stalin's nationalities policy in the Soviet Union. In 1928, Stalin decreed that American Negroes were entitled to self-determination in a sort of Negro SSR to be carved out of parts of several Southern states where African-Americans constituted a majority. The CPUSA balked at accepting this policy, which was obviously inapplicable to the American situation. The notion was eventually adopted as party line in 1931, but there never were attempts to work towards its actual implementation. The concept nonetheless was discussed in Party circles and fostered anti-integrationist, black power, black self-sufficiency ideas among African-American CP members, including Sam Parks.

Hungry for personal power, Parks used the union and the CP to promote his own advancement. When he was fired during the 1948 strike, he made no effort to get the job back. "I stayed out and became a local business agent, and I wore my good suits. Good clothes. And I wore 'em because down in Memphis I never did get 'em. Going to live good." The following fall he ran for political office. "I ran on the Progressive Party ticket against Congressman [William] Dawson. I was the only candidate on the Progressive Party ticket in the whole state of Illinois when Henry Wallace ran."

Parks was jealous of the workers' devotion to Pa. Even with his loss of an official role, Pa was still an influential and revered figure. Utilizing the black power concept in the CP's party line, Parks began to conspire with Richard Durham, another Party member in UPWA's employ, to have Pa expelled from the union's Party cell. Durham was a writer and well-known radio producer in Chicago. His "Destination Freedom" radio series was one of the first broadcast series to promote black history and challenge stereotypes of African-Americans. Durham had been hired to produce pamphlets for the Anti-Discrimination Committee. Inspired by the Party's black self-determination line, Durham evolved into a fervent black nationalist. A few years later he became the editor of *Muhammed Speaks*, the newspaper of the Nation of Islam.

Pa recalled that one day at work at the Local 347 office, Leon Beverly, the local's president told Pa that they needed to go to a secret meeting of the Party cell. Pa was disgusted by how they reached the meeting place. They left the union hall in Pa's car, driving to a building where they went in the front door, then slipped out the back into another car waiting in the alley and finally arrived at the meeting site. "I didn't go for that cloak and dagger bullshit," Pa commented wryly.

Sam Parks informed Pa that he had been expelled due to his "white chauvinism," because Pa had opposed a Party directive that all leadership positions in Chicago-centered District 1 must be held by blacks. Pa advocated that whites should be represented in proportion to their portion of the membership. Pa noticed the hangdog expressions of Leon Beverly, Charlie Hayes and other friends in the group. It was clear they were chagrined but they wouldn't dare speak up for him.

"Don't I get to have a trial?" Pa queried.

Parks responded, "Oh, you've already had a trial, a good trial, and you were found guilty." An active anti-racist and civil rights crusader since his teens, Pa was expelled from the CP for white chauvinism. The words of Sam Parks himself, in an oral history interview, only add to the irony. "I think Herb March made a hell of a contribution to the advancement of blacks in this union. He made a hell of a contribution. If it hadn't been for guys like Herb working with guys much like myself and other blacks, then the Packinghouse union wouldn't have had the progressive policies and programs that it had."

With his expulsion, Pa decided to resign from his job at Local 347 and leave Chicago. The idea had been percolating for a while. The previous summer we made a months-long cross-country road trip seeing friends and relatives along the way. Mom and Pa had a knock-down drag-out quarrel in San Francisco. At age seven I had no idea what they were hollering about. Decades later Mom told me that Pa, in his pride, refused her request to ask Harry Bridges for a job in the ILWU, the International Longshore and Warehouse Union. She was sure Bridges would hire him.

Little Brother Buddy

Early in the Difficult Decade I was added to the family, making my appearance on Christmas Eve, 1946. On the snowy evening of December 23, Pa was making the rounds to union offices making an appearance at the locals' Christmas parties. At the Ingleside apartment Mom was mixing up batter for a holiday cake when she went into labor.

Mom telephoned a union office. Yes, Herb had been there but had already left. She called another office, got the same reply. A third time, same result. She was starting to feel contractions and becoming desperate. She phoned Vicky who in minutes picked her up and, braving a snowstorm, conveyed her to Michael Reese Hospital where I was born in the wee hours of the morning.

When I was a week old I got my family nickname, Buddy. It was New Year's Day. The University of Illinois football team was playing the UCLA Bruins in the Rose Bowl. Pa and my two brothers had the game on the radio. Considering Richard too formal for everyday use, my brothers argued about a nickname for me. Bobby wanted Ricky, Billy supported Dickey. Annoyed that the boys' dispute made it hard to follow the radio play-by-play, Pa came up with a suggestion. Claude "Buddy" Young, an African-American Chicago native and star halfback for the Fighting Illini had just scored his second touchdown in the game. "Why not call him Buddy?" Pa suggested. "He's the star of the game, and besides, Buddy means little brother." So I became little brother Buddy, as family members and close family friends still call me.

Mom was 34 when I was born, the last of her three children, almost 13 years younger than Bob and 7½ years younger than Bill. With my siblings out and about engaged in their own boyhood activities, I had Mom to myself. She walked me in a stroller to nearby grocery stores. She spread crayons and watercolor sets on the dining room table. Together we created artwork on the blank back sides of leaflets urging a boycott of "unfair" Wilson meat products.

In 1947, the family moved a couple miles east to a "co-op apartment" on Lake Park Avenue. A co-op was an arrangement similar to a condominium, so my parents became homeowners for the first time. The three-story brick building constructed in the 1910s had two large apartments per floor plus a basement apartment. The "railroad apartment" floor plan was linear and long. As a child I explored it thoroughly. By the time I was five, I enjoyed riding my scooter down the long hall from the living room up front to the distant kitchen at the back—to the annoyance of the terrifying Mr. Tapper who lived in the apartment below. The building had once been the residence of wealthy people. The "butler's pantry" was a narrow, diagonal room off the kitchen with a separate entrance from the back porch. It was teenage Bob's bedroom. There was also a "powder room," a small pass-through space between the master bedroom and the bedroom Billy and I shared. It had a sink and a big mirror. Mom sat there to fix her hair and apply lipstick. I thought it odd; it was like a bathroom without a toilet. In the dining room there was a small panel covering a cavity in the floor that once housed a bell to summon servants. There was a fourth bedroom for Nona. A large back porch was accessed from the dining room. It was painted battleship gray, like the wooden structures attached to many Chicago brick buildings. From the back porch there was a commanding view of the Illinois Central railroad tracks behind our building. The back yard was bounded by a sturdy limestone wall, about five feet high that bordered the raised embankment of the railroad lines. I was accustomed to the clatter of trains, day and night. There were still black steam locomotives which gave off the shrill blast of a whistle. I learned to identify box cars, flat cars, hopper cars, tank cars, the new diesel engines that blew horns instead of whistles, the dark green, electric-powered IC commuter trains and the shiny streamliner inter-city passenger trains.

In the summer, Mom lifted me atop the limestone wall when she carried watering cans to her vegetable garden on the sunny slope below the tracks. She always planted tomatoes and a couple other crops. Mom had an obligation to plant *riga*, a spicy variety of arugula from Nerezine. Nona brought the seeds with her in

1921 and because we knew no other Americans who ate *riga*, we collected seeds each fall and replanted them every spring. Despite the availability of arugula at my local farmer's market, I still plant Nona's variety in my back yard 95 years later.

Mom had to rinse away dust on the garden plants from red cinders that lined the railroad tracks above. The parking lot next to our building was paved with those same cinders. We'd push them aside to make a flat dirt circle on which to shoot marbles or for the girls to play jacks. I had countless of these prickly cinders pulled from scrapes on my knees from inevitable tumbles on the lot while wearing short pants.

Our building had hissing steam heat radiators powered by a big coal-fueled furnace in the basement. On a couple occasions with David Hoselitz, my across-the-hall neighbor and constant playmate, I sneaked into the coal room and climbed the mountain of coal near the furnace, all the way up to the basement window into which coal deliveries were dumped. Then we slid and rolled down the coal slope, setting off avalanches. It was so much fun we dared do it once more even after we had been severely scolded by our mothers who firmly scrubbed us clean in our bathtubs. The second scolding was even more severe, but the reason we never did it again was that spring arrived and the coal mountain was so diminished it wasn't worth playing on the remaining coal mole-hill.

The flat roofs of the buildings on our block were sealed with tar. Roofers came with trucks of hot tar and hoisted buckets three stories up and spread it around. There were inevitable stray globs of tar on the pavement that we kids collected and treasured. A shiny tar glob on whose brilliant black surface rainbow colors shimmered was a rare prize. A few big boys chewed the stuff, proudly displaying their hideous black teeth, but I never dared put the poisonous-smelling goop in my mouth.

Our apartment was a frequent gathering place for my parents' friends and associates. Friends like Les and Hermione Orear, Mary and "Sippie" Siporin, or Ed and Vicky Starr came over frequently, usually bringing their kids in tow. Also there were "caucus meetings" in our living room. Five or six of Pa's union brothers would assemble to discuss matters. I was under firm orders not to make noise during the meetings. Sometimes I crawled under the chairs of the caucus members and pondered their incomprehensible discussions.

For a long time during 1954, Friday night meant my brother Bob and his wife Georgie would be over for supper and an evening of singing folk and political songs from the *People's Songbook*. Bob and Georgie, like my parents, married at the young age of 19 while students at the University of Chicago. To Bob's banjo and Georgie's guitar we sang union songs like "Joe Hill," bluesy songs like "Midnight Special" and Spanish Civil War songs like "*Si Me Quieres Escribir*."

In the building across the parking lot was the barber shop where John, a barber with a thick European accent, cut my hair. There was also the Meineses' "School Store," a Mecca for us neighborhood kids. Not only could you get school supplies—pads of coarse lined paper with a cover sheet photo of Roy Rogers or the Lone Ranger, pencils, crayons and paste—but also glorious candy. There were waxy black moustaches or little waxen bottles filled with colored sugar water, bubble gum that came with a tiny folded comic or you could get your gum in a pack of baseball cards. If you were lucky you might get our White Sox heroes Nellie Fox, Sherm Lollar or Chico Carrasquel. I got my first musical instrument there, a little harmonica. Mom told me that the Meineses, the gray-haired couple who ran the store, were Jewish refugees who got out of Germany "just in time."

Directly across Lake Park Avenue was Kenwood School, an imposing three-story brick edifice where I went to Kindergarten, and First through Third Grades. Since I became an adult, it is amazing how much the building seems to have shrunk! The entire schoolyard was paved with asphalt. We'd dash around at recess playing tag, or if we had a rubber ball, we could play "penner," bouncing it off the foundation of the school. During class time, we were allowed to place the ball in the hole in the corner of our desks where in times past there had been an inkwell. Girls brought jump ropes to school and seemed to know interminable rhymes chanted while skipping rope all through recess. "Gypsy, gypsy, tangerine, who in the world can your boyfriend be?..."

Next to the school was the Blackstone Public Library, an elegant Neo-Classical structure with a central dome flanked by symmetrical wings. Like the school, it seems to have shrunken lately. When I was old enough to safely cross the street, the library became my home away from home. The librarians got to know my interests, suggesting books I might like. Next to the library was a tall apartment building with "The Blackstone" emblazoned in big letters across the top. I was never in there. I heard it was occupied by rich elderly ladies, a remnant of the era when our street was stylish. There wasn't much stylishness left on our side of Lake Park. Our proximity to the noisy railroad tracks made it less desirable.

Over the course of my years on Lake Park, I sensed our block's rapid decline. Scruffy alcoholic street people appeared. On the sidewalk we kids found paper bags with empty liquor bottles, sometimes broken. It became my duty to take our loyal black mongrel Chico for walks down the block. There was a courtyard building that seemed prosperous, and the most amazing structure was the Harding Museum, a replica of a Scottish castle that a wealthy Chicago businessman built to house his collection of medieval weapons. I was inside only once. In the dark confines, the pikes, swords and especially the suits of armor were really creepy.

Along the block, ordinary apartment buildings like ours were growing bedraggled—more litter in front; there were broken and boarded up windows and hangers-out on the stoops. I hadn't been taught to categorize people by skin color, so I didn't understand that our block was "in transition." And though I didn't know it, the end of the block, 47th Street, was supposed to be one of segregated Chicago's neighborhood boundaries. That didn't seem to faze our family. Mom routinely took me with her shopping at 47th Street stores and our family patronized a restaurant there. After he married, my big brother lived near 47th. To me it was just part of my neighborhood.

African-Americans from the overcrowded area just a block away sought better housing. Owners of the tracks-abutting buildings on our block found it profitable to divide the big flats into small kitchenette apartments that they rented to blacks. They could get away with neglecting maintenance and reap three or four times the rental income.

I didn't realize it was a racial issue at the time, my parents did a good job of making me "color-blind." I remember when a couple new girls came into my 2nd Grade classroom. They must have come straight from a Mississippi tenant farm. I was amazed at the girls' long skirts hanging to their ankles and they wore earrings. I was startled when the boy in the next desk groaned, "Oh no, more colored!" The girls had pretty light brown skin. I was puzzled that my classmate found them offensive.

Later, Ronald Jones, a little black kid, began to harass me. He threatened me and chased me home. He snatched and ripped up a spelling test I was bringing home to Mom. The next day he pursued me again and I decided to stop. "Why are you chasing me?" I demanded. He didn't say anything; he took the copy of *Weekly Reader* from my hand. "You're not gonna tear that up!" I said emphatically. "No, I won't," he said. "Do you wanna play?" We became playmates. I also met his sisters. The girls were good at Chinese jump rope. They had a long string of rubber bands and could execute complicated jumps between its strands while chanting "Shimmy shimmy koko pop..."

When the University of Chicago was founded back in the 1890s, Hyde Park was an elegant, classy neighborhood. As the Black Belt enlarged, the University became concerned that its environs might turn into a slum their graduate students and faculty wouldn't live in. To keep Hyde Park white, the University had quietly encouraged restrictive covenants, but those restrictions were now illegal, and black residents found homes in sections of the area. By the 1950s, as slumlords expanded their Hyde Park holdings, the University used political clout in City Hall and the State Legislature to fund an urban renewal plan to remove the "blighted" areas. Understanding it was no longer possible for Hyde Park to remain lily white, they undertook to assure it would remain middle class, albeit integrated.

Our entire "blighted" block eventually was torn down, the street rerouted, obliterating the neighborhood of my childhood memories. Only the Kenwood School building and the public library remain, cast up like old sailing ships tossed ashore by a hurricane.

Despite turbulence and change, my recollections of my first

eight years are mostly positive. I remember digging tunnels in the snow drifts against the IC wall in our back yard, playing ball with friends on a patch of vacant land we called "Farmer's Field," crossing a pedestrian bridge over the Outer Drive expressway to the Lake Michigan shore to climb on the granite seawall. I enjoyed the lake breeze and stared at the watery expanse that stretched to the horizon, our inland sea.

The Red Scare

There was a dark side to those years that my parents shielded me from. Following the 1948 strike, our family was under severe pressure. FBI surveillance became intense. Pa was hauled in front of the HUAC again in February, 1952.

A dozen of Pa's associates in the CP, including Henry Winston, were indicted in 1948 under the Alien Registration Act, a repressive law commonly called the Smith Act. The Smith Act set penalties that included fines or imprisonment for as long as twenty years for anyone who "prints, publishes, edits, issues, circulates, sells, distributes, or publicly displays any written or printed matter advocating...overthrowing...any government in the United States by force or violence...." Efforts to organize or join an "anti-government" group likewise were subject to prosecution.

The nearly year-long trial of the defendants in New York City was heavily covered in the press and had ominous similarities to Stalinist show trials in the USSR. Numerous accounts referred to its "circus-like atmosphere." The prosecution argued the CP encouraged violent revolution; the defendants countered that they advocated peaceful transition to socialism, and that the First Amendment's guarantees of free speech and association protected their membership in the party.

All the defendants were convicted in October, 1949. After sentencing, the defense attorneys also were handcuffed and led to jail for Contempt of Court. This trial was the first wave of a judicial onslaught on advocates of left-wing viewpoints. It coincided with trials of Alger Hiss, a State Department employee, and of Harry Bridges, leader of the West Coast longshoreman's union. Soon to follow were the sensational spy trials of Julius and Ethel Rosenberg, the Smith Act prosecution of Elizabeth Gurley Flynn, the investigation of atomic physicist J. Robert Oppenheimer, contempt actions against folksinger Pete Seeger, playwright Arthur Miller and many more persecutions of American leftists.

The Smith Act cases were particularly terrifying to Mom, who feared Pa could be indicted at any moment. Mom experienced insecurity and privation during her childhood in Nerezine. After a successful adaption to life in America, any security she felt in the 1920s when her family did well was washed away by the Depression. The war years were not free from difficulties. For a while it seemed Pa would be drafted, and Mom faced political turmoil at Studebaker. The onset of post-war anti-communist hysteria was deeply unsettling to her.

Mom's fears had a strong effect on me as a child, as I regressed to more infantile behavior. Miss Rappaport, the child psychologist, concluded that I sensed and was reacting to her fears.

I was disturbed when Mom went back to work outside the home shortly after Pa was fired. With money tight, Mom took a waitress job evenings at O'Donnell's, a nearby restaurant. One evening Ralph Helstein and his wife Rachel came into O'Donnell's with another couple and sat at one of Mom's assigned tables. She had a moment of panic, then composed herself, walked to the table and offered a business-like "Can I help you?" Mom said Ralph, who had fired dad from his union job, turned as pale as a ghost.

Later, Mom began work that more suited her abilities. A friend, Leone Phillips, had established Social Research, a business that contracted with University of Chicago departments like Sociology or Social Work to collect interview data in defined demographic groups. Mom proved to be an able interviewer and her work for Social Research expanded during our last years in Chicago. To facilitate her interviewing work, at age 40, Mom took driving lessons and soon got an Illinois driver's license. Her experience with Social Research enabled Mom to establish her own market research business in Los Angeles in 1956, collecting California data for the East Coast-based market research firms. Through her business she provided interviewing work to blacklisted leftist friends. Later, when I became a folk singing enthusiast I realized Gil Houston, an interviewer who worked for Mom was better known as Cisco Houston, a golden-voiced singer and music-playing partner of Woody Guthrie.

In the spring of 1955 I learned we soon would be moving to California. We would be near relatives we had visited on our trip west the previous summer. They had preceded us by a few years on the trek from the Midwest to Los Angeles. I was distraught about leaving my neighborhood friends and unsettled that some of my stuff wasn't going to come west, like my scooter. Mom said I would soon get a bicycle in California. I met the middle-aged African-American couple who purchased our apartment. It seemed strange that someone else would live in the only home I had known.

The whole family attended a send-off party held in Pa's honor at the union hall. He received a fancy wristwatch in a modernistic square shape and a leather briefcase. I still have it. The built-in combination lock opens when set to 3-4-7, the number of his beloved UPWA local.

Mom, Pa, our pooch Chico and I squeezed into our black Pontiac on April Fool's Day, 1955 for the long trip to California. Brother Bob would remain living in Chicago, while Bill stayed on with friends until his high school semester ended in June. During the trip, I studied the road map, giving my parents updates on the distance to the next town. Later when I heard Louie Jordan's R&B hit "Route 66," I was familiar with all the towns in the lyrics. Pa had the ambitious goal for the pre-Interstate highway era to travel 500 miles per day. He drove with determination, carrying us ever farther from Chicago, making it to Aunt Aggie's and Uncle Nick's house in four days.

LA Livin'

We settled in for a long stay in Aunt Aggie and Uncle Nick Daniels' Spanish tile roofed, stucco house in the Fairfax district of Los Angeles. Viewing the surroundings, I felt we must be in a botanical garden. I was dazzled by the bottle-brush, red-berried pyracantha, flowering hibiscus and oleander bushes and a host of other flowers.

I played under two big shagbark sycamores in front of the Daniels house. Their carpet-like lawn and those of the neighbors were neatly mown and edged, nothing like the scruffy grass mixed with clover and dandelions I was familiar with from "Farmer's Field" in Chicago. I was amazed that Aggie and Nick had an in-ground sprinkling system, its spray so well directed you could walk past them on the sidewalk without getting wet.

In the backyard there were orange trees bearing fruit that seemed sour to me. Aunt Aggie squeezed them for juice. I learned to like avocados from a gigantic tree near the back of their lot. In Chicago we called them "alligator pears" and I had only seen them in the market, an unaffordable luxury. The tree was easy to climb, but it was impossible to get at the fruit, which grew high in its canopy. They didn't seem to be harmed, however, by falling to the ground. I collected a few daily and brought them to Aunt Aggie, who cut spears of avocado for me to taste.

Aggie and Nick had a comfortable standard-of-lining in an inviting upper-middle class neighborhood. My parents slept in the extra bedroom. I had a couch in an enclosed porch overlooking an outdoor sitting area that I learned was called a "patio."

With lots of war work for his machine shop, Nick had prospered in Detroit. In 1948 he sold his interest in that business, and, foreseeing a boom in aviation in southern California, with a new partner named Howard Jarvis opened Fedco, a machine shop in Redondo Beach. Nick and Jarvis were an odd couple—Jarvis a right-wing Republican activist and Nick a true-believing communist. Somehow they managed to keep business and politics separated.

Jarvis, born in Utah and raised a Mormon, had fallen away from that abstinent religion, becoming a heavy drinker and a cigar smoker. He entered politics as an anti-tax crusader, running and losing in elections for Los Angeles mayor and the US Senate. In 1978, several years after he and Nick sold Fedco and dissolved their partnership, Jarvis became notorious for spearheading Proposition 13, a measure that severely limited property taxes and gutted municipal services in California.

The day after our arrival in LA, Mom and I walked several blocks to Carthay Center School, with Mom calling attention to street signs and pointing out landmarks so that I could walk there by myself the next day. I was assigned to Miss Saunders' 3rd Grade class. My new teacher greeted me warmly. She was a pleasant woman, a little plump with short brown hair. Nonetheless I felt very out of place. Miss Saunders called roll by chanting "*Buenas dias*, Johnny" and the student dutifully replied "*Buenas dias*, Miss Saunders." I couldn't make out what they were saying. When she got to my name, I approximated the words as I'd heard them, "Gwen as tee oz," which made the kids laugh.

When we were dismissed for recess, I was amazed the school provided big inflated rubber balls. There were yellow stripes on the asphalt demarking courts for games like dodge ball and four-square. There were wooden free-standing walls for handball and tetherball poles. It was a far cry from playing tag or penner in my Chicago school's bare asphalt yard. When the bell rang and the kids charged back into the building, I remembered neither the room number nor the way back to my classroom. When the tardy bell rang, I was still searching. A teacher saw me wandering the halls and asked what I was doing. "I'm looking for my ruhm," I replied, using my Chicago pronunciation of room. "Looking for what?' she queried. "For Miss Saunders' ruhm," I stressed. "Oh, roooom," she responded, demonstrating how I should be pronouncing the word. She took me there.

The next morning I set off for school carrying my brown bag lunch. I'd memorized the streets: 8th Street to Ogden, then Orange Grove, cross Fairfax at the light, etc. and made it to school without a hitch. When I arrived, however, things seemed strange. There were no other kids in sight. I walked down the abandoned hall to Miss Saunders' room and sat down at my desk. There was nobody around. After a few interminable minutes, Miss Saunders rushed into the room, out of breath. She was surprised I had come to school. "Today is Passover," she explained. I gave a blank look. "It's a Jewish holiday, a very important holiday. Most of the kids here are Jewish so they stayed home. Even the teachers who are Jewish didn't come to school today." She led me to the principal's office. After a brief consultation, Miss Saunders took me to the school library, where the librarian helped me find books and I had a whole day of free reading.

When I arrived at the house after school, I confronted my parents. "How come you made me go to school today? It's Passover. I was the only kid there." They looked surprised. Mom said, "Buddy honey, we didn't know. We don't celebrate religious holidays so we didn't know today is Passover. We're sorry if you had a bad time."

"It was OK. I read books. But I don't like this school. The kids are weird. They don't play anything I do. They don't understand what I say. I hate it here. I want to go back to Chicago."

"Buddy honey, we're going to live in California now. We can't go back to Chicago. Tomorrow the other kids will be back. You'll have a better day." For a long time, despite its allures, I remained dubious about California and loyal to Chicago. I was used to many more nearby playmates on Lake Park Avenue. There were eight kids in our building alone, and plenty of kids, black and white, in adjoining buildings. During the three months we stayed with Aggie and Nick, I befriended only one boy and I must have begged to return to Chicago every day.

I kept up the "return to Chicago" complaint even after we moved to our next residence. In June, 1955 the folks bought an old house on Crenshaw Boulevard. They notified movers to bring the furniture we had in storage in Chicago. Unexpectedly the deal fell through. With the furniture arriving in a couple days, the folks were desperate to find something, so they rented a little shack on 90th Street in South-Central LA. Pa delighted in telling visitors that, "this is the best-constructed cracker-box in the City of Los

Angeles." Then he would grab the beam in the ceiling between the living and dining rooms and shake it, making the whole house quiver.

At that time most of the neighborhood's residents were white southerners who had settled in LA, referred to as "Okies" pejoratively. Here I made friends with several kids and we played the rough and tumble games that I was used to. I was puzzled by their devotion to the military and their hero worship of a couple members of the Marine Corps from the neighborhood. We played "war" most of the time, pretending to be a Marine. The dialect of these kids reminded me of the accent of my black playmates in Chicago.

In January, 1956 we rented a moving trailer and hauled our stuff to a spacious house the folks had bought on Gower Street in Hollywood. Bob and Georgie were visiting us for the holidays and helped us move. This was where I grew up.

An important reason for choosing the house was its central location in the LA metro area. Mom was about to launch her market research business. She could send interviewers in all four directions—north to the Valley, south to the South Bay, east toward Pasadena and west to the beach towns. For much the same reasons they had moved to Hyde Park, the folks figured in Hollywood they would find a congenial social atmosphere. There would be people with values and political persuasions like ours. Indeed, the artsy and cultural communities connected to the motion picture and entertainment businesses in Hollywood tended to be liberal, and there were a significant number of fellow radicals.

To supplement our tight family budget, Mom rented the two upstairs bedrooms that had a separate side entrance. The first tenant was a deaf man who did construction work at nearby Paramount Studios. Mom felt he was an ideal tenant because he paid the rent on time and couldn't hear the commotion our family might be making. Another tenant had very good hearing. Jozef Puszkas, a Jewish immigrant from Poland, was a violinist and violin maker who had an instrument-repair shop nearby on Melrose Avenue. I was in the school orchestra at Van Ness Elementary, so Mom had him give me violin lessons. During the couple years I was his student, I was scared to death of Mr. Puszkas. Despite his diminutive 5' 2" stature, he was as stern and intimidating as a good European music teacher should be. He informed me that in Poland, when he was my age, if he made a mistake, his violin teacher would rap him on the fingertips with a ruler. "I figured I'd better not make any more mistakes or my fingers would be so sore I couldn't press them down." Mr. Puszkas never did that to me, but just hearing about it was intimidation enough.

As time went on, my music interests broadened beyond the classical strings. Mom took me to St. Anthony's Croatian Catholic Church to play with the youth tamburitza orchestra. But I only went three or four times. We discovered that right in our neighborhood, Joseph Budrick, an elderly immigrant from Lithuania, was forming a balalaika orchestra. I could walk to his place, saving Mom the trouble of driving me and waiting for the rehearsal. One whole living room wall in Mr. Budrick's cramped apartment was a pegboard hung with instruments for balalaika orchestra. He had four sizes of triangular balalaikas and two sizes of oval-shaped domras. Seven or eight of us crammed in there for rehearsals. I usually played domra, but occasionally filled in on the cello-sized balalaika. We played a few performances at a Russian restaurant and in park gazebos.

In Hollywood, our section of the city turned out motion pictures the way Detroit manufactured cars. The neighborhood was full of studio lots and sound stage buildings, big factory-like structures. Our street had acquired the nickname "Gower Gulch" because of the cowboy-attired actors often seen on the street as they headed to the studios. One block up Gower Street abutting Paramount Studios were the enormous RKO Studios. The corner of the building at Melrose and Gower was decorated with a 3-D rendering of the RKO logo: a huge radio tower with a flashing light on top. RKO cranked out scores of movies: "King Kong," "Little Women," "The Bells of St. Mary's" and numerous Tarzan films.

A few years after we moved there, the RKO facilities were bought by Lucille Ball and Desi Arnaz to become Desilu Studios. They turned out popular TV shows. We took out-of-town guests to be in the studio audience. I caught a glimpse of Lucy and Desi once or twice, coming or going from the building. Later I learned that Lucy once shared our values. In the 1930s she registered to vote listing "Communist" as her party and hosted leftist meetings in her home.

Pa found a little work in the movie industry doing carpentry at Paramount. Alfred Hitchcock was going to make "Torn Curtain," an espionage thriller with a theater scene. Paramount's old set for "Phantom of the Opera" comprised just the right half of an "opera house." Hitchcock needed both sides for his film, so Pa was on a crew that built a matching left side.

As a youth I became blasé about Hollywood, but in retrospect it was a very stimulating place. There were interesting people right on our block. Two doors down lived Mr. Cassidy, a friendly retired stuntman. He told us kids he was adept at falling off a horse without injury. He generously loaned us hats from his collection to play in.

In 1955, Pa worked out a plan for his next employment. But sadly, unlike Mom, who blossomed in California, Pa never found personally satisfying work that compared to his packinghouse days in Chicago.

In Los Angeles he had a few ex-Party friends, Henry Giler, Pat Haggarty and Marlowe Booth, veterans of the Abraham Lincoln Brigade who fought Franco in the Spanish Civil War. After World War II, they became sheet metal workers in southern California. In the 1950s the construction business in LA was booming. With their sponsorship, Pa was able to get into the apprenticeship program of the Sheet Metal Workers Union, Local 108 and learned the trade sufficiently to become a journeyman.

When he joined the union, the president of the local informed Pa that the FBI had visited him to warn against admitting a dangerous communist to his union. "I told them to go to hell." He assured Pa, "as long as you do your work, mind your own business, and don't get involved in union politics, you can be a member and work through this hiring hall."

Before long he was fabricating and installing heating and air conditioning duct at construction sites all over the LA area. He was one of the workers to install the metal awnings on the cylindrical Capitol Records Building at Hollywood and Vine. When the Pacifica community-supported radio station KPFK acquired their new studio building, Pa installed the heating and air conditioning systems. For a while he worked in other California cities, even in Nevada and Arizona for a company that put up filling station buildings. He'd be gone from home for a week or two. But he soon settled on working only close to home, turning down a lucrative construction job in Thule, Greenland.

Construction work is seasonal. Even in the mild California climate there were frequent lay-offs. While drawing unemployment compensation, Pa began to think that he would soon turn 50 and strenuous construction work might become too physically demanding. He thought he might study law. It was an occupation through which he might advance the rights of workers. He registered for night classes at Southwestern Law School, a community-oriented college in downtown Los Angeles. They provided legal education to non-traditional students. In his first semester Pa signed up for two evening courses, Torts and Contracts.

Around that time, Pa succumbed to the temptation to engage in Sheet Metal Workers Union politics. He helped assemble a progressive caucus that ran a slate of candidates. "Vote rank and file" was the slogan. When the insurgency failed, the incumbents knew who had been the sparkplug for the challengers, even though Pa wasn't on the slate. The president of the local felt Pa had failed to heed his warning and retaliated. The union notified Pa that they had "recently learned" he was in violation of the union's anti-Communist prohibition. Therefore he was expelled forthwith. Pa filed a petition with the union's internal appeals board that dragged on for over a year.

Pa continued working in sheet metal and attending law school evenings while the appeal was pending. By the time he was expelled, he could complete law school in one more year, attending full time. So he buckled down, took a heavy load of courses, graduated Cum Laude, and passed the difficult California Bar Exam on his first try.

But his travails were far from over. Despite his demonstrated knowledge of the law, with FBI instigation, the California Bar Association refused to admit him on the grounds that he was not of "good moral character." By this time, in the 1960s, the McCarthyite smear of communist affiliation alone wasn't adequate, so the Bar Association contended his bad morals were indicated by the fact he lied to the HUAC in 1939 and more recently lied to his

Sheet Metal "union brothers," concealing his former Communist ties.

Pa went to work as a law clerk for Margolis and McTernan, a well-known left-leaning firm that handled civil liberties cases in southern California, including Pa's own suit against the California Bar Association. In 1967, in a lop-sided decision, the California State Supreme Court ruled in his favor, ordered the Bar Association to admit him and Pa became a lawyer.

For about a year, he ran an office for Margolis and McTernan in the LA Harbor area, but when he was offered the opportunity to become a "junior" partner in the firm, for considerably more money, he turned them down and instead became a lawyer for AFSC-ME, the public employees union. I had just returned home then after graduating from college. On a walk to run some errands, Pa apologetically explained his reasoning. "I never figured to make that much money...," he trailed off. "Sure, Pa, it's OK," I told him. My thinking in 1968 was that we were on the verge of our New Left revolution. Money was irrelevant to me and if we had our way, it soon would be irrelevant to everybody else too.

But Pa became disillusioned with representing an AFSCME local of LA County probation officers. He felt that they had it good financially and were not necessarily conscientious workers. "Try to get a hold of one of them on a Friday," he said. "They're all 'in the field.' Yeah, in a corn field, maybe!" So he went to work for the United Food and Commercial Workers (UFCW), the conglomerate union of packinghouse workers and retail clerks that the UPWA had merged into. There, as a lawyer, he was doing much the same work that he had done as a union official—negotiating contracts and handling grievances.

One day in 1971, Pa was in Firebaugh, California, a dismal little agri-business town in the Central Valley, negotiating a contract for packing shed workers. During the parley, he felt ill and asked to be excused. In the men's room he swallowed a whole roll of Tums and returned to finish negotiating the contract. When he got home, he told Mom he thought he had the flu and took to bed. It took Mom two days to get him to see a doctor, who promptly informed him that he had suffered a heart attack and sent him to a hospital.

In his weakened condition, Pa was restricted from working much. So, about to turn 60 in 1972, Mom sold her business, they sold the Hollywood house, pulled up stakes and departed for a long stay in Nerezine where the cost-of-living would be low. Hav-

ing enjoyed a visit to Mom's birthplace in 1967, Pa had pushed the idea to escape to the sunny Adriatic, but once there, in her childhood village, Mom adjusted much better to their surroundings than Pa did.

By 1974 they were ready to return to the US. Without any pensions from employers, they were now eligible to receive Social Security, making life in the States affordable. To supplement their income, on a case by case basis, Pa took work on grievance arbitration cases for the UFCW.

Herb March with author, last photo together, 2001

Mom and Pa found their retirement paradise at last in San Pedro. Lots of our relatives and old friends were nearby. They bought two low-priced old houses that were built on a single lot. They had a view of the LA Harbor and a strip of open ocean. Located on the Point Fermin peninsula, a neighborhood then replete with shipyards workers, longshoremen and maritime workers, it was the last still-inexpensive place to live near the ocean in the whole LA area. They rented out the bigger house and remodeled the smaller. Except for a long sojourn in Madison, Wisconsin, to be near my kids, they lived the rest of their years in that house until their lives came to a peaceful end.

California Dreamin'

During our first years in Los Angeles I drove my parents crazy with pleas to move back to Chicago. I went so far as to write a letter to brother Bob and his wife Georgie, asking if I could live with them in their cramped apartment. I got a gentle, diplomatic rejection letter from Georgie. After two years in California, Mom responded to my unflagging pleas by proposing that the two of us fly to Chicago for a visit. Neither of us had taken an airplane trip before.

We stayed with the Hoselitz family, who had been our neighbors on Lake Park. They were now living in a different apartment on Hyde Park Boulevard. We went by our former residence. The building looked as bedraggled as the ones up the block. In the back yard I met the kids who lived there. They were all strangers to me. I was dismayed that the sandbox we had constructed in the back yard and filled with pure clean sand we hauled from the Michigan dunes was now more dirt than sand, with scrawny weeds growing in it. It was a symbol: my Chicago was gone. I flew back to LA resigned to adjust to our new home.

Pa also sought closure with Chicago a couple years later, making a visit to his former domain:

It was about 1959, I think. I was between jobs, laid off, so I took the opportunity to go to Chicago. I hadn't seen it in four years. I decided to take a look at the stockyards and it damned near broke my heart to see what had happened, you know, the yards torn down. At that time, Armour & Company wasn't completely torn down; they were still operating a lard refinery. There were a few plant guards and one was an old Irishman who had formerly been an officer in the Livestock Handlers local and we felt very kindly towards each other. Well, this guy spotted me walking around the yards and he said, "Herb, you've got to visit what's left of our plant." So he stepped into the booth and called up the visitors' entrance, said, "I've got a gentleman here who wants to visit the lard refinery; can you take him through?" They said yes, certainly, so I walked over there. They were brand new people, all except one who recognized me. They got all excited, contacted the Armour brass and a sergeant of police who was currently the captain of the skeleton police force in the plant accompanied me on the visit. He told me on the side, "Herb, I want to tell you something. This is not my idea. I think you should be able to go in here and shake hands with these people. Everybody here knows you. But look, I follow orders and they told me to go along with you and keep an eye on you." I said, "Why the hell do you have to keep an eye on me? Is there anything that I could do that would be worse than what Armour seems to have done here?" I just waved my hand at a demolished area there. It looked like a bombed-out city. "No, I guess you're right about that," he said. And that was my last visit. I saw some of the old-timers in the plant. The lard refinery was closed down shortly thereafter. There's nothing there now.

If Pa and I retained wistfulness for Chicago, Mom scarcely did so. She kept in touch with old friends in Chicago, some visited us and a few of those families moved to LA as well. In California she came into her own. Her market research business thrived. With Southern California's population exploding by the mid-1950s, its significance as a trend-setting market was apparent in the world of business. Moreover, there was a rising emphasis on data from market research to formulate business strategy.

Mom's business became our reliable family income. Shipments of mimeographed questionnaires regularly arrived at the house. Crews of interviewers came over for briefings. I was put to work tabulating data from completed questionnaires.

Sometimes we received generically labeled products to place with respondents, like boxes of toothpaste in plain white tubes labeled type A, B or C, or after-shave lotions or deodorants. I was thrilled by a study of flavored yogurt and was even interviewed about it.

In the late 1950s and early 1960s, the public eagerly awaited the new cars each fall. This was Mom's busiest time. She sent squads of interviewers to auto showrooms. During this rush, Pa frequently helped Mom with the surveys. By my teens I was pulled into service, hired to "screen" potential respondents as they entered the dealerships. If they fit a demographic, I sent them on to adult interviewers. Once during "new car time," I woke up for school and found Mom and Pa awake and disheveled. They had worked all night tabulating results and packing boxes of completed questionnaires for an early morning pick-up by Railway Express.

Mom never lost track of other interests. She turned our front, back and side yards into vivid flower gardens and a cornucopia of fruits. She added grape vines, guava bushes and a fig tree to the peach and apricot trees that had been planted by a former owner. A sweet-scented jasmine bush perfumed our front porch in the evenings. A passion fruit vine on our back fence produced exotic blossoms and fragrant colorful fruit. As a boy, on pruning days, I grumbled when dragooned into making bulging bundles of brush. From the street you could scarcely see our house between the date palms and the hibiscus bushes out front.

Mom also revived her interest in art. Sister Aggie had become an avid oil painter. The homes of friends and family all had a couple of Aggie's paintings on their walls. She took Mom to art camps. I spent a week with them at Idyllwild, an art school in the San Bernardino Mountains. Mom attended art shows and classes at Barnsdall Park in East Hollywood, where I enjoyed kids' art activities.

It frustrated Mom that by family consensus her sibling rival Aggie was the better painter. Mom could never quite finish oil paintings. Then she discovered silk screen prints. After running the planned set of colors, the print was done, there was no going back. They soon equaled sister Aggie's works in friends' and relatives' homes.

Even with her business, gardening and art, Mom continued some political activity. Pa's CIO colleague Bob Travis and his wife Helen moved to Los Angeles and Helen drew Mom (and me) into leftist California politics. At the beginning of the 1960s Helen got involved in the movement to ban nuclear weapons. During the "arms race" between the USSR and the West, citizens of atomic powers lived in constant fear of nuclear war. In the 1950s we school children were subjected to "duck and cover" drills, while ordinary people outfitted "fallout shelters" in basements and backyards.

We were reminded of the threat everywhere by the yellow and black Civil Defense fallout shelter signs in every public building.

The Campaign for Nuclear Disarmament (CND) spearheaded a "ban the bomb" movement. Inspired by the British movement, American peace groups and pacifist-oriented religious denominations took up the issue.

Helen became active in one of the most effective peace groups, Women's Strike for Peace (WSP), a woman-led organization. WSP organized a protest against nuclear testing in 1961, where 50,000 women demonstrated worldwide. Helen persuaded Mom to attend the Los Angeles demonstration, but Mom's involvement with the WSP protest proved to be her last effort of that type, she was weary of FBI harassment.

There had been relentless FBI surveillance of our family in Chicago. We always assumed our telephones were tapped. We assumed that when we were away from home the FBI routinely broke in to clandestinely search our home. There had even been an attempt to recruit brother Bob to spy on his own parents.

The surveillance did not diminish when we moved to California, even though Mom and Pa were no longer active in leftist organizations. A few times a year, an agent would park across the street from our house and sit in the car all day, every day, for a whole week. When I was a smart-ass junior high kid, I tapped on the agent's car window. "Hey mister, could you tell me what time it is?" The agent ignored me, pretending to be intent on reading his newspaper. When Mom saw me doing this, she shrieked from the front porch, "Buddy, get away from there!" I was sorely tempted to organize my friends to make a dirt clod attack on the guy's car, but Mom persuaded me to leave him alone. We remained under FBI surveillance until J. Edgar Hoover died in 1972.

Mom volunteered to tutor elementary school children with special education needs. She worked with community groups on local issues, opposing a new road through a neighborhood park. She helped the elderly and immigrants navigate complex bureaucracies, assisted families in cases of illness and death. Pa teased that she was a "private social worker."

If Helen did not succeed in "hooking" Mom, she did play a crucial role in fostering my budding interest in leftist activism.

When I started high school she linked me with the high school group at the First Unitarian Church. I liked the radical bunch, having already made a good start in activism in middle school.

In the Spring of 1960 during the lunch counter sit-ins against segregation at a Woolworth store in Greensboro, North Carolina, my older brother Bill, then a UCLA student, brought me to a protest in front of Woolworth's on Hollywood Boulevard. I was 13 years old—my first demonstration. Northern student organizations had sprung up to support the sit-ins of black students in the South.

I took a paperboard sign tacked to a stick which read "Freedom Now!" and joined a score of college students circling on Hollywood Boulevard's star-studded sidewalk. We encountered hecklers who made anti-Semitic catcalls or called us Reds. A hefty middle-aged man with a blonde crew cut in a tacky, checkered suit confronted us. He held up a Holy Bible with a golden cross on the cover like he was trying to frighten away vampires. I thought he was funny, but the student marching in front of me took it seriously and angrily shouted at him, "Was Christ a bigot?"

After a half hour of circling, three of my schoolmates from Le Conte junior high came walking up the sidewalk. They were tough guys who displayed their "bad" image by wearing un-tucked Sir Guy shirts over baggy khaki pants. Their hair gleamed with Brylcreem. I had a flash of panic. At school we had to deal with their intimidation; these kids carried sharpened metal shoe horns. Should I duck into the store's entrance and hide? In a second, that impulse passed.

"Oh my God, we know one of these creeps," Tony Santolla snarled when he caught sight of me. I stopped and jauntily held up my picket sign right in front of the three toughs like the Bible guy was doing to us. They sheepishly said hi and walked away. It was exhilarating! On Monday in Industrial Drawing class, Santolla respectfully asked me about the picket. Now I was really hooked. I couldn't wait for the next opportunity to protest.

Inspired by the 50 mile marches to Aldermaston in England, peace activists in LA planned a peace march on Easter Saturday from MacArthur Park, near downtown, along busy Wilshire Boulevard to the Santa Monica Civic Auditorium, sixteen miles away.

There we would hold a disarmament rally with famed peace activist, scientist Linus Pauling as the featured speaker.

At Le Conte, we kids of leftists had sniffed each other out, hearing each other argue with our red-baiting Social Studies teachers or seeing the political buttons we'd sometimes wear. By the 8ᵗʰ Grade we had established a dozen like-minded friends. Some of us were learning guitar and playing folk songs. We started wearing buttons with the "peace sign." The symbol is a superimposed graphic of signal flag positions for the letters N and D (for Nuclear Disarmament). Joan Kramer, a chum from that junior high lefty group told me that a classmate asked her "Why do you people who drive Volkswagens wear buttons with their logo?" It was hilarious, but an honest mistake. Both logos feature black lines in a circle, and a lot of peaceniks drove Volkswagens.

Several of us lefty 8ᵗʰ graders decided to participate in the disarmament march. I had a crush on Carol Zelman, one of the bunch, and we dared each other to make the whole sixteen-mile trek. My mother dropped off the two of us at the park that morning saying she would find us in the evening at the rally. It was my first date with a girl, setting a pattern for "dates" at demonstrations that became the norm through my youth.

I picked up a sign with the slogan "No More War." We early arrivals headed west along the Wilshire Boulevard sidewalk. Soon some people started the chant. "Hey hey, what d'ya say, let's get that bomb and throw it away." Then the group switched to singing "We are marching for disarmament, disarmament, disarmament..." which highlighted our cause better. We sang or chanted, "We shall not be moved..." "Last night I had the strangest dream I ever dreamed before, I dreamed the world had all agreed to put an end to war..." Our numbers swelled as we headed west. I saw and greeted Loren and Mona, a young couple who were in the balalaika orchestra with me. I should've figured they'd be peaceniks too. By the time we reached the Miracle Mile district, marchers were filling the whole width of the sidewalk for longer than a block. A few more schoolmates found me and Carol and joined in, it was a movable party.

We heard no catcalls or jeers. Shoppers heading in or out of the department stores stared quizzically; a few even smiled and nodded. We passed a movie theater showing Stanley Kubrick's "On the Beach," a film dealing with nuclear holocaust. Because of the holiday, many marchers were carrying Easter lilies. I joined a group who decorated the theater's box office with lilies and placed a sign reading "Ban the Bomb" among them.

By mid-afternoon we reached a park on the east edge of Santa Monica, where hundreds more joined the march for the last two miles. By the time we reached the Civic Auditorium our ranks were spilling into the street, the singing was loud and people who only came for the rally were arrayed in front of the auditorium cheering us. It was the emotional peak. We less than full-grown school kids were swallowed in the crush. Carol urged me, "Richard, hold your sign up high. It's a high ideal." We were so corny.

A couple months later the Democratic National Convention was held at the LA Sports Arena in Exposition Park. Outside the facility, I joined a picket line organized by the Congress of Racial Equality (CORE), a leading civil rights organization. Our signs read, "We demand a strong civil rights plank" (in the Democratic platform), and "Freedom Now." The singing was great. There were several African-Americans in the picket line who sang well. We sang "Oh Freedom," "Ain't Gonna Let Nobody Turn Me 'Round,'" and of course, "We Shall Overcome."

The NAACP had organized a rally at nearby Shrine Auditorium, within easy walking distance. I sat with my CORE friends on the balcony of that cavernous hall where previously I had seen the Moiseyev Dancers and Bolshoi Ballet. A few Democratic politicians and a star-studded line-up of black leaders delivered speeches. Though each speaker had been assigned a 10-minute slot, many of them spoke only a minute or two, then dramatically intoned, "I yield the rest of my time to the Reverend Martin Luther King." I hadn't heard him speak yet, so I wondered what was up. New York Congressman Adam Clayton Powell, Jr., not yielding any time, delivered an impressive fiery oration. But next I heard the sonorous voice of Dr. King. He eloquently took us through a half-hour sermon replete with metaphors and florid Biblical language on the necessity to end segregation and gain voting rights. I had heard the master orator of the Civil Rights Movement.

We peaceniks and civil rights advocates were urging the

Democrats to draft Adlai Stevenson to run again in 1960. The two-time loser to Dwight Eisenhower was firm about not running. Backers of non-candidate Stevenson were not allowed to appear on the convention floor. Foreshadowing much more significant struggles at forthcoming Democratic conventions, we Stevenson backers sneaked onto the convention floor with a group supporting New Jersey Governor Robert Meyner. We pulled "Draft Adlai" signs from under our shirts and delivered our message before being ejected.

When I started at Hollywood High, Helen Travis picked me up every Sunday to go to the First Unitarian Church for meetings of the Starr King Fellowship youth group, which shaped my beliefs, character and future actions.

Because of the welcoming attitude of the church's minister Stephen H. Fritchman, First Unitarian became a gathering place for radicals cast adrift during the stormy McCarthy era. The many ex-Reds who became active members thoroughly enjoyed the "respectability" of working for progressive causes in a socially reputable church.

I relied on Helen to take me until my older cohorts got driver's licenses and could give me a lift. Mom and Pa weren't interested in attending, although some of their friends did. Pa said he once took a call from a recruiter for the church. "No I'm not interested. I'm an atheist," he answered. "Oh that's all right, we have lots of atheist members," the caller replied. "So I asked him," Pa said, "why the hell are they messing around going to church when they're atheists?!"

First Unitarian was founded in 1877 by Theodoric and Caroline Severance. Before moving to California, Caroline had been a noted abolitionist and campaigner for woman's suffrage, an associate of Susan B. Anthony and Elizabeth Cady Stanton.

Unitarians have no dogma, not even the existence of a supreme being, hence the participation of atheists. Drawing from teachings of all world religions and philosophies, they have stated principles, among them: "justice, equity and compassion in human relations," "the guidance of reason and...science," and "earth-centered traditions."

For ex-Communists weary of Party dogma, the tolerant Unitarian approach was more than attractive. In fact, during the

1950s, this congregation delivered a significant blow to anti-Red hysteria.

In 1954, California made recognition of non-profit status contingent on a loyalty oath. Church leaders struck out the offensive oath and returned the paperwork, resulting in loss of their tax-exempt status. They sued Los Angeles County to recover property tax charges and won four years later. In a 7 to 1 decision, the U.S. Supreme Court invalidated the loyalty oath requirement. In 2013, First Unitarian became the lead plaintiff in a lawsuit against the National Security Agency over the NSA's wiretapping program.

Moreover, they made successful efforts to recruit members from the black community located near the church. In the turbulent 1960s it was African-American congregants from First Church who pushed the Unitarians' cautious national association to fund a Black Affairs Council.

In the early 1960s, Starr King Fellowship was an inter-racial group of high school students active in the peace and civil rights movements. Half of the group's 40 or 50 members were "red diaper babies" like me, children of communists. At our frequent parties, the black and mixed-race kids became arbiters of what was cool in music, dance and dress styles which we whiteys lamely tried to emulate.

We adored Ken Lipscomb, the youth worker who led the group. Tall, lean and handsome, Ken was a former basketball player on the Harlem Globetrotters. He also was a DJ on a Rhythm & Blues radio station, spinning our favorite music. Every Sunday Ken invited a representative of a "movement" group to speak. There were college student freedom riders or voter registration workers, pacifists from the War Resisters League. We had World Federalists and even a representative of the Black Muslims speak. After hearing about it at Starr King, a few of us joined an after-school sit-in in the hallway of the LA school district offices protesting *de facto* segregation.

Much as my parents had become involved in the YCL as teenagers, Starr King played a similar role for me. But the eclectic mix of progressive viewpoints we were exposed to and discussed contrasted sharply with the narrow party line of the 1930s Communist movement.

During the summer of 1963, about 20 members of our group

participated in a service project at *Escuela Granja*, a Mexican orphanage in the village of Huejotitan, Jalisco, 25 miles south of Guadalajara. It was a life-altering experience. *Escuela Granja* (the Farm School) had been founded eight years earlier by Hugh and Susan Hardyman, members of our church, and administered by Mercedes del Campo, the resident director. In a 200-year-old hacienda, they provided a home and education to two dozen boys. All the boys learned agricultural techniques. On seven hectares they raised much of their food: corn, beans, milk, pigs and chickens. There were a dozen boys who went to grammar school in the village, about ten older boys who boarded at a high school in Guadalajara, returning weekends, plus four or five college students who were home for the summer when we "*Nortes*" were there.

Our project was to construct an irrigation system for an orchard on a former polo grounds. Using the hacienda's swimming pool as a reservoir, we built brick-lined channels to each fruit tree. Assisting the surveyor Jesus Navarro, we excavated, mixed mortar and fitted bricks to make the channels.

We gringos also helped with daily farm chores. During our months in Huejotitan, we gained a deep understanding of life in a developing country. Although we worked hard, our sojourn was far from drudgery. A few of us brought guitars, and we shared music sessions with *Escuela Granja* boys. Manuel, the school's agriculture director, was an accomplished mariachi musician. One evening he donned his charro suit and performed for us.

On Sundays we took a "third class" bus, actually a flatbed truck with high wooden railings, into Jocotepec, the nearby market town on Lake Chapala. We bought snacks and soft drinks and with the local young people, strolled in the *paseo* around a park gazebo, boys and girls in separate circles.

Riding horseback still was a significant form of transportation in that part of Jalisco. One morning a few of us rode horses borrowed from local villagers. I rode a gentle white mare aptly named Gringa. A few boys asked about making a hike to the summit of a nearby mountain. A couple of the Mexican college boys led the hike. We camped in the open, under orchid-laden trees, unnerved in the dark night by the screech of mountain lions and the glowing eyes of animals reflected in the light of our campfire.

We learned about rural Mexican traditions. Our girls were subject to rigid chaperoning and weren't allowed on the rides or hikes. Most of the time we were segregated by sex; boys, Mexican and *Norte*, slept on cots in a vacated turkey shed; the girls occupied indoor bedrooms in the hacienda under the watchful eye of the resident director. We boys did the digging with picks and shovels, the girls did farm chores and maintenance of the hacienda. Only in the dining room did we sit intermingled. The sexual segregation did not prevent, however, a few girls in our group from having summer romances with the Mexican college boys.

We discussed Mexican politics and social issues with the engineer Jesus Navarro. He explained that the ruling PRI party had been revolutionary in its inception but had become corrupt and authoritarian. It was from Jesus that I first heard the term *machismo*. He described it as a bane to the advancement of Mexican men. Macho men scorned education, Jesus said, and behaved irresponsibly, drinking, fighting and mistreating women. We noticed that many young men in the area wore broad-brimmed hats and vaquero-style clothes, and many openly wore sidearms. It seemed like we had stepped into a cowboy movie.

One day returning from Jocotepec on a third-class bus, we got a lesson about messing with a macho. Our friend Doug had bought a length of rope to use on our camping trip. He formed it into a lasso and leaning over the railing of the flatbed, whirled it, playfully threatening to rope pedestrians, men and women bearing bundles or leading donkeys on the shoulder of the road. It was an obnoxious trick; some of the people were startled. The truck approached a young man on horseback in vaquero gear. Seeing Doug and his lasso, he whipped out his pistol and pointed it at us. The boys near me hit the deck; I witlessly remained standing to see the vaquero laugh heartily at the frightened boys.

Over the course of our stay, Jesus took us to visit Guadalajara, where he showed us impressive murals by Jose Clemente Orosco and explained the historical meaning of the images, such as Fr. Miguel Hidalgo's Grito de Dolores, Mexico's declaration of independence. After the art tour, we had free time to explore Guadalajara's open marketplace on our own.

The summer in Huejotitan and our high school years active in

Starr King made us world citizens and strivers for justice. Though college and post-college life scattered us in many directions, that shared experience produced a group of progressive people who worked to advance the causes of peace and racial justice.

I Lived Three Lives

In the mid-1950s, there was a hokey TV drama titled "I Lived Three Lives" loosely based on the dishonorable career of FBI agent Herbert Philbrick, who "infiltrated" the Communist Party. It was schlock. The scripts were outlandish, including one episode in which Communists attempted to convert vacuum cleaners into bomb launchers. The show may have been terrible, but recently it occurred to me that its title seemed to apply to me.

I had three lives. I was a school kid from Hollywood who played folk songs and became an activist in progressive causes. I was a Croatian-American in a bilingual household with three immigrant members. My third life was summers spent working Bob and Beth Pepper's farm.

During our years in California, my family became increasingly drawn into ethnic activities. Mom's family gradually picked up stakes from Chicago and moved to LA, while more European relatives joined us in California. The family had long had a western foothold. Mom's two eldest sisters Christina and Lena having lived on the West Coast after leaving Nerezine.

Initially based in Portland, Oregon, Lena and husband Dominic relocated to San Pedro in the 1930s. Her widowed sister Christina, after spending many years in her old Portland house, moved in with Lena. Never learning much English, the sisters and their husbands remained firmly ensconced in the Croatian immigrant community, living in neighborhoods where they could use their native language to shop, socialize, and worship. When the men worked on fishing boats, Croatian was the language of the crew. Christina remained childless, but Lena had four kids, Anthony, Albert, Mary and Joe. They assimilated, married non-Croatians, but remained close with the large Croatian community of San Pedro. When we drove down Normandie Avenue to visit our San Pedro kin, it felt like entering another realm where my uncle and cousins mended fishing nets on docks or welded steel in ship-yards, and my aunts took seasonal work in a tuna cannery. The Sunshine Market sold Croatian groceries and the Ramona Bakery vended Croatian treats.

After World War II, my sophisticated uncle Krešo settled in San Pedro, opening his pharmacy only a few blocks from Lena's house. In 1948, Aggie and Nick continued the family's westward relocation project. In 1954 Nona traveled by train from Chicago to stay with them. Mom's brother Joe, a plumber, knew he'd have plenty of work in LA's construction boom, so he, Aunt Kate and their kids moved west in 1952. By the time we arrived in 1955, there was a large family contingent in California.

A couple years later, Aunt Maritza arrived from Italy, moving into our home to help care for Nona, who was back with us. Then Maritza's son Virgilio, with wife Lina and their two young daughters, arrived from Europe in 1961. A few years later, Lina's younger sister Gemma came from Nerezine. The family group was growing fast, speaking Croatian and practicing Old World customs.

Aggie and Nick were active in the LA Croatian community. Uncle Joe remained an energetic fraternal lodge member and sang in Croatian choirs. The Detroit Croatian choir "Slavulj" relocated to Los Angeles in 1948 after its director moved west. Aggie and Joe promptly joined, as did Mom. We attended performances of ethnic choirs or folk dance ensembles and enjoyed lamb roasts and dinner-dances at San Pedro's Yugoslav-American Club or at the Ford Boulevard Hall and picnic grounds in East Los Angeles. Ford Boulevard was operated by leftists. We brought family friend Paul Robeson to one picnic, where he visited with folks and stood on a picnic table to deliver a short *a capella* performance in his booming voice.

In that era, to participate in our progressive ethnic organizations became an act of militancy and bravery, a stance in defiance of dangerous foes. After the War, divisions and tensions in the American South Slavic communities sharpened. Thousands of "displaced persons" entered the US from refugee camps in Europe. Some of them had been supporters of the Ustaši, Hitler's quisling regime in Croatia, or of Serbian royalist Četniks. In the Cold War, these former fascist supporters now were welcomed to the US for their support of the post-war anti-communist hysteria.

The *starosjedioci,* meaning "old settlers," i.e. the earlier wave of immigrants, had been miners and industrial workers and leaned left politically. They had been through union organizing drives and strikes, and supported FDR and the New Deal. A struggle for control of Croatian- and Serbian-American organizations developed between the left-leaning *starosjedioci* and the right-wing "DPs" as we pejoratively called the newcomers. The rightists gained control of many ethnic churches and their parish organizations, but the Croatian Fraternal Union, the largest national organization, remained firmly in the hands of the "old timers."

The key dividing issue among Croatians was support for or opposition to Yugoslavia. With Tito's break with Stalin in 1948 and his easing of Stalinist repression, the *starosjedioci* developed a favorable attitude towards Tito's regime.

A founder of the "non-aligned" movement, Tito refused to take sides in the implacable Cold War stand-off. In Yugoslavia, he fostered market-based "self-governing socialism" and opened the country's borders, allowing in a flood of Western tourists to the sunny Adriatic coast, and allowing out a stream of Yugoslav "guest workers," who earned hard currency for their families back home by laboring in West European industries.

My family became Tito supporters. Even non-political organizations like the Croatian Fraternal Union increased friendly ties to Yugoslavia, promoting cultural exchanges and visits to the homeland.

Among Croatian nationalists it was forbidden even to utter the word Yugoslavia. The most extreme of them, unreconstructed Ustaši supporters, maintained a network in Argentina, Franco's Spain, Australia and West Germany, forming Croatian "national liberation" armies, fronts or movements. They carried out terrorist attacks, bombings, the assassination of the Yugoslav ambassador to Sweden and the hijacking of an American airliner. A group of heavily armed Ustaši commandoes from Australia tried to incite an uprising in the mountains of Bosnia but were hunted down and killed by police.

In the emigrant communities, a clandestine war raged between violent Croatian separatists and UDBA, the Yugoslav secret police. UDBA agents carried out assassinations of key leaders, including Ante Pavelić, the "Führer" of the Croatian quisling state. The separatists attacked both Yugoslav targets and immigrant group leaders friendly to Yugoslavia.

In the Los Angeles area we were in the thick of the battle. A strong contingent of Croatian separatists settled in southern California. Andrija Artuković, the former quisling Minister of the Interior, had a well-fortified residence in Seal Beach, California a few miles from San Pedro. He had overseen the operations of concentration camps and was described as "the Croatian Adolph Eichmann." Shielded from extradition by the State Department for 36 years, finally he was sent to Yugoslavia and convicted of war crimes. His followers in California represented a constant threat.

Over the years there were right-wing attacks: attempts on the life of the president of the Yugoslav-American Club of San Pedro and bombings of the club's hall. When our groups sponsored concerts by touring artists from Yugoslavia, or when Pittsburgh's Duquesne University Tamburitzans came to town, it was common to receive bomb threats. This community level battle was unrelenting until the 1991 disintegration of Yugoslavia, when the core issue dividing us became moot.

Our family restored connections to the Old World. In 1957 brother Bill took a break from college to travel to Europe with cousin Joe Gerbac. They participated in the International Festival of Youth and Students in Moscow, organized by the World Federation of Democratic Youth (WFDY). The Federation, founded in London in 1945, is a still-active, UN-sanctioned organization, a self-described "anti-imperialist, left wing" NGO that promotes peace and friendship among young people worldwide. Their most recent 18th festival was in 2013 in Quito, Ecuador. In 1957 Bill was among 34,000 youth from 63 countries attending. Many delegations had governmental support. The US government, on the contrary, condemned the event, made the WFDY the target of CIA spying and tried to prevent Americans from attending.

At the close of the Moscow festival, the American delegation was invited to tour the People's Republic of China as guests of the government. Because the United States still refused to recognize China, it was illegal for Americans to visit that country. Bill embraced the opportunity to go to China but Cousin Joe declined.

The group traveled east on the Trans-Siberian railroad, enjoying a long tour of Chinese cities and rural regions. They were addressed by Chinese Premier Chou En-lai, and at trip's end returned to Moscow. Perhaps the Chinese government was hoping for the diplomatic breakthrough that happened 14 years later when the US table tennis team visited China.

From Moscow, most of the Americans flew to the US, where the government confiscated their passports and charged them with violating the travel ban. Bill, however, decided to stay in Europe longer to visit Nerezine. Before leaving Moscow, at Mom's request he went to the office of the Soviet Red Cross and asked for information about our lost uncles and where they might contact us. This led later to the postman bringing an astonishing letter from our cousin Edik, Uncle Tony's younger son, establishing reconnection with him and other relatives in Russia.

When Bill got to Nerezine, he met our many cousins in Mom's village. 18-year-old Bill had to reject avid suggestions that he should pick out a Nerezine girl to marry. He returned home, crossing the ocean as a passenger on a merchant freighter. The ship landed in Montreal and he passed through Canadian customs without a hitch, re-entering the US unnoticed with his passport still in his pocket.

During his half-year of international travel, Bill discovered his innate ability to learn languages. At UCLA he switched from Geology to Slavic Languages and after graduation in 1961, he returned to Yugoslavia to study at Zagreb University. There he met and married a spirited, artistic local woman, Ljubica Miković, and moved from his dormitory into his in-laws' apartment. In 1963 their son Borislav was born. Seeing Bill's letters and pictures from Zagreb, and corresponding with Russian cousins, Mom developed a yen to travel.

In July, 1963 a deadly earthquake hit Skoplje, the capitol of Macedonia in southern Yugoslavia. Mom got involved with relief efforts. While assembling emergency supplies at a Serbian church in San Gabriel, Mom's group was routed from the hall by a stink bomb thrown by Četniks.

In the summer of 1964, Mom joined a delegation of earthquake relief workers invited to Skoplje to view recovery efforts and receive thanks from the Macedonian people. After touring with the group, Mom headed for Zagreb to meet Bill's in-laws. By that time, Bill, Ljubica and son Bobo were in the United States, but Ljubica's parents received her warmly, showed her around Zagreb and took her to their favorite vacation spot on the Dalmatian coast.

Mom then made her return to Nerezine, 42 years after her departure. For her it was an emotional return. She was delighted to be recognized by Nerezinci after so many years. When she left at age nine, she had been blonde but was now chestnut brown. Referring to her hair, a relative exclaimed, "*Ma, još si bila strižica*" (Oh my, you're still a little white witch). Mom didn't explain that her frosted dye job covered darker hair than the blonde tresses she had back in 1921.

Once the ice was broken, our family visited the old homeland with greater frequency. We took charter flights, which made crossing the Atlantic cheaper. A non-profit organization would book a plane for group travel and divide up the costs per seat. In 1967, while Pa was awaiting the California Supreme Court's decision on his suit against the Bar Association, Mom decided that rather than sit on pins and needles at home, a long stay in Europe was better. Brother Bob, a physics professor, with wife Georgie and son Tom, was in Geneva, Switzerland, working at CERN, the European nuclear research center. Bill and Ljubica were back in Zagreb living at the Miković apartment. Mom and Pa bought a Volkswagen in Germany and made the rounds from Geneva to Zagreb to Nerezine.

For a long stretch of that year I was the only immediate family member still in the US. It was my junior year at UC-Berkeley, where I was immersed in political activism. At Mom's urging, that summer I booked a charter flight to London, then hitch-hiked to Zagreb. I frequented rock shows at the Studentski dom, (Student center), meeting lots of young people. I had a chance to jam all night with young Croatian musicians in a Baroque Era building in the Old Town. The Zagreb youths were amused by my accent. A year of literary Serbo-Croatian at college hadn't erased Nona's archaic island dialect from my speech.

I took a train, a boat, then a bus to Nerezine; my parents, Bob's wife Georgie and son Tom already were there. When I got off the bus, an elderly man, a stranger to me, without being asked, directed me to my cousin Antonija's house where the folks were staying. Something similar happened to Bob when he drove down from Switzerland to join us later. He got out of his car, began to stroll on the piazza where an old man addressed him in accented English, "Your people are up there," he said, pointing the way. "How do you know who I am?" Bob asked. "You walk like a Grbac," he stated. We have a family tendency to throw our left leg outward when we take a step. That's the intimacy of village life for you!

As brother Bill did a decade earlier, I disappointed my elder cousins, who wanted to match me with a Nerezine bride. I hung around with *"furešti"*—foreigners, tourists, mostly urban teenagers from Slovenia. Before hitch-hiking back to Amsterdam for the return flight, I thumbed rides through Bosnia and Dalmatia, became enchanted with Yugoslavia and promised myself to return sooner or later to study as my brother was doing then.

Farm Boy

If it was unusual for me as the Hollywood activist kid to have this second life as a Croatian ethnic, it was even more unusual that soon after our arrival in California I became a summertime farm boy. A year after our arrival in LA, while driving to the Bay Area to visit friends, we stopped at a farm near Watsonville to visit Bob and Beth Pepper. Bob Pepper had worked as a business agent for the UPWA in St. Joseph, Missouri. Bob had been inspired by Pa's speeches and was glad to get better acquainted.

Bob and Beth had accepted an offer from Grace McDonald, a wealthy progressive widow, to operate a farm she owned and maintain the vacation cottage she and her friends used as a country get-away. In return they could live there rent-free and derive whatever income they might from the 17-acre farm. They did classic forms of subsistence farming: had a milk cow, always raised a steer and a couple of hogs for the family's meat, and planted a big household garden.

They built chicken houses. At its peak, their egg-production operation had 3,000 Leghorn laying hens. The farm had several acres of aging apple orchard, more than a dozen beehives, and rows of boysenberries.

In 1956 Bob and Beth, still childless, were providing a home for Bob's nephew Marvin Pepper. They eventually adopted the boy and the next year, Beth gave birth to their daughter Janie. Marvin was about a year older than me. Through him I met other local kids. When I wasn't gathering eggs and feeding livestock, we prowled the manzanita-covered hills and forested valleys in the area. .

When the visit was over and my parents were climbing in the car, I begged to stay on at the farm. Bob and Beth noticed that I was a willing worker. "I figure he can do enough work around here to earn his room and board," Bob declared. "We'll put him on the Greyhound bus to home when he's ready to go." So stay I did, and for the rest of my boyhood I wound up riding the 'hound up to Peppers' to spend most of every summer there (except for the 1963 Mexico sojourn).

I felt right at home with them, despite their being old-stock Americans from Missouri. Their speech was Southern dialect. Suppers were Southern classics: cornbread and beans or fried chicken. We had plenty of fresh vegetables from the garden. For dessert, if Beth hadn't baked a pie, we slathered thick layers of home-made jam on bread. We had milk from our cow and churned our own butter. Once I counted the number of turns I had to crank the spinning paddles in the churning jar until the milk "turned." It was over 3,000 times.

Spending the summer at Peppers' seemed like attending an educational seminar. Bob Pepper was a brilliant man. His people were poor dirt farmers, while Beth was from a more sophisticated Missouri town. They both were thinkers and readers and avid debaters on every topic that came up. We discussed books. They had read philosophers and historians and novelists. Living adjacent to the Salinas Valley, they read John Steinbeck, a local. During World War II, while Bob was living in Los Angeles, he persuaded his roommate to take a long streetcar ride with him to the Revolver Bar where W. Somerset Maughm hung out. Bob met and chatted with the elderly writer.

During those summers it was fun to finish a book and discuss it with Bob and Beth. One summer I read the whole Bible just to discuss it with them. Whether we were arguing or just talking, the conversations lasted all day. That's a little-known secret of farm life—you can talk during much of your daily work. We'd discuss the problems of the world at breakfast, the nature of humanity while we gathered eggs, then American history through cleaning and grading eggs. At the big mid-day meal Bob might narrate funny tales from his hometown Dearborn, Missouri, or he'd tell about his wartime days in the merchant marine. Sometimes we'd realize we had been sitting at the table jawing our way well into the afternoon and that we'd better get back to work driving wooden stakes and tightening up wires in the boysenberry patch. We could still talk while doing that job or while making repairs on sheds and chicken houses, or while mucking out chicken manure, hoeing rows in the garden, or filling the chickens' feeders with a wheelbarrow.

Soon the children of other friends, some of them radicals, joined our informal work brigade, the Fuller kids, the Simcich kids, Chris McDonald and Ann Baxter. We worked every day and only took monetary pay for piece-work fruit picking, same as the other hired pickers.

Beth Pepper, with a lot of farm chores to do, still had the ambition to commute to college at San Jose State to become a schoolteacher. Owing to the gendered division-of-labor on the farm, I was around Bob much more, so he was the bigger influence on me. He was a surrogate father, despite my good father-son relationship with Pa. That bond with Bob has carried over to my ties with his daughter, who seems like a sister.

During the summer of 1962 when I was 15, Bob wasn't around his own farm very much. Efforts to unionize California's migrant farm workers were just beginning to find traction. Bob had taken a job as organizer for the Agricultural Workers Organizing Committee (AWOC). He operated from the AWOC office in Modesto, in California's San Joachin Valley, staying weeknights in a rundown motel. He suggested I come to Modesto to spend a couple weeks with him. As usual, being with Bob was very educational.

While working as an organizer, he did not wear his everyday

farm work denim bib overalls. In Modesto he wore a khaki work shirt and matching pants, a khaki canvas fedora covering his bald head. With his ruddy face and prominent nose, he looked exactly like a typical Anglo grower or ranch foreman. That appearance camouflaged him from the authorities, helping his organizer work. But it cut both ways. Until they got to know him, to Chicano farm workers Bob looked just like a boss.

We made the rounds to work sites looking for opportunities to speak to laborers. Bob explained how various crops are grown and the nature of the labor required. One day we drove to the Stockton AWOC office, picked up Larry Itliong, a veteran unionist from the Valley's Filipino community, and drove out to look at some asparagus fields. Larry explained how the skilled seven-man Filipino "grass" cutting teams worked.

In the Modesto area, Bob and I made the rounds to peach orchards. Bob handed me a batch of leaflets, in Spanish and English, announcing a meeting of peach pickers in a hall in town. We split up and passed out as many leaflets as we could before we were chased away by the foremen. We repeated the process at a couple more orchards.

On the evening of the meeting, there was a decent turnout, forty or fifty men and women, all Mexican. Conducting the meeting along with Bob was a Mexican-American woman who translated Bob's remarks and also made a speech of her own. I was embarrassed when Bob identified me as a boy from Los Angeles who was the son of a great union leader.

I was glad to get back to the pleasant coastal climate of Watsonville after weeks in the blazing San Joachin, but the experiences there whetted my appetite to gain a visceral experience of the work and life of agricultural laborers beyond the Peppers' farm. During the summer of 1966, I rose early and drove my VW to Salinas, where at 5 AM I would stand on the street at dawn with other farm workers looking for day labor. Contractors pulled up, announced the type of work and we jumped on the truck or bus. Near Salinas I "tied" cauliflower, wrapping their big green leaves over the white heads to protect them from sunburn. In Gilroy I pulled up garlic, and I picked apricots in Morgan Hill. The contractors paid us in cash at the end of the day. It wasn't big money, but I was much luckier than most farm workers, since I could drive back to Peppers' for food and lodging.

Every crew was different. Sometimes I wound up on a "wino" crew, black and white middle-aged alcoholics. These were usually garrulous guys with great stories, plus useful advice about how to get by on the bum: which Salvation Army missions had the least preaching before coming across with a "hot and a cot," (supper and a bed), or which towns had the most comfortable jails for a "thirty-day vacation." At age 19, I wasn't brave enough to accept their invitations to go in on a jug of cheap wine after work.

On one crew there were a couple young Navajos about my age. We were sitting on crude benches in the back of a pickup truck under a camper shell traveling to a Brussels sprouts field when I noticed their eyes light up; smiles blossomed on their faces. Through the yellowed plexiglass of the camper shell the Pacific Ocean was visible. "Is that the ocean?" one asked. "Sure is," I replied. I racked my brain. Was there any way I could take them to a beach, let them put their desert country toes in the cold Pacific? Not really. Unlike me, they needed to work every day, and the contractors hauled us from a skid-row street in Salinas out to the fields and back again. That was it. The Navajos kept on smiling at the blue expanse and I was too shy to ask them, "Do you want to go there?" The wonders of the Golden State were so near yet so far for those young farm workers.

As the spring of 1964 began and high school graduation loomed, I faced a difficult choice. Many of my closest friends, including my high school sweetheart, were going to attend UC Berkeley in the fall. To our cohort of leftist students, Berkeley was the cool place to go; there was plenty of political ferment that soon would lead to the Free Speech Movement (FSM). My free-spirited friends were willing to endure the humiliation of having to live in regimented dormitories as freshmen, still a requirement then.

The cost of dorm living was more a factor for me than their ban on opposite sex visitors or 10 PM curfews. If I went to UCLA I still would have free room and board at home. Moreover, I had it really good in my parents' household. They gave me complete freedom; we didn't have boarders anymore, so I used the big upstairs bedroom. I had the side door to come and go, plus the full-time use of our beat up 1952 Dodge.

The deciding factor, however, was that my musical hopes were growing. It was not until later that the Bay Area psychedelic music scene emerged. Hollywood with its record companies and the magnificent Ash Grove folk music coffeehouse scene seemed the advantageous place to "make it" in music. It caused a break-up with my girlfriend, but I decided to stay home, play music and attend UCLA.

One of my closest chums from Starr King, a member of our budding rock band, Ted Gustafson, began to attend nearby Los Angeles City College. His family home was distant, in South Central LA, so he rented our other upstairs bedroom and took his meals with our family. The March and Gustafson "apartment" became a frequent hang-out for our friends, relatively quiet gatherings—acoustic guitars only. My parents had an amazing tolerance of my music interests. My parents agreed to use Nona's former bedroom. We brought in amps and an upright piano and converted their master bedroom into our band's rehearsal studio. The band was conscientious to rehearse afternoons and early evenings.

Our hopes to "make it" didn't seem unreasonable. One of our close friends from Starr King, Kenny Edwards, had formed a band, the Stone Ponies, with a Mexican-American woman recently arrived from Tucson, Linda Ronstadt. For decades he made his living as her bass player. Some other Ash Grove regulars had formed The Byrds and had a hit record on the radio, as well as a regular gig at Ciro's, a night club on Sunset Strip.

With so much focus on rehearsing, writing songs and playing gigs on weekends, my heart wasn't really in college. I did, however, have to maintain full time student status to retain my 2-S deferment from the Draft Board. More and more US troops were being sent to Vietnam, increasing the monthly draftee numbers. We lefties opposed the war from the start. We viewed the struggle of the Vietnamese people as a legitimate anti-colonial uprising. Wanting none of it, we took the practical way to stay out of the Army and remained in college.

I never identified much with UCLA, not even with Coach Johnny Wooden's championship basketball teams. I commuted to Westwood, parked the old Dodge on a residential street far from campus and trudged to my classes. Because of an inspiring biology teacher at Hollywood High and my scientist brother Bob, I signed up as a biology major. I made a hash however of Chemistry 1A. Too sloppy in the lab, my experiments never came out correctly. Even in high school I had been no whiz at math, so college calculus proved too challenging. I wound up on academic probation and dropped the biology major. After a flirtation with art, I settled on anthropology.

As the fall 1964 elections approached, I worked on the "No on 14" campaign, opposing a retrogressive ballot initiative to repeal a recently passed fair housing statute. Known as "the Realtors' Initiative," it would allow housing discrimination to continue. Proposition 14 did pass, but was ruled unconstitutional three years later by the US Supreme Court.

I was one of a group of students who set up a table outside the campus union building with literature opposing Proposition 14. It was in an area where campus peace, civil rights and religious organizations could promote their causes. This activity did not become an issue at UCLA. However, student political activity soon became a big political football in Berkeley.

The arch-conservative editor of the *Oakland Tribune*, ex-Senator William Knowland, raised a hue and cry about the political activity of UC students on Sproul Hall Plaza. A number of students had participated in the 1964 Freedom Summer civil rights drive in the South, and now, back in college, they wanted to protest racism in the Bay Area.

Student activism on social issues was incompatible with the university "mission" espoused by UC President Clark Kerr (whom Pa had encountered on the War Labor Board over twenty years earlier). Kerr had written *The Uses of the University*, a book which depicted universities not as an ivory tower, but as an institution to turn out well-trained, compliant employees for corporate America. We laughed when Bay Area singer-songwriter Malvina Reynolds parodied and Pete Seeger popularized Kerr's program in the song "Little Boxes."

Kerr hated college students organizing for change on campus. Facing bad publicity about radical student organizations, the administration banned political information tables on Sproul Hall Plaza, the entrance to the historic campus. This led to sanctions against violators, protests, and sit-ins involving thousands of students. In December, 1964, over 1,000 students demanding free speech rights occupied the administration building. After 36 hours, the administration called in the Oakland police to arrest them. More than 800 students were jailed. The incident was a major spark igniting the militant student movement of the 1960s. In the turmoil that followed, the faculty supported free speech, and in 1965 the administration relented, allowing political activity on campus.

At UCLA our groups did not attract the attention of powerful outside forces. The tables in front of the student union were tucked away in the heart of campus, seldom visible to outsiders. When students participated in politics in the LA area, it was rarely obvious that they were associated with UCLA, bringing little pressure on the administration to suppress us. As a result, our attempts to create a UCLA version of the Free Speech Movement

(FSM) fizzled.

In January, 1965, our Students for a Democratic Society (SDS) chapter reserved a lecture hall at lunchtime for a founding meeting of UCLA's FSM. We wanted to show support for the students arrested in Berkeley, and to discuss free speech on our own campus. The meeting was totally stampeded by a group of fraternity boys who, on signal, stood up and shouted, drowning out the speakers. "Let's get the hell out of here," one frat boy hollered and most of the crowd stormed out the doors. In the calm that followed, only our committee and a handful of others were left in the hall.

At the beginning of my sophomore year, farm workers in the National Farm Workers Association (NFWA) and AWOC went on strike in Delano, California during the table grapes harvest. I got involved in SDS efforts to support the strikers and urge a consumer boycott of grapes. I identified with this issue as a continuation of Bob Pepper's AWOC organizing. We targeted areas with significant, sympathetic Latino populations for picketing. A few members of our group entered the stores, filled grocery carts with grapes, pushed the carts to a far corner, then walked out. We solicited contributions of non-perishable food, sacks of rice, dry beans and flour, canned goods and baby food, for the strikers.

By the fall of 1965, President Lyndon Johnson had escalated the war in Vietnam, sending tens of thousands more American troops. The war became a national issue. In November, we assisted the Vietnam Teach-In organized by UCLA faculty members. The marathon event featuring panels of anti-war politicians and professors was held continuously from noon to midnight in the Grand Ballroom of the Student Union. For most of us, the presentation by popular philosophy professor Hans Meyerhoff was the highlight. Dr. Meyerhoff's anti-war position was grounded in his horrible experiences during World War II. His impassioned speech received a standing ovation. Sadly, it was his last appearance. The very next week he died tragically in an automobile accident.

In March of 1966 I crowded into a car with a bunch of friends to make the day-long drive up Highway 101 to San Francisco to participate in the "Days of International Protest," one of the largest marches against the Vietnam War. At night we "crashed" in sleeping bags on the floor of friends in Berkeley, talking intently into the night. I became persuaded that our movement activities in LA could not attain the degree of public notice in the vast and diffuse LA metro area that the Bay Area efforts were achieving. By the time we were ready to head home, I was ready to transfer to Berkeley in the coming fall.

I spent the summer based at Peppers' and did migrant farm labor much of the season. In addition to working near Salinas, I made my way up the west coast as far as Hood River, Oregon picking fruit. By fall I was back at Peppers' farm. Passing through Berkeley on the way down from Oregon, I rented a furnished room in a former residential house on Grove Street that had been converted into offices for Turn Toward Peace, an anti-nuclear weapons organization. At the start of the fall session Bob Pepper in his bib overalls took me and a couple boxes of belongings to Berkeley in his pick-up.

One block north on Grove Street was a duplex where my good high school friends Joan Kramer and Janie Corey lived with a third roommate, Connecticut native Laurie Baumgarten. They had a big ground floor apartment with a spacious living room-dining room area. It wound up being the frequent setting for SDS or other New Left meetings. Lacking much legroom at my own digs, their place became my "living room." I had no record player, so I left my treasured LPs there. I had no television, so what little TV I watched was there with my friends. They had an upright piano, so their apartment also became a place to make music.

At the apartment on Grove we hatched plans for upcoming movement actions that historians would write about decades later. Our group was fluid and participatory, without formal structure. We never had a meeting that followed Roberts' Rules. The individuals that the mainstream press (and later historians) focused on, Mario Savio, Jerry Rubin, Steve Hamilton, Stew Albert, had no special status or rank as far as we were concerned. They were a few years older than us, which might have diminished rather than enhanced their authority.

We were a tight group of mostly undergraduate students, several of us red-diaper babies who had known each other since high school. Of the SDS media stars Mario Savio was the most thoughtful and articulate so his opinions carried weight. On the other hand, Jerry Rubin was the most suspect. He was eight or nine years older than us, was a recent arrival in California, and his flamboyant suggestions for actions seemed designed to put himself in the spotlight. That he was not from a radical background seemed suspicious to our red-diaper core group, having spent our childhoods under FBI surveillance. At the time, I had a strong suspicion that Jerry might be an agent.

Neither did the national SDS leaders like Carl Oglesby or Tom Hayden exercise much sway over our opinions. They were off in remote places like Michigan or New Jersey, the boondocks according to our California-centric universe. Their treatises, drawing on the writings of scholars like C. Wright Mills and Herbert Marcuse, seemed boring and superfluous. We red-diaper babies had received the basic principles of Marxism with our mothers' milk. We didn't need a sociologist or a philosopher to tell us that there was a Power Elite, that racism was a strategy to divide workers, that colonialism/imperialism was capitalism's super-exploitation of Third World working people, and that war was the capitalists' means of grabbing from their competitors more of the world's wealth and disposing of excess workers as cannon fodder. Struggle against these evils and for a socialist society was the purpose of life. I may have been arrogant, but the SDS leaders' need to construct ideological treatises seemed pompous and redundant.

In 1966 Tom Hayden visited us in Berkeley. We met in a classroom and he showed a film about his community organizing efforts in Newark. He received a fairly cool reception. Hayden seemed old and bossy. We felt we already knew what we were doing and we didn't need directions from him.

The first big project of our SDS group in the fall of 1966 was the Black Power Conference held on campus on October 29. The university administration viewed it as provocative and keenly wanted to ban the event. Owing to the gains of FSM the previous year, the conference fell within the university's guidelines, so it took place despite their unhappiness. They probably wouldn't have been so opposed had we not scheduled Stokely Carmichael, the recently elected leader of SNCC, to deliver the keynote address. He was sure to draw negative attention from mainstream media. Since Carmichael split with Martin Luther King during the Selma Marches and called for Black Power over Integration, the mass media elevated Stokely to epitomize the most threatening bad-ass black man since the death of Malcolm X the previous year. With violent uprisings proliferating in urban ghettos, the media distorted Carmichael's advocacy of self-defense and the Black Power slogan as a clarion call to violence.

Besides the administration there were others who opposed the Black Power Conference. The Afro-American Student Union initially called for a boycott of the event, objecting because the largely white SDS chapter had organized it. In a meeting with Stokely they argued without success that he should not waste his time speaking to a mostly white audience.

The 1966 California gubernatorial election pitting incumbent Pat Brown against conservative challenger Ronald Reagan was looming only a few days after the conference. Democrats were horrified that a Black Power Conference at the state-supported university handed Reagan a highly inflammatory issue.

Indeed, Jerry Rubin and Stew Albert had been advocating for our movement to facilitate Reagan's election. Their argument, which I found totally unconvincing, was that a conservative, repressive government would make things worse for everyone, heightening dissatisfaction and hastening the anticipated revolution. Our concrete red-diaper experience did not support this notion. In the 1950s our families had the visceral effects of repression. The blacklists, ruined careers and lives, the many jailed and executed comrades led to a decimation of the leftist and trade union movements in America. Moreover, we viewed as far-fetched the notion that a successful revolution might be imminent. That had been our parents' mistaken idea in the 1930s. Many years of work lay ahead to build a mass coalition that might change the system.

Despite opposition, the Black Power Conference was a great success, with the highlight being Carmichael's keynote address. In moving oratory he characterized as irrelevant the goal of integrating blacks into an otherwise unchanged, unjust American society. He challenged gross economic inequality and the aggressive imperialist stance of the United States military. He supported the right of blacks to defend themselves from racist attacks. Most relevant to us was Carmichael's plea that white activists concentrate efforts on organizing in white communities to oppose racism, war and injustice. He suggested a suitable issue around which to organize:

The only power we have is the power to say, "Hell no!" to the draft....And this country will only be able to stop the war in Vietnam when the young men who are made to fight it begin to say, "Hell, no, we ain't going." Now then, there's a failure because the Peace Movement has been unable to get off the college campuses where everybody has a 2-S and not going to get drafted anyway. And the question is, how can you move out of that into the white ghettos of this country and begin to articulate a position for those white students who do not want to go.

Carmichael spoke clearly about a way forward, with a concrete strategy that might advance the movement. For me it fit my parents' mass organizing emphasis. The recommendations in Stokely's address to take our efforts off-campus to young working-class whites became the main item of discussion in our Grove Street meetings.

But events on campus seemed to have a momentum of their own. Later that same fall, a group of anti-war students attempted to block access to Navy recruiters who had set up in the student union hall. In ensuing days we crammed the hall around the Navy recruiters' table, loudly singing "We shall not be moved...." When we were ejected at last, we set up a PA system the next day and used it to call for a student strike. I was one of the speakers at the "illegal" microphone and was cited for it. An AP photograph of the moment was transmitted as a wire photo to newspapers across the country. It gained a prominent place in the *Chicago Daily News*, so Mom received two or three clippings of the picture from Chicago friends with approving notes that "Buddy seems to be following in his father's footsteps." Actually, when it came to being a public figure for the movement, nothing could be farther from the truth. I wished to avoid the limelight so as not to allow my easily traceable communist connections to harm the movement.

The student strike ended inconclusively. After a few days of turmoil, we assembled in a large lecture hall and voted to end the strike. One speaker, as a face-saving rationale, commented that the strike effort had enhanced our cohesiveness. To make the point he quoted from the Beatle's recent hit "Yellow Submarine." We all belted out the chorus, "We all live in a yellow submarine, a yellow submarine..." and the event became known as the Yellow Submarine strike. The metaphor, however, only emphasized our isolation and insularity. While the national SDS leaders were recommending just this sort of on-campus confrontation to radicalize college students, we were dissatisfied with such tactics and intent on ways to get out into the wider community.

One day Luis Valdez of the farmworkers union and his Teatro Campesino came to campus to perform skits on Sproul Hall Plaza. Entranced, I sat down with Luis and a few friends to ask how to initiate a street theater group. "Keep the plays short and simple," he asserted. "Only one main point per play." He suggested plays should be metaphoric, like living political cartoons. And use eye-catching costumes and props whenever possible.

Richard March, 1967

Several of us soon gathered at Grove Street to found an anti-draft street theatre group. We would work in collaboration with an emerging Bay Area Anti-Draft Union to encourage draft resistance and offer resisters advice. We aspiring dramatists selected the Soviet-inspired name Agit-Prop Theatre. In addition to Luis' advice about play structure, I suggested that we emphasize songs.

Soon, to the strum of my guitar, we used group process to create satirical anti-draft lyrics to familiar melodies. One of the first used the tune of the theme song for "Rawhide," a Clint Eastwood TV western. We chanted, "Movin', movin', movin', though they're disapprovin', keep those draftees movin' Draft Board...." Then on the chorus we shouted, "Call 'em up, ship 'em out, call 'em up, ship 'em out, Draft Board!" We created dozens of songs, linked to the content of our plays.

We created several skits about five minutes in length. The purpose of their brevity was not only to keep it simple, but also because we made hit-and-run performances on community colleges and high school campuses, where we would be promptly chased off. We swooped onto a campus, usually at lunchtime, quickly piling out of a car or the converted hearse that one of our members drove, sang a song to draw a crowd, then quickly began the skit. We utilized themes from current pop culture. For example, the Warren Beatty movie "Bonnie and Clyde" was all the rage, so in a skit, an Army recruiter tries to enlist Clyde Barrow to use his submachine gun on the Vietnamese instead of on the banks.

One of our group had the assignment to argue with and stall school officials who would appear to chase us off. We brought leaflets promoting the Anti-Draft Union. At some schools we already had contacts who passed them out, or otherwise we did it ourselves. About the time the school official tired of arguing and headed inside to call the cops, the play would end and we would pile in our vehicle to make a swift getaway.

After a foray in the East Bay town of Hayward, we stopped at a café for lunch. When we came outside, we saw that our hearse had been vandalized with thick letters in white paint. "Fuck hippies," and "Go to Hell" were among the painted slogans. We joked that we had done a successful job of organizing the locals...into action against us! A couple of times local cops issued our driver unwarranted traffic citations. We chipped in to pay his fine, but the moving violations remained on his driving record.

Sometimes we were asked to perform at rallies on Sproul Hall steps, providing a little variety between speakers. One of our earliest performances there received a strange recognition. In the play we portrayed a line of underwear-clad draftees proceeding through their physical exam at an Army induction center. Worried about being busted for indecent exposure, I wore a tight bathing suit beneath my white boxer shorts. But I needn't have bothered, we weren't hassled. The play was well received by the crowd and we were amazed to see a political cartoon in the next day's student paper depicting our line of draftees followed by a pair of copulating dogs. "Future Dogfaces" read the caption. Weird!

Agit-Prop Theatre became a familiar part of the Berkeley movement. We'd enter a crowd in a public place chanting our theme song to the tune of "When Johnny Comes Marching Home." It contained our claim, "When Agit-Prop come on the scene, the power structure starts to lean..."

The Black Power Conference had been the big Berkeley movement project at the start of the 1966-67 academic year. The next fall, in response to Stokely Carmichael's urging, opposing the draft became our primary issue. We began to plan a huge action, Stop the Draft Week, to take place in Oakland in October, 1967. Rifts over strategy emerged while planning the protest. The ardently pacifist faction, which had singer Joan Baez as its best-known spokesman, advocated completely passive resistance—a peaceful sit-in in front of the Oakland Induction Center. Inspired by the assertive stance of the Black Panthers, many of us favored a more active form of non-violent resistance. We wanted to use hit and run tactics to blockade downtown Oakland and prevent the busses bringing draftees from reaching the Induction Center.

Stokely Carmichael at Black Power Conference, Berkeley, 1966

A compromise was reached that the "Baez Faction" would have free rein on Monday, we would stay away while they sat in and submitted to arrest. On Tuesday our group swarmed the downtown. The construction of the Bay Area Rapid Transit (BART) system was in process. We barricaded key intersections using trash cans as well as I-beams or other construction materials from the BART project. The buses were kept at bay for hours. It was national news. The Oakland Police were criticized for their failure to control the situation. We relished our success, rested two days then returned on Friday to repeat the same type of action.

Much as tactical differences in the movement were sharpened in Stop the Draft Week, rifts began to appear in our small Agit-Prop group. Early in 1968, Art Napoleon, of Jana Films, a producer/director of low-budget B-movies, came up from Hollywood to watch a Grove Street Agit-Prop rehearsal. Perhaps Mike Smith, one of our regular actors the media focused on as a leading activist, had invited him. Mike had a beautiful statuesque girlfriend Lesley Gilb whose conventional good looks fueled her acting ambitions. Art Napoleon explained he was interested in making a feature-length movie about a Berkeley activist with a focus on Agit-Prop Theatre. We quizzed him about it. He explained that his most recent film had been about the pastoral life of West Coast surfers, but now the time was ripe for a movie about activism in Berkeley.

After Art left, we had a spirited discussion. He would pay the group some much-needed money that could help cover expenses for props and gasoline. It would be an opportunity for a big movie audience to see our plays on the silver screen. I was convinced we should cooperate with the filmmaker. Laurie Baumgarten, the chief spokesperson for the other opinion, argued there was no way that this Hollywood producer would create anything other than a sensationalized, distorted depiction of us and the movement. The Hollywood movie industry was not about to present our genuine anti-war, anti-draft message. She would have nothing to do with it. Of course she was right.

There followed a number of film shoots, "on location" on Telegraph Avenue. Art's crew filmed our induction center play and a couple others. We learned that sound for those visual shots was to be dubbed in afterwards. Art created an improvised studio in an apartment. With my guitar and a couple actor-singers we set about recording the songs that went with the filmed plays. The induction center play began with a mournful parody of "I've Been Workin' on the Railroad." "I've been waitin' to be drafted, since I've been eighteen. Now they've got me and I'm shafted by the US war machine. Oh my goodness I am worried, I have no disease. I don't want to die for Wall Street or kill Vietnamese."

In the course of the recording session Art made what he presented as a minor innocuous request. "How about changing just a couple of words? Can you substitute "nothing" for "Wall Street" in the last line of the verse?" To be agreeable we just did it, we sang "I don't want to die for nothing..." instead.

When Laurie heard about this change, she confronted me about it. "Oh my God, you are right, Laurie. He conned us into plucking out a key anti-capitalist message." I was mortified. The shooting of our Agit-Prop plays already had been completed. Art was through with me, there was nothing I could do. The rest of the shoots mainly involved Mike and Leslie, who had been cast in the two leading roles as "The Activist" and "The Girlfriend." More disturbing aspects leaked out. Art had requested they film a scene in which they relaxed nude in the bathtub together, smoking a joint. While it may not have been an unrealistic depiction of something we might do, it was the sort of personal behavior we thought should remain private; it might be used to smear our movement.

Then we learned that Art had recruited some good-looking young women unconnected to the movement to portray the girlfriends of other supposed activists. In the movie, these women accurately depicted grievances of movement women: being expected to carry out all the drudge work, like mimeographing leaflets or assembling mailings, and being expected to clean up after and feed their activist boyfriends. Their desired redress of the grievance, however, was an abominable distortion. The movie girlfriends just wanted their boyfriends to give up this activist nonsense, get good jobs and marry them! The only comfort is that the film was a little viewed flop. Now, except for a brief clip on YouTube, only one videotape copy of the whole film remains in an archive on the Berkeley campus.

Seriously wounded by the rift over the movie, one more issue remained to break up Agit-Prop Theatre. After presenting a skit at Berkeley High School, we stopped at a nearby grocery to pick up some fruit and sandwich fixings for a picnic lunch in a nearby park. Mike Smith portrayed a Viet Cong fighter in the skit. He was dressed in black pajamas and had a toy submachine gun. While we were in the store we started goofing around. Mike went running from aisle to aisle and we chased him, playing "war." The store was nearly empty, but suddenly we realized that the few shoppers present had been seriously startled by the playful depiction of violence, so we cut it out. The checker was decidedly cool towards us.

There ensued discussions at our next rehearsal about doing more unannounced "freak out" plays. Proponents argued that when we frightened people, it "brought the war home." Once people realized they weren't in danger, they would think about how it must be for the Vietnamese enduring an actual deadly war. I didn't like the idea at all. I doubted that people really would think about the Vietnamese, they would just be pissed off at us. I refused to participate in such "guerrilla" acts. Soon the cohesiveness of our group dissipated.

A few months earlier, the grievances of women about movement leaders' blatant sexism in the movement had burst into open discussion. When Stokely Carmichael was asked, "what is the position of women in SNCC?" he supposedly quipped, "Prone." The Black Panther Party emerged in 1966, influenced partly by Carmichael's advocacy of armed self-defense at the Black Power Conference. Bobby Seale became a familiar figure on Bancroft Avenue at the edge of Sproul Plaza, selling copies of Mao's Little Red Book. The Black Panther male members strutted in leather jackets and black berets, and posed for photos brandishing rifles. Eldridge Cleaver soon arrived in Berkeley to join Huey Newton and Bobby Seale in the Panther Party. Cleaver, in his book *Soul on Ice* explicitly justified the rape of white women by blacks as a revolutionary act.

Sexism was so pervasive that we unconsciously fell into it, even in some Agit-Prop creations. In a rehearsal, male and female group members were making up an anti-LBJ song to the melody of the Everly Brothers' "Bird Dog." One verse was: "Lyndon has a wife, she's a bird." The line seemed perfect, the first lady's name was Lady Bird. "The pride of his life, what a bird." Then things got ugly. "Take a closer look now, she's a dog. Bet you're really shook now, what a dog. Is it any wonder that he's the biggest killer in town?"

The verse is disgusting and sexist, and to my shame, we actually performed it in public. We were still blind to the sexism of mocking a woman's appearance because she didn't conform to some Hollywood standard of beauty. And we suggested that her supposedly horrible appearance was so revolting to LBJ that he would be so sexually deprived he'd become a killer.

At that time many of my good friends were women developing a strong feminist consciousness. I also am fortunate my mother was a proto-feminist who, as the only female in our nuclear family, refused to be saddled with all the traditionally female tasks and insisted that I learn to do my share of them.

The Grove Street apartment became the site of female gatherings to discuss grievances concerning men in the movement. With their help I soon "got it" about our ingrained sexism. I had to own it and change it. I saw male comrades shamefully erupt during meetings when our sisters confronted them about sexism. The tug of war between our emerging feminists and the recalcitrant male chauvinists was going on in the summer of 1968 when remarkably enough, I graduated from the university.

For me, graduation was a mournful occasion. It represented losing my 2-S draft deferment at a time when the US had half a million troops in Viet-Nam. The hungry draft boards were scooping up more young men. I had some friends who escaped to Canada but I didn't want to do that, my devotion to jazz and blues was a powerful disincentive to going to Canada. I had frequented Esther's Orbit Room, an R&B club in Oakland, and the 5-4 Ballroom in LA. I wanted to visit Memphis and the Delta country of Mississippi to encounter the lands that originated the music I loved to play. Canada's Great White North sounded like a bleak exile. I had to find a way to stay in the USA yet not be drafted.

The prospect of going to prison also was bleak. Then I heard about a program to recruit teachers for schools in the black ghettos of South Central LA. Grasping at straws, I speculated that the draft board might deem such a necessary job worthy of granting me a deferment. I bid what I hoped would be a temporary farewell to my Berkeley friends and headed down Highway 101 to LA.

Radicals, Hippies and Avoiding the Draft

Agit-Prop Theatre had been an ideal project that allowed me, the troupe's guitarist, to pursue my musical interests, especially the group process of fashioning plays and songs. We had to think up cheap-to-produce, portable but eye-catching props. The most outlandish of them was made from a cardboard shipping tube, eight feet long, the red, white and blue "atomic harpoon" wielded by Captain Elbie (LBJ) in our parody of Moby Dick.

When the vandals in Hayward castigated us as "hippies," we disagreed: we were radicals, not hippies. As far as we were concerned, hippies just wanted to drop out of our repressive society, anesthetize themselves with mind-bending drugs, and retreat to an isolated "hippie commune." We radicals were dedicated to the serious business of making a revolution. The hippies would counter that they were making a revolution, too, by changing society, one blown hippie mind at a time. Berkeley was the hotbed of radicals, while across the Bay Bridge, San Francisco's Haight-Ashbury district was home of the hippies.

The Hayward vandals weren't so far off target. There were areas of overlap that an outside observer might fail to grasp. We all commonly used marijuana, although the hippies experimented more with LSD and other drugs. The sexual mores of both groups were pretty loose. All sex wasn't necessarily "serious." In terms of dress and grooming, we distinguished a paisley-clad, sandals-wearing hippie with a flower in his long hair from a radical wearing patched jeans, work boots and a snap brim cap, but to outsiders, we all were scruffy and unconventional.

There was an overlap in musical tastes as well. The hippies tended toward overtly psychedelic bands that played at the Avalon Ballroom, while more of us radicals favored the Fillmore, where blues bands predominated. But hippies and radicals listened to much of the same music: Bob Dylan, Country Joe and the Fish, the Grateful Dead, Jefferson Airplane and others.

In January, 1967, my taste for the Bay Area rock bands lured me and a few friends across the Bay to the "Human Be-In" in Golden Gate Park, the first of the big hippie gatherings. We found a place to sit on the grass near the stage and enjoyed the sunny afternoon. The poetry recitations by Alan Ginsberg, Lenore Kandel and Gary Snyder seemed a bit pretentious, and it was evident that Timothy Leary had fried his brains with LSD, ceaselessly repeating "Turn on, tune in, and drop out." But the bands were good, Big Brother and the Holding Company, the Grateful Dead and Quicksilver Messenger Service. Owsley, the "hippie chemist," had produced a quantity of LSD and was passing it out. It was fun to dance on the grass surrounded by a lot of tripping age-mates.

After the program, we walked from the park to Haight Street and stopped in a Mexican restaurant for enchiladas. When we came out, a tall young man was standing on the corner loudly playing Ornette Coleman riffs on a tenor saxophone with several impromptu percussionists banging on metal trash cans. A crowd gathered, some spilling into the street. We had only lingered to listen a short while when a police car slowly drove past blasting a murky, unintelligible announcement in the din. Moments later, police cars zoomed into the intersection from all four directions, a squadron of blue-clad San Francisco police waded into the crowd swinging clubs, randomly grabbed people from the crowd, and flung them into cars and police wagons. In the street I saw three blue coats beating the shit out of the struggling saxophone player, obviously using excessive force.

In Los Angeles, since the investigation following the 1965 Watts riot, which faulted police misbehavior for sparking the disturbance, it became legitimate for citizens who observed police misdeeds to get an officer's badge number and report him to the civilian police review board. Not realizing it might be different in San Francisco, I approached the nearest of the trio whaling away at the sax player. "Officer, I'd like your badge number," I shouted. He straightened up and faced me; I looked into the round, pudgy visage of the policeman I later learned was named Tom Sully. "You want my badge number? Come over here, I'll give it to you," he said walking toward the sidewalk. I followed. As we neared a squad car parked a few strides away, he threw open the rear door, agilely flung me into the back seat and slammed it behind me. Reflexively I tried to open the door and was startled to find no handle. In front of me a wire mesh restricted access to the front seats. "Hmm, am I under arrest?" I wondered. I turned, looked at the other prisoners in the car and was amazed to see Dave Kast and Mike Sweet, two of my Berkeley friends with whom I'd come to the Be-In.

Moments later Sully and his partner got in the car and drove to the nearby Park District station. We were led into a barred holding cell and soon, police wagons arrived. We were joined by dozens of other prisoners, crammed like New York subway passengers at rush hour. I started a conversation with the fellows closest to me, our bodies pressed together. One was a diminutive, scraggly hippie who was clearly still tripping. He told me that some months ago he had sown marijuana seeds on a forested hillside. When he returned weeks later he mistook the poison oak growing there for marijuana, picked leaves and smoked them! "Oh, that was bad!" he groaned. The guy next to him said during the wagon trip to the station, the little hippie kept chanting, "They're taking us to the Avalon." His love trip included loving the cops.

Officers removed us one by one from the holding cell to process us. When his turn came, the hippie asked the cop, "Do you turn on?" "Yeah sure, all the time," he replied sarcastically. "Now I know 'cop' is only a name," the hippie gushed and hugged the officer. Taken aback and embarrassed, the cop shoved him along the hallway.

While I was still in the crowded holding cell, Sully approached the bars and gestured for me to come close. I squeezed over to him. In a muffled, hesitant tone he asked, "Now, is this going to cause problems for you at the university?" He had confiscated my wallet and must have seen my student ID. With a pathetic lack of quick thinking, I replied honestly, "I don't think they'll even know about it." Sully seemed relieved and moved away.

I was processed, charged with "Failure to Disperse," and loaded into a wagon headed to jail downtown. Perhaps the police were disappointed the Be-In had come off without a hitch. At Alan Ginsberg's urging, the crowd even picked up litter on the grounds.

Unwilling to let the event pass successfully, the cops inflicted violence and arrests.

Downtown we were herded into the drunk tank, a spacious chamber the size of a basketball court. I milled around the room late into the night. In a while the little hippie went into a bad trip, screaming incessantly. Some guards quickly dragged him off. As the evening wore on, we were joined by conventional drunks, congenial fellows, mostly our elders. There was a jovial sense of jail comradery. The drunks said they hoped to get bailed out in time to watch the big football game the next day; the Green Bay Packers were taking on the Kansas City Chiefs in the very first Super Bowl.

Sometime after midnight they took me to a cell with no mattress. I tried to get a little rest lying on the cold enameled metal bunk attached to the wall. About dawn a prison employee came around carrying a tray with tin bowls of mucky oatmeal. "Would you like to buy a carton of milk for it?" he inquired. "Hey, they took my wallet and my money," I complained. "Oh, that's too bad," he responded and moved along. I didn't have a chance to choke down much of the oatmeal before an officer opened the cell and led me down the hall to a spot where a telephone was mounted on the wall. "You can make two calls," he informed me.

Without any thought, I dialed my parents' number. It was still early on a Sunday morning. My mother answered groggily. "Mom, I'm in jail in San Francisco," I blurted. She groaned, "Talk to your father." Pa got on. "What's that, Bud? You in jail? What have they got you in for?" "Failure to disperse." "That sounds like a bunch of bullshit. Well, see if you can get bailed out. Call me back if you need to." I felt foolish for bothering them.

Taped to the wall near the phone were ads for several bail bondsmen. "Which one should I call?" I asked the cop standing by my elbow. "Barrish has been takin' 'em," he replied laconically. I got the number from a card with the slogan "Don't perish in jail. Call Barrish for bail." Before long I was released. I made my way across the street to the storefront office of bondsman Jerry Barrish to complete some paperwork. The room was packed with hippies, standing, crouching, sitting on the floor. Several had hats, bags or baskets brimming with coins and small bills. "We are the Diggers," one informed me, a group known for rounding up food donations for hippie events. I was bailed out thanks to the generosity of hippies.

I was supposed to appear in court for arraignment in a few days. Prior to the date I received a call asking me to come to a meeting with attorneys at the Vincent Hallinan law offices. The name sounded familiar. I realized that the Hallinans were old lefty friends of my parents. Hallinan had in fact run for president as a third party candidate in 1952, the first elections that I can remember. Sitting around a conference room table, we met Michael Stepanian, a young lawyer recently graduated from Stanford. He was passionate about our case and would handle it *pro bono*, for no fee. He was a player on an amateur rugby team. On Saturday they played a match in a nearby section of Golden Gate Park. Most of the rugby players sneered at the long-haired revelers, but Stepanian was curious. After the game, still wearing his rugby jersey and cleats, he wandered into the Human Be-In. "I looked like I was from a different planet, but nobody seemed to give a shit. The sun was shining, the kids were beautiful, the music was magic. That was the beginning of my education."

I learned that ten out of dozens who were arrested in the post-Be-In bust would be the first to go on trial. John Keskulla, the sax player was in the group. My Berkeley friends and I were selected because our student status lent us a degree of respectability, at least more than a Haight-Ashbury street person. Stepanian along with Brian Rohan, another young Hallinan firm lawyer, would represent us at the arraignment and trial. They asked us to dress respectably, or at least less outrageously than usual when we came to court.

I made a good faith effort, consistent with the Agit-Prop creed to be eye-catching. I wore a checkered sports jacket from Goodwill and a necktie emblazoned with a Technicolor photograph of Plains Indians by a teepee. Most of the defendants made sartorial gestures for the honor of the court. One of us even got a short haircut and dressed like a stock broker. There was among us, however, one defendant who refused. He wore grungy clothes, walked in and out of the courtroom with a hipster's swagger and a carnation in his hair. In a voice audible beyond our table, he made rude comments about the prosecutors.

The press called our case "The Hippie Trial." A photograph of us at the defense table with Stepanian appeared on page one of the San Francisco Chronicle. The trial took a week. We wound up with an all-white, middle-aged jury.

On the initial day of prosecution testimony, the first arresting officer to testify made a serious error. He told the truth. He admitted he could not remember arresting the defendant in question or what he was doing. The cops grabbed people so fast, I'm sure none of them could remember each arrest. The defendant in question was Mr. Outrageous with the flower in his hair. The instant the cop made that admission it was like a brick tossed in a goldfish bowl. The attorneys approached the bench and huddled with the judge. A recess was called.

When we came back, our lawyers asked Mr. Flower Power to sit in the most conspicuous spot, at the end of the defense table. Stepanian made a motion to dismiss charges against him. The judge concurred. The exonerated hippie swaggered out of the courtroom taking a long cut passing right in front of the jury box.

Now we were nine.

When testimony continued, all of the cops displayed amazing powers of recall. The police riot became re-characterized as a sit-in—they warned us to move on, pleaded with us, and reluctantly had to arrest us. Keskulla viciously attacked them-with his saxophone. Tom Sully greeted me pleasantly in the hallway before he went in to testify. I was momentarily deceived that he might be honest, but he lied, too. I was dogging the cops' footsteps, pestering them; he warned me repeatedly but I refused to go away.

The jury was out for a long time. After a few hours they came in. The foreman said they were deadlocked. The judge sent them back. Late in the evening the jury emerged again with what seemed like a 50-50 compromise–four convicted, four acquitted, a hung jury on one. The convicted were Keskulla and me, obvious troublemakers, along with my angelic-looking buddy Dave Kast and Mr. Stock Broker! Why them? We'll never know.

Apparently the prosecution wasn't happy with only four convictions out of ten and dropped charges on everybody else! We got a $100 fine, (at a time when average pay was less than $500 per month), a 30-day suspended sentence and 6 months' probation. At our sentencing, another lawyer offered to file an appeal for us *pro bono*. We signed some papers. Years passed. I finished college, moved to Los Angeles, then to Wisconsin. It was the last I ever heard about the case. Maybe he won the appeal, maybe I'm still a wanted man in San Francisco.

# # #

During my sophomore year at UCLA I car-pooled to campus with Tommy Siporin. Tommy was a brilliant guy who had recently finished a double major at Harvard in Mathematics and Philosophy and was in Law School at UCLA. He was the son of my parents' friends Mary and "Sippie" Siporin from their Back of the Yards organizing days. I'd known Tommy and his brother Mickey since our childhoods and now fate had thrown us together again.

Tommy also was a cartoonist and writer. His work combined those skills in symbolic works that joined social commentary with appreciation for the absurd. During the year we were commuting together he penned a novel titled *The Avoider*, about a young man whose existence was defined only in the negative. He existed to avoid the draft. After graduating from Berkeley, I realized, I had become Tommy's Avoider. Now I began draft avoidance by teaching in a poor black neighborhood school.

When I was the scruffy guitarist/actor in Agit-Prop, I couldn't have imagined that by the summer of 1968 I'd be donning a dress shirt, tie and sports jacket each morning and heading from my Gower Street home to an elementary school in South Central Los Angeles. I had signed up for the Los Angeles Unified School District's "Talent Search Program." My reason was a hope that this essential occupation might help me avoid the draft. Anyone with a bachelor's degree could qualify if you were willing to teach in segregated schools in LA's ghetto. I took some training, orientation and practice teaching during Summer School, then at the start of the fall semester I was assigned to a 6th Grade class at Manhattan Place School, not far from where I had lived on 90th Street in 1955. There was a supervising teacher who oversaw three Talent Search teachers in the building. Each morning he'd look over the lesson plans we prepared the night before. He sat in to observe each of us about a third of the time, sometimes presenting a demonstration lesson in class.

On my first day I had a private meeting with the principal, an African-American who avoided black speech so much that his diction sounded like an affected English accent. "Mister Maaach, the most important thing to teach these children is discipline. If you have to spend 90% of your time on classroom control, I want you to do it. If you have to spend 100% of your time on classroom control, you should do it."

To the principal's consternation, I kept blowing it. The school's routine when the morning bell rang was for students to line up with their classmates, in order from tallest to shortest, in front of the school building. Then the teachers would lead their classes into the building. They were to walk in silence one arms-length from the right side of the hallway. After a few days of this routine, without consulting anybody, I spoke to my class before dismissal one afternoon, "OK, you kids are 6th Graders, the oldest kids in this school, right? You know how to come in by yourselves, right? Tomorrow, you'll come in quietly, no noise, no trouble, right?" I got a chorus of "Yes, teacher" after every question.

The next morning the bell rang. I remained at my desk in the classroom. My students filtered into the room in a fairly orderly fashion. After a minute or two, because the intercom was broken, the principal's secretary appeared to summon me to the office. I got quite a dressing down and had to return to the usual routine the next day.

I soon discovered that in my slow reading group I had a few boys who were completely illiterate. How could they be in 6th Grade? I learned from my supervising teacher that it was policy to keep them with their age level, as long as they were not disruptive. To try to accommodate their deficit I was allowed to use the 5th Grade Reader. They couldn't read that either. The World Series between the LA Dodgers and the Detroit Tigers was going on. I had an idea. I signed up to use the school's television and managed to have the kids watch part of the game. The next day I brought the sports section from the LA Times. We went over the account of yesterday's game, beginning with the captions to the photos. By the next day I was busted again for deviating from the approved curriculum.

I finally was fired about a week later. We had a couple rainy days and the kids had to stay inside for recess. With rain predicted the next day, I suggested they bring their favorite records, I'd get the school's record player and they could dance during recess. I resisted the kids' challenge to get up and show them my moves—they were much better dancers than me. Before long, the principal's secretary made another appearance to summon me downstairs. The principal informed me I was "not working out," that I could leave immediately, my supervising teacher would take over the class for the time being. I guess I wasn't so essential after all.

I was getting advice on the draft issue from Bill Smith, an attorney active in the left-leaning National Lawyers Guild. Bill had been skeptical that the ghetto teaching strategy could work. He advised two simultaneous strategies: that I file for conscientious objector status, and that I see a doctor who Bill claimed was "good at finding things wrong with people who don't know there is anything wrong with them."

Dr. E quizzed me about my recent medical history. Late in 1967 I had returned from Europe with no money, so I accepted a friend's offer to live on his sailboat in the Berkeley marina. Lacking a refrigerator I ate some spoiled hamburger and wound up in the hospital with ptomaine poisoning. The doctor ordered an Upper GI (gastro-intestinal) x-ray. After viewing it he declared I had an ulcer and should start drinking Maalox.

Meanwhile my request for CO status was rejected—I was classified 1-A, fresh meat for the Army. Every letter I received from the Selective Service stated I had 30 days to respond. On Bill's advice, I waited 29 days, then sent a registered letter on the 30th. saying only, "I appeal my classification." I soon received a letter informing me my local draft board was forwarding my case to the California State appeals board. Bill asked, "Do you have any place to go in another state? The California appeals board is turning everybody down except for Quakers and Jehovah's Witnesses." "I could stay with my brother in Wisconsin," I said. "Go there," he replied.

By the time another 29 days passed and I had to respond, I

was ensconced in Madison in the home of Bob and Georgie, my brother and sister-in-law. In accordance with Selective Service regulations, my next registered letter to the Draft Board requested that my appeal be handled in the state of my current residence, Wisconsin.

While waiting for the wheels of the Draft Board bureaucracy to grind on, I looked for a job. I landed a job as custodian at the Madison Metro School district central offices.

At the offices I met Mary Bruce, the daughter of one of the clerical workers who was working there during her winter break from college. We started dating, she became my girlfriend, and a year and a half later we married. We were fascinated by each other's differences. To her I was an exotic Californian. She had grown up in a village, population 300, in northern Michigan. When we took a ferry across the lake to Bear Lake, it seemed exotic to me.

Unrest seemed to be happening wherever I went. In 1969, soon after my arrival in Madison, strife broke out on the University campus. The Black Student Union called a strike to demand an Afro-American Studies program and to protest that activist black students were expelled at regional campuses. The governor called out the National Guard. I went to demonstrations, but as an outsider, it proved hard to gain acceptance in radical student groups on campus.

Then I discovered another outlet for my activist impulses. Martha Smith, a friend of Bob and Georgie's, was a leader of Measure for Measure, a Madison group that supported the efforts of civil rights leader Fannie Lou Hamer in Sunflower County, Mississippi. Martha, a tall, flamboyant redhead from Texas, lived in a rural A-frame west of Madison that became a gathering place for civil rights supporters.

Mrs. Hamer had become known nationally at the 1964 Democratic convention as a leader of the Freedom Democratic delegation that challenged the official all-white Mississippi delegation. It made national news when she eloquently rejected the party's miserable offer to allow two non-voting observers from her group to attend the convention.

She was a charismatic leader in Ruleville, where she initiated practical efforts to improve the lives of African-Americans. She opened a thrift store to raise money for their organization and provide inexpensive goods to local people. We Measure for Measure activists solicited donations from Madison's large, well-off liberal community to supply the thrift store. Whenever we accumulated sufficient rummage to fill a U-Haul trailer, a few of us piled in a car and hauled it down to the Mississippi store.

In 1969, before the Interstates, the drive from Wisconsin to Mississippi took nearly two days. To make the trip worthwhile, we'd stay in Mississippi about a week. I always stayed in Pap and Fannie Lou Hamer's house, since "outside agitators" would have been unwelcome at the Ruleville motel.

On my first trip down, with Martha Smith and another woman from Madison, the Hamers lent their own double bed to the two women and I made a pallet on the floor in the same room. When I laid down, I was a little startled to see a shotgun handy under the Hamers' bed. They were not violent people, but contrary to a stereotype about the non-violent Civil Rights movement, like other activists, they faced constant threats and had to be prepared to defend themselves.

On my first trip to the Hamers', I asked where there might be a telephone booth. I wanted to call my girlfriend in Madison. "Oh, you can just use our phone," Mrs. Hamer offered. "No, I don't want to run up a long-distance charge for you," I countered. In those days long-distance calls were expensive. "Don't worry about that," Mrs. Hamer replied, "Harry Belafonte had this phone put in and he pays the bills." Sandy Stark, a friend of our family in LA, was Belafonte's secretary; she probably wrote the checks for those phone bills.

After I finished the call, Mrs. Hamer recalled that when she first got the telephone a couple years earlier, "I didn't know nothing about getting an unlisted number. So I's just in the phone book, 'n all. 'N you shoulda heard the phone calls I was a-getting'. They said some horrible things. Now 'scuse me for what I'm 'bout to say, but one guy called up and he says, 'I got my ass up to the phone and I'm a-fartin' in your face.' Well, I just told him, 'You know, I feel powerful sorry for you. You must be terrible deformed if you got both ends up to the phone!'" She cracked me up.

We tried to make ourselves useful during our stay in Ruleville.

On one trip we transported Mrs. Hamer and other Ruleville women to a conference of black women activists in Gulfport. On the drive from the Delta to the Gulf Coast, the station wagon resounded non-stop with gospel and civil rights songs. Another time Mrs. Hamer was granted an honorary doctorate from Tougaloo, a historically black college in Jackson, Mississippi. Mrs. Hamer and her cohort set out for Jackson, but we Measure for Measure people stayed behind. We made a run to the grocery store with some local folks to purchase supplies for a gala party welcoming Dr. Hamer home. We got a long roll of butcher paper to make a banner, and while local women were preparing barbecue, pecan pies, greens and potato salad, I got some paint, unrolled the paper and huddled with a couple Hamer family members to brainstorm a message. Pap mentioned that this would be Fannie Lou's third honorary doctorate. So it hit us: on the paper that wound up stretching along the entire length of the front porch we painted "Just call me Dr. Dr. Dr. Hamer, Jim Eastland!"

It was a slap at the long-serving US Senator James Eastland, a notorious racist and a local resident. He was probably in Washington, DC just then, but he had a 6,000 acre cotton plantation down the road. Upon their return, the group that went to Jackson got a big laugh from the banner. Martha Smith fretted, however, "I hope none of Jim Eastland's sheriffs drive by and figure they ought to do something about it."

At that time I was keen on the Delta blues and learning to play bottleneck guitar. On a couple occasions I got to jam with neighbors of the Hamers. I couldn't come near matching their expressive singing. My romantic notion that the Delta was frozen in time, a world apart musically, was corrected. Stopping by legendary Beale Street in Memphis, celebrated in jazz and blues songs, I was disappointed to find a largely abandoned commercial strip with boarded up storefronts. I made a pilgrimage to Rosedale, a hamlet on the Mississippi River famous for its barrelhouses and mentioned in one of legendary bluesman Robert Johnson's famous songs. The bars were still there but there was hardly any blues on the jukeboxes.

On one trip I brought my bulky Wollensack tape recorder, the common machine in those days. We wanted to record music for

PR about Measure for Measure. We taped Mrs. Hamer's gospel group the Hamernette Singers performing at the Sweet Kingdom Missionary Baptist Church. As usual, wherever we went in Mississippi, we were the only whites around, and the people in the church seemed apprehensive about us. To put the congregation at ease, Mrs. Hamer said, "I want to say something about these people here. I stayed at Martha Smith's house in Wisconsin, and let me tell you, it wasn't no different than I was staying in my own sister's house." You could feel the tension evaporate. We experienced a joyous evening of singing, preaching, praying.

The tape recorder was a big hit with local teenagers. In those days, it was an expensive item, and living in poverty-stricken rural Mississippi, most of them hadn't yet heard a recording of their own voices. The Hamers' daughter Lynne was particularly intrigued. She recorded her unaccompanied version of a current Marvin Gaye hit, "Too Busy Thinkin' 'Bout My Baby," and "We Shall Overcome."

While I enjoyed the trips to Mississippi, I was becoming disenchanted with Wisconsin. The Selective Service appeals board re-classified me 1-Y, making me eligible for the draft. They rejected my conscientious objector claim and rejected my request to be made 4-F, physically unfit for service, due to my "ulcer." But they just didn't want me for the army just yet. Perhaps all my manipulation of the bureaucratic rules made them figure I'd be a problematic serviceman.

I missed my friends in California. Aside from my girlfriend Mary and the Measure for Measure bunch who were mostly about a decade older than me, I hadn't made friends. In December of 1969 I got laid off from my job. My second consecutive Wisconsin winter seemed bleak. By February, I managed to persuade Mary to move with me to California. From a company in Chicago we got a "drive-away car," an auto that someone needed to have transported to Los Angeles. We jam-packed the small sedan with our stuff and headed for the Golden State.

In LA I reclaimed the old Mercury I had left behind over a year earlier. We decided to move to San Jose, where my friend Ted Gustafson was working as a carpenter. We got an apartment in a mostly Mexican neighborhood near the old downtown and enjoyed the local culture. In the center of the city, we awoke to roosters crowing, discovered a fine Mexican bakery, a carñitas stand, and enjoyed the community's celebrations of Cinco de Mayo and Mexican Independence Day.

I got a second-shift job at Container Corporation of America where they manufactured paperboard boxes for familiar products like Cheerios and Tide. Most of the time I was a hand-stripper on a press that made frozen food boxes. Every couple minutes, the press spit out a stack of 50 big sheets, about six feet square, of 16 flat boxes each. With a partner across the table, it was our job to use rubber-tipped hammers to break the paper tabs connecting the boxes, pound out the waste chips and stack them in eight cardboard boxes for shipping. After five repetitions, with the press still going, we had to run like hell to do a "seal up," tape the full boxes shut and carry them to a pallet near the end of the table.

It was hot as hell in the factory and the air was filled with paperboard dust. After a couple months my right hand went numb from constant pounding. I couldn't feel if I had any coins in my pocket and worst of all, I couldn't play the guitar. The company nurse told me she was "ashamed of this company" and directed that I be on "light duty" for a while. They put me on a gravure press that turned out cereal boxes. This machine stripped the chips automatically so I didn't have to pound anything. I only had to grab flat boxes from a conveyor and stack them neatly on a nearby skid. The boxes were printed with colored ink and had passed under heating elements to dry them so they were literally hot off the press. The air was hot in the factory during the warm Santa Clara Valley evenings, so I sweated prodigiously doing this job. The legislation to create OSHA (The Occupational Safety and Health Administration) had recently been passed. One evening a government inspector came, watched me work for a few minutes then wrote something on a clipboard. A couple days later when I reported to work, the foreman pointed out a salt tablet dispenser installed on the wall near my work station, saying "If ya get dizzy, take a tablet."

After a few months working there, I started to scan the want-ads for a different job. With my building maintenance experience, I was hired by the City of San Jose as a custodian. After a few weeks working evenings at the City Hall, they transferred me to the main police station. For me it was a hostile work environment, hearing the racist and sexist patter of the police officers. One evening I came in the room while a group of cops were listening to a speech by Chicano movement leader Corky Gonzales that a police agent had taped. At this time, the Chicano movement was gaining momentum.

I admired Corky Gonzales and lingered surreptitiously to hear his speech. The cops, however, commented venomously. Most of his speech was in English and a Mexican-American cop sitting with them explained the occasional Spanish words and phrases Gonzales employed. The cops muttered how they'd like to "blow away the little brown bastard."

Remaining cautious not to betray my viewpoints, my nights in the station made me ever more paranoid. When I had to go into the narcotics agents' office to sweep and empty wastebaskets, if the narcs were there, they'd hastily close drawers and the air smelled like weed. After a few weeks working, somebody decided I ought to be fingerprinted. I started to worry what they might find out. Then there was another worry. In 1970, the Weathermen, a terrorist splinter group of SDS, was bombing police stations. Sometimes the victim was a custodian who happened on the bomb. What an irony I thought, for me, an SDS member, to be killed by a radical bomber.

I knew I had to get out of there.

At home, things were becoming tense between me and Mary, who was pressing me to get married. I dragged my feet a while, then agreed to it. We arranged for a wedding at Aunt Agnes and Uncle Nick's place in Malibu in August. It was a big gathering of family and friends. At the wedding, Uncle Nick offered me the job of manager at an apartment building he owned in Santa Monica in return for free rent. I was so fried by my San Jose job that I jumped at the chance. We moved the next month.

The Santa Monica apartment was on a hill with a view of the ocean from the kitchen window of our second floor apartment—straight down noisy Pico Boulevard. It proved difficult to find steady work, but with no rent to pay, we didn't need much money. It was pleasant in the mellow beach town. Mary attended

Santa Monica City College, a few blocks away and worked part-time tending bar in a Venice joint on Lincoln Boulevard. I got odd jobs, working in the greenhouses of an elderly German florist who raised cyclamen. I did landscaping work for my aunt and uncle's neighbors in Malibu and market research for my mother's business. My parents made it known in their wide circle of friends that I was available to do house painting which landed a few additional jobs.

Although I missed the Berkeley crowd, I enjoyed my circle of friends and relatives in southern California. It was time, however, to figure out what should come next. I jammed informally with musician friends, and occasionally filled in on gigs, but I decided I really disliked working clubs in a cloud of cigarette smoke, having never been a smoker.

My two big brothers were professors, so I thought about further studies. I had taken undergraduate courses in Folklore at UCLA and Berkeley, and visiting Yugoslavia in 1967, I attended the International Folklore Festival in Zagreb. The folk cultures of that country were fascinating. I visited a couple professors in the Folklore & Mythology program at UCLA, who received me coolly. I was turned down for admission there. In 1971 Zagreb University became my goal.

At six AM on the morning of February 9, our second floor apartment began to sway. Things flew from shelves and cabinets, dishes crashed to the kitchen floor. Mary leaped out of bed and crouched under the door jamb, the recommended thing to do. I had been raised in earthquake country, but nonetheless I just laid there like a rock. In a minute it was over. We quickly surveyed the minor damage and turned on the television. Non-stop news of the quake already dominated the airwaves. It was 6.6 on the Richter scale. The Valley had it worst. Out there the freeways fell, and there were a few fatalities downtown. It seemed in Santa Monica we had come through it pretty well. All the tenants in the apartment building were OK and the stucco-covered frame building seemed undamaged.

The earthquake unleashed a communitarian outpouring: everyone talked to everyone. We all cringed as after-shocks struck. Was another big quake starting? As time went on, the frequency of the after-shocks gradually decreased, though they kept us on edge for days.

A couple of days after the earthquake, my friend Zucky, Robert Zuckerman, stopped by. I had known him since high school days at the Ash Grove. In Berkeley he was in a rock band and he sometimes helped out with music for Agit-Prop plays. His old '51 Chevy was barely running and he needed to make it more reliable. He needed transportation for a steady gig playing guitar in a country rock band in a club in El Monte, a working-class suburb about 30 miles to the east.

I knew a little more about engines than he did, so at his request we got to work in the apartment carport. We cleaned the points, set the gap and changed the spark plugs. But his heap wouldn't fire up. We got a can of gas, took off the air filter and tried to adjust the carburetor. We primed it with a splash of gas, all to no effect. The day was fading fast, it was late afternoon. Zucky despaired of fixing the twenty-year-old Chevy and decided to junk it. So we removed everything from the jalopy and put it in the trunk of my Mercury.

It was about time for me to take Mary to work at the bar in Venice. Zucky lived nearby, so we hatched a plan. We'd drop off Mary, then go to his apartment to fetch his guitar and band uniform. I would drive him to his parents' house in Hollywood where he could borrow their car to get to El Monte.

The back streets of Venice are really quite a maze. Early in the 20th Century the town was laid out to be a tourist attraction, "the Venice of the West," with canals and arcades to resemble its Italian namesake. The tourist business tanked during the 1930s, most of the canals were filled in and turned into a confusing warren of streets and alleys.

After dropping Mary at the tavern, since Zucky's apartment building was close to the beach, I cut through back alleys figuring on saving time. I didn't know exactly where I was going when to my surprise, the alley led me into a parking lot filled with LA Police cars. It was the back way into the Venice police station. I threw the car into reverse, but we were quickly boxed in by police cars, in front and behind us. We heard the order, "get out with your hands up." With our knees wobbling, we climbed out.

Cops instantly shoved us spread eagle against the car and patted us down. A big blonde cop asked me for the key to the trunk. I muttered something about a warrant. "A warrant!" he bellowed. "Well, we can just arrest you now and then search it without a warrant, so give me the key." I complied. I heard the cops start to exclaim about my trunk's contents. "Hey look, here's a can of gas!" I also had some glass pop bottles that I planned to return for the deposit, and of course there were some greasy rags from working on Zucky's Chevy. Plus Zucky had several books of matches. They were printed with an ad for the club in El Monte where he was gigging. He gave them to friends saying, "Come see us play."

They read us our Miranda rights and led us in the jail. As soon as we entered the back door, shouting cops shoved, poked and knocked us around as we made our way down the hall. Once inside a room they ordered us to strip naked and bend over. A rubber-gloved finger indelicately searched my anus. Zucky remained in that room, but I was led, still naked, to another room down the hall. I was shoved onto a wooden bench and metal handcuffs were slapped on each wrist, the other end latched to the bench's armrests. For a few minutes I was alone there. Suddenly the silence was broken by a large after-shock from the recent quake. The whole building shuddered and I did too. "Oh my God," I thought, "this ratty building is going to collapse. They'll find me chained up here, naked and dead."

After a few minutes, a steady stream of cops passed through the room. They relished humiliating me. "So you're the big brave bomber," one said derisively. "Well you don't look so tough now!" Another muttered menacingly, "It's not too smart to attack cops. Your mama won't even know you when we get through with you." The big blonde cop who had arrested me was in a much breezier mood. He chatted almost jovially with me. "Hey, you know it's pretty cool that I arrested you. Y'know, Jack Webb's TV show 'Adam-12' asks us to turn in ideas for shows. They just might like this story." I never responded to any of this talk. My naked thighs were sticking uncomfortably to the hard lacquered bench. The metal cuffs were pinching my wrists. And every few minutes I was startled by another after-shock.

At last a cop threw my clothes at me and unlocked the cuffs.

"Get dressed," he barked, "You're gonna chat with Inspector Haggarty." He shoved me down the hall and into a room where a weary-faced detective sat behind a desk. He gestured for me to sit down. The questioning began slow and easy. He asked my name and where I lived, his tone like pleasant chat. Then suddenly his manner changed. "Do you know any blacks?" he shouted. "Absolutely not," I lied. I'm not telling you, I thought, and get friends of mine in trouble too. He asked me to repeat every detail of that evening. We went over it multiple times. I just told the truth, so my story was consistent.

Haggerty called for a cop to take me to a cell. They led in Zucky as I went out. He would be the next one on the grill. We caught each other's eyes. Wordlessly, I tried to convey, "Just tell the truth." Zucky seemed to get it.

I spent an hour or more alone in a cell. Mentally I was bemoaning my fate. Why hadn't I left for Zagreb already? Now I'm bound to be in prison for years. I'll never get to go there. My life is ruined.

At last a cop came and got me. The mood had changed. He didn't shove me as we went down the hall to a room where they took full-length felony mugshots of Zucky and me. They led us to a counter where they returned our wallets and pocket contents. They told me that they had impounded the contents of my trunk as evidence, but incredibly, they were going to turn us loose. "Just don't try to leave town," the cop warned. We staggered out the door, scarcely able to believe our good fortune. Zucky looked at his watch. It was half past ten. "Hey man, let's get me to my gig; we play 'til 2 AM."

For the next few days, wherever I drove, I noticed stereotypical unmarked cop cars. Driving east on Pico Boulevard, I suddenly decided to double back. I turned around, but in my rear view mirror, the Chrysler that had been following me eastward was now tailing me back west.

After a week, there appeared a small article in the newspaper. "Possible Bombing Averted by Police" the headline read. The chief of the Venice station was quoted. "They had all the ingredients for Molotov cocktails, but they were not assembled yet, so we could not hold them." He went on to speculate, "It might have been a dry run or a probe of our defense," and reported that we were known radicals who had been associated with SDS in the Bay Area.

Oh my god, I thought. I had supposed that the cops had concluded that we were not up to any mayhem. But from the article it seemed they thought we were planning a bombing. Probably they thought we were little fish and would lead them to the bigger masterminds, Weathermen or Black Panthers. When that didn't pan out, the DA probably concluded the case against us wasn't strong enough. Feeling like a marked man, I was ready to get out of the country. In my idealized notion, Yugoslavia seemed like a refuge.

Three months later, when moving day came, as we loaded the rented trailer, I had the familiar experience of seeing an FBI man parked across the street. Damn, how did they always know when I was going to move? What was their point?—to let me know, "We're still watching you."

Rambling Around

I spent the next two years at Zagreb University studying Ethnology, a field close to Anthropology, while Mary took the Croatian-language course to prepare foreign students for study. Her classmates were from a variety of Arab and African countries Yugoslav leader Marshall Tito was building relationships with in the Non-Aligned Movement.

I had a steep learning curve to comprehend the formal language of my university lecturers. The professors read from notes and the students copied down the words verbatim. It seemed senseless, but proved excellent for improving my language skills.

I found lucrative opportunities to play music. To European blues and jazz aficionados I was a real American "Blueser." They seemed impressed that I had blues harp lessons from Sonny Terry and I had been to the Mississippi Delta. I formed a jug band with a few musicians who had experience with Dixieland jazz, and Mary, who has a good voice, sang some Country songs with us. I was surprised at the good gigs we were able to get. Instead of playing noisy, smoky clubs, we were treated like a chamber music group, playing to rapt audiences. I had a couple well-paying television appearances and concert performances. I gave guitar lessons and Mary tutored students in English. Our standard of living was modest but OK.

I made many friends. In those days people in Croatia invested real effort in socializing. Home phones were rare, so it was customary to drop by to visit, or to look for your acquaintances on the "*korzo*," the downtown street where young people strolled every evening. Movies were inexpensive, mostly two or three year-old sub-titled Hollywood releases, but there were a few domestic films as well. Three or four friends would go together—one person always treated, which assured we would do it again so that everyone could reciprocate. After the movie, we'd have Turkish coffee or a glass of wine and discuss it. Croatians love to deliberate and debate.

There were hot issues developing in Zagreb at the time. My notions of Yugoslavia as an idyllic oasis and just society soon were disabused, although not nearly so violently as what befell my uncles in Russia. The spring of 1971 became known as *Hrvatsko proljeće*, the Croatian Spring. Leading Croatian intellectuals, including many members of the League of Communists, were pressing for more Croatian cultural and economic autonomy. Croatian Communist leaders, Savka Dabčević-Kučar and Miko Tripalo spearheaded a movement to democratize the party and redress grievances for a fairer distribution of money generated by the Croatian economy. Since Croatia had more tourism and industry than elsewhere in Yugoslavia, Croats felt too much was tapped by the Belgrade government and funneled elsewhere.

Student leaders organized a protest strike to press these demands. On Zagreb's main square, I joined a crowd chanting "Savka-Tripalo." We soon were routed by riot police. I recollected our resistance to the Oakland police during Stop the Draft Week in 1968 and was surprised by the relative civility of this melee. The Zagreb students scattered at the first police onslaught. Moreover, the police were armed with short rubber billy clubs, nothing like the yard-long riot batons we faced in California.

The serious part of the crack-down came later. The central authorities decided the Croatian reform movement had gone too far. Overnight, popular Croatian Communists were removed, old hard-liners were installed, Savka and Tripalo were put under house arrest; several political figures and two prominent student leaders wound up with prison terms for their political "crimes."

Ironically, many of the demands of the Croatian Spring were enacted two years later in a new Yugoslav constitution. It enshrined self-governing socialism, decentralized power and created an elaborate decision-making process that in theory started in workplace and grassroots residential councils and rose step by step to the Federal Assembly. Paradoxically, this constitution which proclaimed a democratic structure also decreed Josip Broz Tito president for life.

The political climate was repressive for the rest of that stay in Yugoslavia, but I focused on my studies and my music. I taped the songs and tales of the oldest people in Nerezine and did research in other villages. My brother Bill brought a group of American students to Zagreb for a summer language seminar. I met a couple grad students from Indiana University who were dumbfounded that I was doing these studies "on my own." "Don't you know people get fellowships to do this sort of thing?" they asked. No I didn't. It was my turn to be dumbfounded when I received a package of catalogues and application materials for the Russian and East European Institute (REEI) at Indiana University. The students had told their professors about me. The institute spent over $12.00 on air mail postage, a tidy sum back then. I figured they must be serious.

Ultimately I applied and was accepted into the IU Folklore grad program plus the REEI offered a Ford Foundation fellowship that paid my tuition plus a living allowance. It seemed too good to be true. Soon I was in grad school in Bloomington, Indiana. I thrived in the grad school environment, loved the heady discourse with my classmates and professors. As a bonus, many of the Folklore students were also excellent musicians. The Ford Fellowship was renewed for a second year and afterwards I became a Teaching Assistant and Research Assistant in a team fieldwork project in the vicinity of Gary, Indiana. In 1977, after finishing my classwork and exams I received a Fulbright-Hayes fellowship to return to Yugoslavia for dissertation research on Croatian tamburitza music. I spent a rewarding year working out of the Folklore Research Institute in Zagreb. When it was time to return to the US, Mary requested that we move to Milwaukee where she could be near relatives.

In Milwaukee I toiled on my dissertation, worked part-time at a community center in a low-income neighborhood, and taught Croatian in evening community education classes. I began to be offered consistent contract work to do folklore field research in projects funded by the National Endowment for the Arts (NEA).

A few years earlier, in 1975, the Smithsonian Folklife Program hired me to develop part of the Bicentennial production of the Smithsonian Folklife Festival. When first approached, I was apprehensive. This was work for the Federal Government. I likely was on some blacklist as an untrustworthy commie. On the other hand, J. Edgar Hoover had died while I was living in Zagreb and in Indiana there were no more signs of FBI surveillance. My federal work contract was signed and I breathed easier.

My assignment was to identify and recruit South Slavic folk artists for the big festival. I discovered I had a talent for landing in an unfamiliar city, Cleveland or Detroit, figuring out how to find folk artists, documenting their work and persuading them to showcase their traditions on the National Mall in Washington, DC.

When I returned from my second Zagreb sojourn, I informed Bess Lomax Hawes, the folk arts director at the NEA, I was available to do contract work. I became one of her cadre of public folklorists who could reliably provide assistance to arts organizations on folk arts projects.

Bess was working to entrench the folk arts among the forms of culture supported by the Arts Endowment and State Arts Agencies. Her ardor to democratize the cultural policies of the US stemmed from her days as a radical. Born in 1921 in Austin, Texas, her father was the pioneering American folklorist John A. Lomax. Her elder brother Alan Lomax was a prodigious field collector of folk music, an ethnomusicologist, archivist, and political activist. Six years older than Bess, Alan became involved in radical politics as a college student. It seems she soon acquired similar views.

At the beginning of the 1940s Bess came to New York City, where she became a member of the Almanac Singers, a folk music group that supported labor and leftist causes. Bess married fellow Almanac member Butch Hawes in 1942. Although I am uncertain if Bess ever was a Communist Party member, two famous Almanac Singers Woody Guthrie and Pete Seeger certainly were.

During the 1940s the Almanac Singers traveled the country playing for CIO rallies. Bess' own composition "UAW-CIO" praises wartime auto workers (which incidentally included my mother) who turned out the "jeeps and tanks and airplanes every day." The Almanacs' experiences confirmed Pete Seeger's belief that folk music could be an effective force for social change. In 1946 he founded People's Songs, an organization to disseminate songs for political action. When Seeger convened People's Songs' founding committee in Greenwich Village, it included Bess and her brother Alan, as well as folk music notables Woody Guthrie, singer Lee Hays, bluesman Josh White and labor songster Tom Glazer.

Bess broadened her folklore credentials by earning an M.A. at Berkeley in the early 1960s, one of the first students of program founder Alan Dundes. A few years later, Dundes was my faculty advisor at Berkeley. I had yet another thread of connection to Bess. We first met when she performed at the Ash Grove in Los Angeles.

Bess fostered my public folklore career. Whenever I was the appropriate specialist, she referred me to arts groups needing a consultant. As a strategy to ensure the survival of public folklore in the nation's arts infrastructure, Bess encouraged state and local arts agencies to put a folklorist on staff by providing start-up funds for the positions. To have a folklorist in every US state and jurisdiction was her goal.

In 1982 Bess made a crucial intervention in my career. I was living in Milwaukee during the economic downturn known as "the Reagan recession." I had been laid off, and jobs were scarce in a "Rust Belt" city like Milwaukee. I was weary of needing to leave Mary and my toddler son Nikola for two or three weeks at a time to work folklore contracts in places like Ohio and Nevada. There was talk that a state folklorist position might be created at the Wisconsin Arts Board, but months dragged on with no news about it. Los Angeles where I had family and friends beckoned. At the fall, 1982 American Folklore Society convention in St. Paul, I told Bess I was sinking financially in Wisconsin and contemplating a move back to southern California. Her eyes flashed. "Don't you do it!" she commanded. "You stay in Wisconsin where you're needed." I just gulped and told her I'd think about it.

In the summer of 1983 I finally landed the newly created Wisconsin state folklorist position. When I was in Washington a couple years later, I noticed a USA map on a bulletin board above Bess' desk with multi-colored push pins stuck in the various states. The red pin marking Madison, Wisconsin designated me.

From my office at Wisconsin Arts Board, I telephoned Bess nearly every week, seeking advice on how to strengthen the folk arts program and how to navigate an arts agency where, as was typical then, elitist attitudes imbued my colleagues' thinking. My father also gave good advice on how to develop supporters in key constituencies.

At a meeting in Kentucky I got acquainted with the other important public folklore guru Archie Green. Born in 1917 in Winnipeg, Archie moved to Los Angeles with his parents in 1922. After finishing college in Berkeley, Archie did a stint in the Civilian Conservation Corps and during World War II he became a shipyards worker in San Francisco. Archie reminded me of my father. His parents, Jewish immigrants from Ukraine, were Socialist supporters of Eugene Debs. As a youth Archie was influenced by the soapbox speakers on Pershing Square in downtown LA. His political views were anarcho-syndicalism, the philosophy of the IWW.

During his years as a shipyards worker, Archie was active in his union. As a mature adult, a passion to study labor songs drew him to scholarly pursuits. Archie earned a Master's degree from the University of Illinois and a Ph.D. from the University of Pennsylvania. He worked for the AFL-CIO Labor Studies Center in the early 1970s and initiated presentation of workers' traditions at the Smithsonian Folklife Festival. His acumen in union politics made him the best lobbyist for the American Folklife Center in the Library of Congress. By the time I started as Wisconsin state folklorist, he had retired and returned to San Francisco. I became one of a coterie of folklorists whom Archie frequently called to urge us to undertake labor-related folklore projects.

In the later 1980s I became concerned that we folklorists in state arts agencies were marginalized in our organizations and undervalued. In some states, the folklorist positions were eliminated. My colleague in New York Robert Baron and I decided we needed to push for the state folklorists to participate in the convention of the National Assembly of State Arts Agencies (NASAA), the annual meeting of our bosses and arts agency co-workers. There we could advocate for our programs. When I broached the idea to Bess, she groaned, "NASAA! They're so elitist. You'll never get anywhere with them." I eventually persuaded Bess to fund travel and lodging for state folklorists to attend the 1988 NASAA meeting, which fortuitously was in San Francisco, Archie Green's home.

Richard March

We were exhilarated to be assembled at our first national meeting, a couple score state folklorists. Archie and Bess attended all our sessions, offering the voice of experience. At that first meeting Archie offered a memorable metaphor; he declared that our developing tight network of like-minded folk culture workers should be our "mad money," the two bucks you stick in your shoe, reserved for when you desperately need it. We could offer mutual support, find ways to collaborate and advance our cause: gaining validation, recognition and support for the traditions of marginalized cultures in our country and the world. Most public folklorists are leftists or left-leaning. As I got to know colleagues, I learned that in their pasts many worked for civil rights and peace, pounded on missile silos, sheltered Salvadoran refugees or sailed on Pete Seeger's environmentalist schooner.

I enjoyed a 30-year career, working with partners, other folklorists and myriad creative people from traditional communities to sustain their cultures and to fight against intolerance, racism and elitism. During 26 years as Wisconsin's state folklorist, I had the opportunities to develop an apprenticeship program in which elders from the state's Native tribes passed on their skills to apprentices of their choosing, to produce 14 years of "Down Home Dairyland," a weekly program on Wisconsin Public Radio emphasizing ethnic music that was largely excluded from the airwaves, to place local folk artists in school residencies and train teachers to organize such residencies themselves, using our on-line database of Wisconsin folk artists.

I took delegations of Wisconsin folk artists to Chiba, Japan, to share their traditions, and then we hosted folk artists from Chiba in Wisconsin in alternate years. My biggest undertaking came in 1998, Wisconsin's Sesquicentennial, when we organized a massive folklife festival, taking 140 Wisconsin artists to that year's Smithsonian Folklife Festival in DC, then seven weeks later re-staging an enlarged festival program around the State Capitol in Madison. The big anniversary freed up funding. I have often quipped that I'll never make a million dollars, but I got to spend a million and a half on the festivals in 1998.

I was fortunate to be able to retire from the Arts Board in 2009 and since then have devoted myself to long-postponed book writ-

335

ing projects: on ethnic musical traditions and this one, about my family's great vision and turbulent journey through more than a century of recent history.

Now seventy years old, I can see how much my choices and actions were influenced by my family's activist traditions, our values and vision. Like my father, I turned down more than one opportunity to be promoted to more lucrative jobs because they would take me away from my public folklore work. That work often incorporated my mother's mode of one-on-one assistance to individuals or small groups.

By the time of my young adulthood I came to the realization that although advances might be possible in the political and economic realms where my family strived, complete reverses also are possible, and even likely. I chose to work in the cultural realm where change is incremental, hoping that the cultural changes might be less susceptible to reversal. My public folklore work has been like rowing a bulky rowboat across a choppy lake in a headwind. Stroke by stroke you may feel that you're making little progress, that you're getting blisters on your hands from pulling the oars. But at a certain point you look up and realize you've rowed a long ways from the dock and you can look over your shoulder, over the bow of the boat and realize you've come closer than you realized to that other shore you were heading for.

I'm proud of the accomplishments my public folklore colleagues and I achieved. We have made inroads against elitism. I hope we have chipped away at intolerance enough that future generations, deep in their consciousness, will be ever more receptive to progressive ideas. If humanity can survive the difficult crises ahead, a better world akin to our great vision still is possible.

During my three decade public folklore career I remained a foot soldier in other progressive efforts, like peace marches, police brutality protests and door knocking for progressive local candidates. In the late 1980s I was active in the campaign to organize my bargaining unit of state employees, one of the very last not unionized, into the Wisconsin Professional Employees Council (AFT). But it wasn't until shortly after I retired in 2009 that I felt compelled to plunge again into full-time activism.

In 2010, as a part of a national reactionary backlash after the

'08 election of Barak Obama, Scott Walker was elected Wisconsin's governor and Republicans swept the state legislature. At the beginning of Walker's term, he introduced Act 10, a far-reaching attack on the collective bargaining rights of public employees, setting off what became known as the Wisconsin Uprising. Spearheaded by organized labor, Wisconsin citizens initiated raucous protest, braving the sub-freezing temperatures of Wisconsin winter, myself among them.

Protestors occupied the state capitol building for 19 days. During this turmoil the 14 Democratic state senators fled to a secret location in Illinois to deny the needed quorum to pass Act 10, but the Republicans ignored the rules to pass the bill, relying on a sympathetic, politicized state Supreme Court to decide that whatever they did was legal.

The next winter I threw myself into the campaign to recall Walker. From a post outside my neighborhood grocery, I collected over 700 signatures. We collected a million signatures statewide forcing a recall election the following summer. The state Democrats made unfortunate strategic mistakes in that election and Walker had unlimited campaign funds provided by reactionary billionaires, so the recall failed.

The Republican government visited upon our formerly progressive state every outrage on the reactionary wish list. Ultimately wife Nikki and I opted to relocate to Portland, Oregon for a better climate, weather-wise and political.

Since the election of Donald Trump in 2016, we face the same challenges on a national level as the citizens of Wisconsin faced under Walker. Now progressives everywhere need to work smart, remain active, resist and not be demoralized. I hope that the story of three generations of my activist family can help the next generation keep up the fight for justice, and win.

Not every member of an activist family becomes an activist. My grandfather Ivan's brother even took the Italian side against the Croatian community. My father's family had socialist views but only Pa dedicated his life to the cause. Inspired by Pa, his youngest brother Irving also opposed racism and supported labor, but his life was tragically cut short by cancer. My mother and her ill-fated brother Gavde were the most passionate activists among their siblings, yet other brothers and sisters in their own ways, in their ethnic affiliations and professions, endeavored to better the human condition.

Most of my relatives have viewpoints that are liberal or farther yet to the left. My two college professor brothers have spoken up and acted for peace and against racism. I had profound activist involvement because in my youth, I recurrently found myself at the right place and time to strive for causes. Then my folklore career afforded an opportunity for progressive action in the cultural sphere.

When it comes to the next generation, my two brothers and I produced eight children, six boys and two girls. They all believe in the basic values of our family's tradition. They vote and they espouse progressive views among friends and associates, nowadays including through on-line social media. There is only one, however, my niece Sara March, who truly became an activist.

Sara was born in 1982 in the college town of Lawrence, Kansas where her father was a Slavic Languages professor. She became a botanist; environmentalism and feminism are her passions.

She attended college in California's redwood country at Humboldt State University, the northernmost and smallest campus of California State University. The campus has a tradition of activism. In 1987 students created the Graduation Pledge of Social and Environmental Responsibility to encourage departing students to be mindful of social and environmental impacts in their life choices.

At the time Sara arrived in 2000, radical environmental activism had been endemic at Humboldt for more than a decade. Provoked by what they considered the sell-out by mainstream environmental advocates, Earth First!, an environmental advocacy group emerged in 1980. From 1987 on, Earth First! emphasized direct action—tree sitting, road blockades and sabotage— to prevent logging, building of dams and other despoilment of wild places. Disruptive direct action was used as a stalling tactic to delay devastation while Earth First! lawyers worked to secure longer-term victories.

The height of the conflict in her area happened in the early 1990s, a time when Earth First! activist Judy Bari was crippled in a car-bombing assassination attempt. But when Sara arrived, tree-sitting still was ongoing. Protesters sit high in a tree, on a small platform to protect it from being felled. They presume loggers would not risk human lives by cutting an occupied tree. Supporters provide the tree sitters with food and supplies.

High above the forest floor, Sara was in the company of another tree sitter, Steve Brown. As they got acquainted, Sara mentioned that her grandfather Herb March was a radical leader in the packinghouse workers' union. Steve rejoined that his grandfather Archie Brown likewise had been a radical union leader, in the West Coast longshoreman's union.

On Sara's next visit to her grandmother in San Pedro, she mentioned she had been tree-sitting with Steve Brown, Archie Brown's grandson. "Oh my god," Mom exclaimed. "Archie Brown was in the YCL with me back in Chicago. In fact, he asked me to marry him around the same time that Herb did. It was no question though," she continued. "I thought Herb was much better looking."

Bibliographic Essay

This is a family history, and thus family sources have been essential to the work. I used items that my mother Jane March squirreled away: files of newspaper clippings, glossy prints of news photos, family snapshots, letters from relatives, bound copies of the proceedings of packinghouse workers union conventions and drafts of her attempts at memoir writing.

I've mentally kicked myself dozens of times that I didn't undertake this project more than a decade ago when Herb and Jane were still living and I could ask them for clarifications and explanations. To augment and cross-check my recollections I had conversations with family friend Vicky Starr, my two elder brothers, Bob and Bill March, my cousins, especially Kathy Grbac, who has a passion like mine for family history, and with friends from my student-activist days, Frank Bardacke, Laurie Baumgarten, Joan Kramer, Julie Miller, Tim Parker, and Janice Ramkalawan.

I obtained and was able to quote extensively from transcripts or tapes of oral history interviews with my father Herb March conducted by Elizabeth Balanoff, Rick Halpern, Roger Horowitz, Les Orear and Molly West.

The searchable on-line database of the *Chicago Tribune* provided me with crucial access to news stories involving my parents and concerning the case of John Bain, the crooked banker who stole the assets of my mother's family.

The holdings of the Neighborhood History Archives at the Brooklyn Public Library proved indispensable to assembling information on my father's childhood home: files of clippings, mostly from the *Brooklyn Eagle*, unpublished manuscripts by local residents and their photograph collection.

Memoirs of radicals about their stirring life experiences or about the twists and turns of the political struggles in which they were engaged informed and sometimes served as models for

A Great Vision

my own work. Especially suggestive were the very few memoirs concerned with family life in a radical household.

History studies and memoirs relevant to my project:

Croatian history:
Stephen Clissold, ed., *A Short History of Yugoslavia* (Cambridge, 1966)

Zvane Črnja, *Cultural History of Croatia* (Zagreb, 1962)

Charles and Barbara Jelavich, *The Balkans* (Englewood Cliffs, NJ, 1965)

-------------, *The Establishment of the Balkan National States, 1804-1920* (Seattle, 1977)

Carlyle A. Macartney, *The Habsburg Empire 1790-1918* (New York, 1969)

Alan Palmer, *The Lands Between: A History of Eastern Europe, 1815-1968* (London, 2011)

History of my mother's home region and village:
Enver Imamović, *Nerezine na Otoku Lošinju* (Sarajevo, 1979)

Michael A. Ledeen, *The First Duce. D'Annunzio at Fiume* (Baltimore, 1977)

Dennison I. Rusinow, *The Liveliest Dying City: Trieste's Spiritual Crisis Over its European Future* (Hannover, NH, 1969)

Julijano Sokolić, ed. *Nerezinski libar* (Rijeka 2010)

Randy C. Wright, *The British Roots of the Trieste Crisis of May 1945* (Madison, 1985)

Eastern European Jewish Immigration and the Brownsville neighborhood of Brooklyn:
Irving Howe, *World of Our Fathers: The Journey of the East European Jews to America and the Life They Found and Made* (New York, 1976)

Alter F. Landesman, *Brownsville; the Birth, Development and Passing of a Jewish Community in New York* (New York, 1969)

Annalise Orleck, *Common Sense and a Little Fire: Women and Working-Class Politics in the United States, 1900-1965* (Chapel Hill, 1995)

The on-line Encyclopedia of Chicago articles:
Encyclopedia of Chicago, "Back of the Yards," "Community Organizing," "Great Depression," "Meatpacking," "Memorial Day Massacre," "Packinghouse Unions," "West Englewood" (accessed April 5, 2014)

Socialism and the populist movement on the Great Plains:
Chester McArthur Destler, *American Radicalism, 1865-1901* (Chicago, 1966)
Lawrence Goodwyn, *The Populist Moment: A Short History of the Agrarian Revolt in* America (Oxford, 1978)
John D. Hicks, *The Populist Revolt: A History of the Farmers' Alliance and the People's Party* (Minneapolis, 1931)
Nick Salvatore, *Eugene V. Debs: Citizen and Socialist* (Urbana, 1982)

The Soviet Union and the presence of Americans there:
E. M. Delafield, *Straw Without Bricks: I Visit Soviet* Russia (New York, 1937)
Miron Dolot, *Execution by Hunger: The Hidden Holocaust* (New York, 1987)
Harrison E. Salisbury, *The 900 Days: The Siege Of Leningrad* (Cambridge, 2003)
Aleksandr Solzhenitsyn, *The Gulag Archipelago*, 1918-1956 (London, 1973–78) (three volumes)
Tim Tzouliadis, *The Forsaken: An American Tragedy in Stalin's Russia* (New York, 2008)
Sidney & Beatrice Webb, *Soviet Communism: A New Civilisation?* (New York, 1936)

American Communism:
Milton Cantor & Eric Foner, *The Divided Left: American Radicalism 1900-1975* (New York, 1978)
Theodore Draper, *The Roots of American Communism* (New Brunswick, NJ, 2003)
Philip Foner & Herbert Shapiro, *American Communism and Black Americans: a Documentary History 1930-1934* (Philadelphia,

1991)

Irving Howe & Lewis Coser, *The American Communist Party: A Critical History* (New York, 1974)

Harvey Klehr, *The Heyday of American Communism: The Depression Decade* (New York, 1984)

Mark Solomon, *The Cry Was Unity: Communists and African-Americans, 1917-1936* (Jackson, MS, 1998)

Randi Storch, *Red Chicago: American Communism at its Grassroots, 1928-35* (Urbana, 2007)

Labor history, especially in the meatpacking industry:

Benjamin Appel, *The People Talk: American Voices from the Great Depression* (New York, 1940)

Frank Bardacke, *Trampling Out the Vintage: Cesar Chavez and the Two Souls of the United Farm Workers* (London, 2011)

Barrett, James. *Work and Community in the Jungle: Chicago's Packinghouse Workers, 1894—1922* (Urbana, 1987)

Robert W. Cherny, William Issel, and Kieran Walsh Taylor, eds. *American Labor and the Cold War: Grassroots Politics and Postwar Political Culture* (New Brunswick, NJ, 2004)

Lizabeth Cohen, *Making a New Deal: Industrial Workers in Chicago, 1919-1939* (Cambridge, 1990)

Cletus E. Daniel, *Bitter Harvest: A History of California Farmworkers, 1870—1941* (Berkeley, 1981)

Dennis, Michael J. *The Memorial Day Massacre and the Movement for Industrial Democracy* (New York, 2010)

Melvyn Dubofsky and Warren Van Tine, *John L. Lewis: A Biography* (Urbana, 1986)

Rick Halpern, *Down on the Killing Floor: Black and White Workers in Chicago's Packinghouses, 1904-54* (Urbana, 1997)

Rick Halperin and Roger Horowitz, *Meatpackers: An Oral History of Black Packinghouse Workers and Their Struggle for Racial and Economic Equality* (New York, 1996)

Roger Horowitz, *"Negro and White, Unite and Fight!": A Ssocial History of Industrial Unionism in Meatpacking, 1930-90* (Urbana, 1997)

Alice and Staughton Lynd, eds. *Rank and File: Personal Histories by Working-Class Organizers* (Boston, 1973)

_____, *The New Rank and File* (Ithaca, 2000)

Leslie F. Orear and Stephen H. Diamond, *Out of the Jungle: Packinghouse Workers Fight for Justice and Equality,* (Chicago, 1968)

Patrick Renshaw, *The Wobblies: The Story of Syndicalism in the United States* (Garden City, NY, 1967)

Cyril Robinson, *Marching With Dr. King: Ralph Helstein and the United Packinghouse Workers of America* (Westport, CT, 2011)

David Rosner and Gerald Markowitz, eds. *Dying for Work: Workers' Safety and Health in Twentieth-Century America* (Bloomington, IN, 1987)

Shelton Stromquist, Marvin Bergman, eds. *Unionizing the Jungles: Labor and Community in the Twentieth-Century Meatpacking Industry* (1997)

Elizabeth Balanoff Labor Oral History Collection, Roosevelt University archives

Herbert March Interview.

Community organizing, settlement houses, working women and other issues relating to Jane March:

Jane Addams, *Twenty Years at Hull-House* (Boston, 1999)

Mina Carson, *Settlement Folk: Social Thought and the American Settlement Movement, 1885-1930* (Chicago, 1990)

Sanford D. Horwitt, *Let Them Call Me Rebel : Saul Alinsky, His Life and Legacy* (New York, 1989)

Susan Estabrook Kennedy, *If All We Did Was to Weep At Home: A History of White Working-Class Women in America* (Bloomington, IN, 1979)

Ruth Milkman, *Gender at Work: The Dynamics of Job Segregation by Sex During World War II* (Urbana, 1987)

Robert A. Slayton, *Back of the Yards: The Making of a Local Democracy* (Chicago, 1986)

Memoirs of individual American radicals:

Bill Bailey, *The Kid from Hoboken* (San Francisco, 1993)

George Charney, *A Long Journey* (Chicago, 1968)

Elizabeth Gurley Flynn, *I Speak My Own Piece: Autobiography of the "Rebel Girl"* (New York, 1955)

William Z. Foster, *Pages From a Worker's Life* (New York, 1970)

Jessica Mitford, *A Fine Old Conflict* (New York, 1977)

Steve Nelson, James R. Barrett, Rob Ruck, *Steve Nelson, American Radical* (Pittsburgh, 1981)

Paul Robeson, *Here I Stand,* (New York, 1958)

Richard Wright, *Black Boy* (New York, 1993)

Works that treat family life in radical or labor movements:

Mickey Friedman, *A Red Family: Junius, Gladys & Barbara Scales* (Chicago, 2009)

Judy Kaplan and Linn Shapiro, eds. *Red Diapers: Growing Up in the Communist Left* (Urbana, 1998)

Gerda Lerner, *Fireweed: A Political Autobiography* (Philadelphia, 2003)

Robert and Michael Meeropol, *We Are Your Sons : the Legacy of Ethel and Julius Rosenberg* (Boston, 1975)

Cheri Register, *Packinghouse Daughter: A Memoir* (St. Paul, 2000)

Later era:

Stewart Burns, *Social Movements of the 1960s: Searching for Democracy* (New York, 1990)

Todd Gitlin, *The Whole World is Watching: Mass Media in the Making & Unmasking of the New Left* (Berkeley, 1980)

Arnold R. Hirsch, *Making the Second Ghetto: Race & Housing in Chicago, 1940-1960* (Cambridge, 1983)

Rik Scarce, *Eco-Warriors: Understanding the Radical Environmental Movement* (Chicago, 2006)

Sincere thanks to all the individuals and authors mentioned above whose work, recollections and advice contributed to this book. And also deep thanks to David Bass for his fine graphics and formatting work, and to Carl Green for his astute copy editing.

About the author

Richard March was born in Chicago in 1946 into a family of committed radical seekers of social justice, his father a labor leader and mother a community organizer. He imbibed the family tradition to become active in the civil rights and peace movements of the turbulent 1960s. He studied at UC Berkeley, Zagreb University and Indiana University, ultimately earning a Ph.D. in Folklore, a field that advances social and cultural tolerance. Richard had a decades-long career at the Wisconsin Arts Board, serving as Wisconsin's state folklorist. He has written extensively about and performed several genres of American ethnic music. In retirement, he resides in Portland, Oregon with his spouse Nikki Mandell, a labor and women's historian, and devotes himself to long-postponed writing projects.

TITLES FROM HARD BALL PRESS

A Great Vision – A Militant Family's Journey Through the Twentieth Century – by Richard March

Caring – 1199 Nursing Home Workers Tell Their Story

Fight For Your Long Day – Classroom Edition, by Alex Kudera

Love Dies, a thriller, by Timothy Sheard

Murder of a Post Office Manager, A Legal Thriller, by Paul Felton

New York Hustle – Pool Rooms, School Rooms and Street Corners, a memoir, Stan Maron

Passion's Pride – Return to the Dawning, Cathie Wright- Lewis

The Secrets of the Snow, a book of poetry, Hiva Panahi (author & translator)

Sixteen Tons, a Novel, by Kevin Corley

Throw Out the Water, the sequel to *Sixteen Tons*, by Kevin Corley

We Are One – Stories of Work, Life & Love, Elizabeth Gottieb, editor

What Did You Learn at Work Today? The Forbidden Lessons of Labor Education, nonfiction, by Helena Worthen

With Our Loving Hands – 1199 Nursing Home Workers Tell Their Story

Woman Missing, A Mill Town Mystery, by Linda Nordquist

THE LENNY MOSS MYSTERIES by Timothy Sheard

This Won't Hurt A Bit
Some Cuts Never Heal
A Race Against Death
No Place To Be Sick
Slim To None
A Bitter Pill
Someone Has To Die

CHILDREN'S BOOKS

The Cabbage That Came Back, Stephen Pearl (author), Rafael Pearl (Illustrator), Sara Pearl (translator)

Good Guy Jake, *Mark Torres (author), Yana Podrieez (Illustrator)*, Madelin Arroyo (translator)

Hats Off For Gabbie, Marivir Montebon (author), Yana Podriez (illustrator), Madelin Arroyo (translator)
Jimmy's Carwash Adventure, Victor Narro (author & translator), Yana Podriez (illustrator)

Joelito's Big Decision, Ann Berlak (author), Daniel Camacho (Illustrator), José Antonio Galloso (Translator)
Manny & The Mango Tree, Ali R. Bustamante (author), Monica Lunot-Kuker (illustrator), Mauricio Niebla (translator)

Margarito's Forest, Andy Carter (author), Allison Havens (illustrator), Omar Mejia (Translator)

Polar Bear Pete's Ice is Melting! – Timothy Sheard (author), Madelin Arroyo (translator), A FALL 2017 RELEASE

Trailer Park – Jennifer Dillard (author), Madelin Arroyo (translator), Rafael Pearl (illustrator) A SUMMER 2017 RELEASE